P9-BXY-655

ECOLOGY, TECHNOLOGY AND CULTURE

edited by

Wim Zweers

and

Jan J. Boersema

The White  Horse Press

Copyright © The White Horse Press 1994

First published 1994 by The White Horse Press, 10 High Street,
Knapwell, Cambridge CB3 8NR, UK

Set in 10 on 12 pt Times
Printed in Great Britain by Antony Rowe Ltd., Chippenham, Wiltshire

All rights reserved. Except for the quotation of short passages for the purpose
of criticism and review, no part of this book may be reprinted or reproduced
or utilised in any form or by any electronic, mechanical or other means,
including photocopying or recording, or in any information storage or
retrieval system, without permission from the publishers.

A catalogue record for this book is available from the British Library.

ISBN 1-874267-11-1 (cloth bound)
      1-874267-12-X (paper)

CONTENTS

PREFACE

Ecology, Technology and Culture is a slightly adapted translation of a collection of essays originally published in Dutch. The book deals with current environmental issues debated in western societies, although the philosophical realm of the essays is thoroughly European. It offers a variety of perspectives on the environmental crisis, in some ways distinct from Anglo-American scholarship, and ranging from historical, theological and hermeneutic viewpoints to scientific, political, economic and technological issues. The introductory article, 'A Framework for Environmental Philosophy', outlines the development and the current situation of the field in the Netherlands.

We should like to thank Miriam Hall for her assistance with the translation, and to acknowledge substantial financial support from members of the Dutch Association for Environmental Philosophy and the Centre for Applied Ethics at Erasmus University, Rotterdam.

Soest/Groningen, January 1994

Wim Zweers
Jan J. Boersema

Chapter 1

In Search of an Ecological Culture: Environmental Philosophy in the 1990s

Wim Zweers

A Framework for Environmental Philosophy

The book in front of you is the result of the conference 'Environmental Philosophy in the 1990s', which was held at the Erasmus University, Rotterdam on the 30th November and 1st December 1990, and was organized by the Pierre Bayle Philosophical Society of Rotterdam and the National Environmental Philosophy Study Group. This conference was the fourth in a series which started in 1984:

— 1984: Environmental Crisis and Philosophy

— 1986: Environmental Philosophy: Theory and Practice

— 1988: Nature: Exploitation or Respect?

— 1990: Environmental Philosophy in the 1990s.

The conferences held in 1984 and 1986 each lasted two days and were held at the International School of Philosophy in Leusden. They centred around discussion of readers which had just been published in preparation for the conference.[1] The reader of 1984 can be seen as a provisional exploration of an area to which almost no attention had previously been paid in the Netherlands, unlike the situation in the United States, for example. It started with a preliminary systematic exploration of the field of environmental philosophy. The reader of 1986, which was already much more comprehensive than the previous one, discussed among other things some questions about the practical applications of environmental philosophy. It was not only philosophers who took part, since attention was also given to ecology (1984)

and to environmental science (1986), two subjects which are closely related
to environmental philosophy. Reports of the 1984 and 1986 conferences
have been published and these include not only comments on the contents of
the readers, but also expansions on the subjects which were treated; hence
one can see them as a type of 'mini reader'.[2] The conference in 1988 was
somewhat different: it consisted of three colloquia, held in March and April
at the Faculties of Philosophy in the Universities of Amsterdam and Utrecht.
These were organized by the Project Group Environmental Philosophy, the
forerunner of the present National Environmental Philosophy Study Group.
The resulting reader, which was published in 1989,[3] contains the lectures
which were given. This 'conference' was different from the previous ones in
so far as a book was made as a result of the conference, rather than the
conference being the result of the book.

   This last approach was also chosen for the conference held in 1990, and
the result is this book. We have reverted to the principle of a two-day
conference because such an approach should lead to greater coherence. Such
coherence was one of the organizers' main aims, because the time was
thought to be ripe for a broad orientation and a general survey; in other words
for a perspective on environmental philosophy as a whole. The fact is that
much has happened since the first conference, and this field of study has
fortunately been receiving increasing attention, even in the Netherlands. A
few examples can be given to illustrate this:

— articles on environmental philosophy are being published with in-
    creasing frequency (especially in the journal *Filosofie en Praktijk*),
    as well as books and even dissertations, which are the *nec plus ultra*
    of academic aspiration;

— environmental philosophers are increasingly being included in gov-
    ernmental environmental advisory committees and councils;

— environmental philosophers are asked to lecture to companies such as
    the Grontmij and the Heidemij, or to institutes such as the Royal
    Institute of Engineers;

— there is a National Environmental Philosophy Study Group, compris-
    ing not only philosophers but also environmental scientists and
    ecologists, and acting as the representative of Dutch environmental
    philosophy. An International Society for Environmental Ethics has
    already been founded which regularly publishes a Newsletter and
    has members in 25 countries;

— environmental philosophy is now a regular philosophical subject that
    is taught at universities, not only in the form of incidental lectures,

but also as an option one can major in (Twente University), and, in collaboration with environmental science, as a full philosophical specialization in which it is possible to graduate at Amsterdam University (started at the beginning of the academic year 1990-1991);

— 'institutionally' financed research programmes at both these universities have an environmental philosophical component;

— environmental philosophy has also been accepted as part of environmental science, even as an officially recognized environmental specialism: thus the last edition of the *Basisboek Milieukunde*, a Dutch standard textbook on environmental science, has its own chapter on environmental philosophy;

— the Agricultural University of Wageningen has recently created a special professorship in humanistic philosophy, on behalf of the Socrates Foundation, which is especially concerned with the relationship between man and nature. At present this chair is held by an environmental philosopher.

One cannot deny the fact that the activities, development and structure of environmental philosophy in the Netherlands are beginning to acquire some weight. Hence ever more importance should be attached to answering such questions as: what is included in the field of study, what is environmental philosophy all about, what can philosophical reflections contribute to the analysis of the environmental crisis? The conference held in 1990 – and hence this book – was intended to begin to answer these questions in a more or less systematic way. This answering process will preserve the original idea formulated in the reader of 1984 of a problem-directed, thematic relationship between the different subdisciplines of philosophy, e.g. not only applied ethics or political and social philosophy, but also fundamental metaphysics and philosophical anthropology, but it will also look at environmental philosophy's openness to the sciences, not only to environmental science and ecology but also, for example, the natural sciences or economics. Hence the book will cover various fields and methods of approach, in order to provide a representative, although not complete, profile of what engages Dutch environmental philosophy.

Six main subject areas have been chosen, each of which includes one substantial article and two shorter papers containing additional, different, or critical perspectives. This ensures that a certain diversity of approach is maintained, which does justice to the existence of different, often rather divergent viewpoints within Dutch environmental philosophy. Besides, as I have noted already, there is also some diversity in the main subjects chosen. Nevertheless, this choice is based on a well defined vision of the systematics of environmental philosophy, a framework in which the different subjects each have their own place (along with others which are not dealt with here) and by which they are related to one another. It seems to me that this framework, this view on systematics, is generally accepted and hardly contested by the specialists in this field in the Netherlands.

The rest of the introduction will include a short explanation of this framework,[4] following which I will introduce each of the chapters. I will also refer to the role of each subject area in the previous readers. This will form a summary not only of environmental philosophy as a whole, but also of the extent to which Dutch environmental philosophy – insofar as it is reflected in these four books – has engaged with the subject.

ENVIRONMENTAL PHILOSOPHY AS AN INTERDISCIPLINARY PHILOSOPHICAL SUBJECT

Environmental philosophy – the newest offshoot of philosophical specialization – is concerned with a systematic and critical reflection of philosophical aspects of the environmental issue; in other words, of the relationship between humanity and nature which in our time has become highly problematic. The subject itself belongs to philosophy, but it is closely related to environmental science and ecology.

The problems which are raised in environmental philosophy are to a large extent related to topics as old as philosophy itself. It seems, however, that these have achieved new urgency in the present environmental crisis. Philosophical analysis can be viewed as a third phase of research into a diagnosis of, and therapy for, the environmental crisis. Initially, the environmental issue was mainly seen as a technical and scientific problem. However, there is growing awareness that here science and technology reach the limits of their range of action: the issues which they are working on have origins extending far beyond their scope. Further research has indicated that environmental problems are not only scientific or technical problems, but especially societal problems. This second phase has led to the recognition that it is impossible to leave our economic and political systems, the position of science and technology, and even the relationships between people out of the analysis.

At the same time a third phase is taking shape: the increasing understanding of the fundamental character of the environmental problem has revealed the necessity of going back to those factors that form the basis of our social structure, especially our ideology and world view and the norms and values which are expressed in them. Though the environmental crisis is above all a result of humanity's actions with respect to nature, these actions are however largely determined by *views* on our place in nature, as well as by our *knowledge* of nature. We can thus, in accordance with the traditional classification of philosophy into the study of being, knowing and acting, develop a classification of the field of environmental philosophy as outlined in Table 1.1.

The following text is an elaboration of these fields, combined with a short discussion of the previous readers and of the book in front of you.

---

1. THE POSITION OF HUMANITY IN NATURE
(images of nature, images of humanity: basic attitudes)
a) Systematic   *(metaphysics, philosophical anthrop-*
                                   ology, philosophy of culture)
b) Historical   *(history of philosophy)*
c) Intercultural   *(comparative philosophy)*

2. KNOWLEDGE OR EXPERIENCE OF NATURE
a) Scientific knowledge: *(philosophy of science)*
    – relationship between environmental crisis and 'classical' natural
    science
    – alternative scientific views
b) Other forms of experience or knowledge of nature:
    – hermeneutics   *(philosophy of the cultural*
                                  sciences and the humanities)
    – ecological aesthetics   *(aesthetics)*
    – religious-spiritual experience *(philosophy of religion and spirituality)*

3. ACTING TOWARDS NATURE
a) Basic assumptions: norms and criteria *(ethics)*
b) Social institutions:
    – politics   *(political philosophy)*
    – social economy   *(social philosophy)*
    – science   *(dynamics of science)*
    – technology   *(philosophy of technology)*

Table 1.1. The field of environmental philosophy

1. THE POSITION OF HUMANITY IN NATURE

Of central importance here is the problem of basic attitudes to nature. These actually form the foundation of everything which is to follow, which is to say that they are always making themselves felt in one way or another: both in the types of knowledge we can have concerning nature, and in human behaviour towards nature. In basic attitudes a particular view of the structure of reality is expressed: an image of the world, a conception of reality (*metaphysics or ontology*), more specifically an *image of nature*, with an accompanying vision of the values of nature, whether only for the benefit of humanity, or also for nature's own sake. At the same time this indicates something about our opinions about ourselves, who we are, the special qualities we possesses, in short an *image of humanity* (*philosophical anthropology*). The images of humanity and nature are closely related, they have a determining influence on one another, and in the present situation of apparent conflict between ourselves and nature, many people feel that a profound *separation between nature and culture* has manifested itself as an essential cause of the environmental crisis (*philosophy of culture*).

The general problem of basic attitudes has already been dealt with in previous readers: see Zweers (1984), in which the so-called 'separation view' is criticized, and in which an ecological theory of culture is proposed; see also Zweers (1988), for an account of how the intrinsic value of nature and the effects that recognition of this can have on 'making' or 'producing' human behaviour are more thoroughly examined.

In general the metaphysical-anthropological-cultural complex of basic attitudes can be approached in three ways: systematic, historical, and intercultural.

a. Systematic.

Which (types of) basic attitudes can be discerned (partly on the basis of historical and comparative research), and to what extent can some of them be seen as being directly or indirectly related to the environmental crisis, and others as possibly directive for the future?

b. Historical.

How has the relationship between humanity and nature developed in western philosophy and culture, which important stages have been passed on the way to the modern world view, based as it is solely on the physical sciences, and what other directions, which could still be inspiring to us, have been blocked or remained undercurrents only (for example, in classical philosophy, or during the Renaissance or Romanticism, or by individual philosophers such as Leibniz, Spinoza, Schelling, or at a later stage by Whitehead, Heidegger, Plessner, Merleau-Ponty)? (*history of philosophy*).

In Chapters 2-4 of this book special attention is paid to these historical backgrounds, with Boersema's article as the starting point. Both the Greek and Jewish roots of our culture, which must certainly not be forgotten, can reliably serve as the basis for a reorientation of our relationship with nature. It goes without saying that Christianity cannot be ignored, even if only because of the charges in relation to the environmental crisis often brought against this world view, which is so important to our culture. As well as being discussed by Boersema, the subject is also raised by Van Dijk, who not only traces the historical position of the church, but also examines some recent theological developments which seem to depart from historical Christianity's presumed hostility towards nature. Finally, Zweers proposes the necessity for a radical reorientation of our relationship with nature, but not so radical that one could no longer speak of links with the past; however, that past should rather be the premodern 'cosmotheological' past, and not that of historical Christianity, which, for the most part, renounced the world (Löwith). This short essay also looks at the systematics of basic attitudes, a subject which is not discussed at length anywhere else in this reader, nor in any of the previous ones.

However, this is not the first time that the historical role of Christianity has been explored in these readers: I refer to the article by Lemaire (1986) where, as part of a consideration of the concept of utopia, Christianity is criticized as an outstanding example of an 'anti-ecological' world view, and to the discussion which provoked Lemaire's analysis, including the lecture by Van Steenbergen published in the conference report, which for the rest concentrated on the 'New Age' paradigm in the light of recent social developments. I would also like to refer to Van der Perk (1988), who, in addition to giving a historical-theological summary, also argued for a new Christian spirituality based on the view of nature found in liberation theology

c. Intercultural.

Which insights can be derived from the basic attitudes that we find in non-western cultures, and what problems does a possible reception of these attitudes in the west bring with it? One may think here not only of eastern, but also of American Indian or maybe even African cultures (*comparative philosophy*).

This subject is not raised in the present volume, but this does not mean that it has been overlooked in the past. I refer to the outstanding critique by Lemaire (1984) which deals with the possibility or otherwise of western society being inspired by the American Indian attitude towards nature, and also with the question whether this attitude was really as positively oriented towards nature as is often believed; for that matter it is interesting to compare the 'hidden' utopian content of this paper with that by Lemaire in 1986, in which utopia has a central position. Westhoff (1988) gives a *tour d'horizon* of almost all the nature religions of the world: the Indians are reviewed, as well as Hinduism, Taoism and Buddhism, and these are taken more or less as an example for western culture.

2. KNOWLEDGE OR EXPERIENCE OF NATURE

a. Scientific knowledge

The key question here is the extent to which the development of the natural sciences since Descartes and Newton has contributed to the origin and continuation of the environmental crisis, and whether initiatives in other directions can be discovered within science itself.

Regarding the first point, attention is often drawn to the analytical-reductionist character of modern natural science, its mathematical-mechanistic methods of explanation, and its dualistic epistemological basis. These together provide the possibility (or the illusion) of complete predictability and hence manageability of nature.

Looking at the second point, in biology there is the discussion about the specific character of animate nature as compared with dead matter, with goal-orientedness and self-organization being the key concepts; then of diversity of nature as it is appears to our senses, compared with the uniformity of only rationally intelligible abstract laws; and finally of the irreducibility of relations postulated in the work of ecologists or systems theorists. As far as physics is concerned, the monopoly of the Cartesian-Newtonian world view has been broken by the theory of relativity, quantum physics and chaos theory, together resulting in the perspective of a world in which dualism and predictability, and thus also complete control, are undermined on a fundamental level (*philosophy of the natural sciences*)

In the previous readers, such aspects were addressed by several contributors. Schroevers (1984) not only looks at the importance of ecology as a biological science, but appeals in particular for a 'social ecology' in which natural values and social values do not take up opposing positions, and in which ecology and economy both turn out to need one another. Verhoog

(1984) also appeals for a 'social biology', or at any rate a view of science which is critical of the social structure; in the same essay he discusses the scientific ideas of Goethe and Steiner, which are nowadays mainly supported in anthroposophic and perhaps in phenomenological circles. There are further examples of similar 'alternative' views of science in the 1986 reader De Groot discusses the possibilities of a 'normative' idea of science, that is, directed at finding solutions for problem situations, as is done in environmental science, a subject he views as 'applied environmental philosophy'. Maas introduces the views of Gregory Bateson, which are difficult to systematize but very important for most of the non-traditional ideas about the biological and anthropological sciences (for example: Morris Berman's well-known book, *The Re-enchantment of the World*, uses mainly Bateson's metaphysics as a basis for a present day participatory understanding of reality).

Hence a fair amount of attention has been paid to 'different' ideas about science in the previous readers. However, what was not tackled before was the 'mother of all sciences' (at least in the traditional interpretation of the notion of science), that is, physics itself. Chapter 5 is concerned with what has hitherto been seen as the foundation of the whole scientific enterprise, and therefore of our whole science based world view, promising far-reaching predictability and controllability.

Tennekes is a physicist and a meteorologist, and so uses his own subject, weather forecast, as a starting point. But it is definitely not only a *bon mot* that the weather is unpredictable and uncontrollable: behind this lies a very general problem, which is seen even more clearly in meteorology than in any other science. This problem has to do with the fundamental impossibilities, firstly of obtaining 'objective' knowledge about systems which we are part of, and then of being able to interfere with these systems from outside – not to mention the unpredictability of complex chaotic but actually self organizing systems. In his paper Chung Lin Kwa also gives evidence for this 'awakening from the dream of reason': it is not as Descartes promised us and as Newton seemed to have proved. We are becoming afraid of our own pretensions, we must show restraint, we will have to question the fundamental presuppositions of our world view: overconfidence is replaced by anxiety, our offensive strategy must make way for a defensive one. But it is naturally true that we should not feel ourselves to be passive and helpless, as Schroevers understandably suggests in his criticism of Tennekes. Instead, we could allow ourselves to be guided by our experiences from the past, using a strategy of 'small steps' such as he recommends, in order to draw up a sensible policy for the future – including an at least limited (one could almost say: controlled) predictability. But that does not alter the fact that the basis of a world view founded on complete predictability and controllability of nature is crumbling under our feet. It certainly seems to me that we have as yet barely begun to realize this mere fact, let alone to be aware that it has already been the subject of philosophical analysis of any significant size or importance.

b. Other forms of knowledge and experience

Hermeneutics of nature. This is a way of obtaining knowledge by conceiving of nature as an expression of meaning which it is impossible to grasp by using reason alone, but for which corporality (sensory perception) and emotionality are also important conditions. The understanding of meaning is hence not limited to human meaning, but is also extended to that of nature (*philosophy of the cultural sciences and the humanities*).

If one ignores perspectives which can only broadly speaking be considered to be hermeneutic (such as deep ecology, discussed in the reader of 1986, which can be categorized as being on the border between hermeneutics and ecological spirituality) then it can be concluded that the issue of a hermeneutics of nature has up to now only been raised once, in Verhoog's article (1988). His paper used the metaphor 'reading in the book of nature' as a starting point to consider the image of nature favoured by Romanticism, especially Goethe's 'phenomenology', and it concludes with a plea for the revival of this type of nature philosophy .

The hermeneutics of nature is discussed again in chapters 8-10 of this book. However, it seems to me that Kockelkoren leads us along a different path from Verhoog's, with his approach based on that of Plessner. Kockelkoren is mainly interested in our ability to understand by a feeling of corporeal solidarity ('Einfühlung') any other individual, including animal organisms, and not just other humans, a view which implies an extension of Dilthey's hermeneutics. The possibility explored by Kockelkoren is critically considered by both Coolen and Lijmbach, albeit in completely different ways. Of central importance to Coolen is the unbridgeable distance between humans and animals, which he adduces from the proposition that humans, unlike other animals, are able to relate to their own bodies and own situations, making any solidarity of the sort proposed by Kockelkoren impossible. Lijmbach limits the concept of hermeneutics to its scientific practice, instead of expanding it as Kockelkoren does to become the object of that scientific practice; on this basis she argues that hermeneutics always plays a role in the practice of science, that the meaning given to it is always cultural, that is, projected by humans, and hence cannot be seen as a meaning of nature itself.

Ecological aesthetics. On the one hand this is concerned with the aesthetic attitude, that is the attitude in which the other – a work of art, for example, but perhaps nature as well – can show itself as what it is in itself (non-instrumentality), in such a way that the senses are given a central part to play. On the other hand it is concerned with the properties of the aesthetic object that nature *is* (*aesthetics*).

This subject is not discussed in this book, and in past readers its absence has been conspicuous too, except for a short paragraph by Zweers (1986). Generally speaking, I think that this is the most serious omission in Dutch environmental philosophy up to now. However, very few people are involved with this subject, and unfortunately it appeared impossible to develop a substantial contribution in the time available for preparation. As a matter of fact, if we were to introduce aesthetics in this context, then we would obviously have to discuss an aesthetics that is less related to philosophy of art, which aesthetics has clearly been reduced to in our days, than to the original meaning of the word. For this reason especially, it seems to me that ecological aesthetics is of great importance, particularly for education in the field of nature and environment, making us receptive to the beauty and hence the value of what we experience through our senses.

Religious-spiritual experience. This is where for some people the meaningful and aesthetic character of nature finds its culmination. In the first instance this is often also known as ecological spirituality, but this can then be developed into a sacral or religious experience of nature as well (*philosophy of religious experience and spirituality*).

This subject was not discussed during the conference of 1990 either, but in this case there is less reason to speak of an omission than in the case of aesthetics. The religious-spiritual approach as it is to be understood here (in other words, besides the historical and theological analyses concerning Christianity) was dealt with explicitly by Duintjer (1984). He mainly considered an alternative for the Cartesian 'separation view', by achieving a Spinozan 'God or Nature' experience through increased bodily awareness and meditative practice. This approach was expounded in Duintjer's introduction at the conference of 1986, which can be found in the conference report. Besides this I would like to refer to the article by Zweers (1986), in which different forms of 'ecological experience' were of central importance, especially the spiritual, aesthetic and scientific. He argued in favour of a connection to be formed between the spiritual-aesthetic and the reflexive-scientific approaches to knowledge of nature.

3. ACTING TOWARDS NATURE

a. Basic assumptions: norms and criteria

The first question concerns the basic assumptions influencing our actions towards nature, assumptions which conform to what has been said previously, which are based on images of humanity and nature, and which are reached by the various scientific and non-scientific pathways for obtaining knowledge about nature. This is mainly the domain of ethics, which is concerned with norms and criteria for actions.

Environmental ethics aims to develop and found (moral) norms concerned with our relationships with nature. This can be developed as *anthropocentric ethics*, in which moral obligations concerning nature are derived from those that we have in relation to other people, not only here and now, but also elsewhere (global justice) and in the future (intergenerational justice). *Extensional ethics* extends ideas concerning humanity to include non-human nature (for example, giving rights to nature, or taking as a starting point a property which has been fully developed in humans, like consciousness or the ability to feel pain). Finally we come to *ecological ethics*, in which the grounds for moral obligations are found in the interest or wellbeing of nature itself, of individuals, of species, or perhaps of ecosystems or maybe even of the earth as a whole, 'Gaia' (ethics).

If we look back at the previous readers, we find that this is understandably one of the subjects to which the most consistent attention has been paid. Achterberg has developed his theories on the subject in the readers of 1984, 1986 and 1988, generally ending in some form of ecological ethics as has been described above. However in 1988 he also explored a specific problem which arises with future generations, that is, the so-called identity problem: briefly, through our actions we not only determine *if* there will be future generations, but we also determine *who* they will be, that is, their identity.

In chapters 11-13 of this book, attention shifts somewhat from a strictly ethical field to a more political-philosophical approach, i.e., to the feasibility and the shaping of specific ethical principles in the policymaking of a liberal democratic government. There seem to be problems here which appear quite serious for the environmental issue. These are partially concerned with the tension between the necessity to limit or make impossible environmentally damaging behaviour, on the one hand, and the desire to restrict the freedom of the citizen as little as possible on the other hand. Achterberg attempts to find a solution to this problem using Rawls' theory of justice, once this has been extended in a certain way. Not everyone agrees with him that this is necessary. Jacobs contends that in this way things tend to become too complicated: sustainable development (a central issue in Achterberg's argument) can be justified just as simply by using the traditional basic assumptions of liberal democracy. Musschenga sees just as few insurmountable limitations for the justification of environmental preservation within a liberal democracy as does Achterberg (or Jacobs). However – differently from Achterberg – he believes that Rawls' theory should not so much be extended as exceeded in the direction of more versatile concepts of the good life, in order to justify a policy for nature and the environment based on the concept of intrinsic value. Anyway, it is also easily possible to categorize this whole issue and argument under the institution of politics, discussed below; but it is apparent that there are also reasons to see it as a branch of environmental ethics.

b. Social institutions

Collective actions crystallize into social institutions. The following are of special importance within the scope of environmental philosophy:

Politics, as the regulated reflection of social relationships between people, especially as far as the division of power is concerned. A few important issues: the accommodation of central policy ideas to ethical principles, the compatibility of liberal-social democracy with effective environmental policy, and lastly the problem of governmental intervention versus decentralization and the citizens' own responsibility (*political philosophy*).

This subject is not mentioned specifically in this book, except in the contributions by Achterberg and his critics. That does not mean that it has not been more or less thoroughly dealt with in previous readers. To start with I would cite the very 'pragmatist' lecture given by the (European and national) politician Van der Lek at the 1984 conference, which was rather sobering for some of the audience, and led to much argument. He was not very much impressed by the philosophical accounts that he had heard, and claimed a straight anthropocentric-positivistic-pragmatist standpoint, partly because of his political experiences. I would refer also to Tellegen who in 1984 clearly argued against less governmental interference, an ideal which he sometimes came upon in the environmental movement (decentralization, autonomy of decision-making for small groups, etc.). With similar results, but using very different arguments, Van Asperen (1986) looked at the well-known Prisoner's Dilemma, applied to the environmental problem. We are much in need of a powerful government to make those decisions that we cannot make ourselves but which would be most advantageous to all of us. One can ask whether arguments such as Tellegen's and Van Asperen's are not directed mostly at the short term – and hence will hardly be contended by anyone – while the so-called decentralization concept, seen as a political ideology, is mainly something for the long term, that is, once the mentality and the basic attitudes of the population have changed fairly fundamentally. I would finally like to refer to Van der Burg (1988), who studied Rawls' theory of state, based on a fictitious social contract, and then discarded it, preferring Dworkin's theory of democracy which starts with a principle of fundamental equality. This issue once more shows the smoothness of the transitions between the development of ethical principles for our actions and the way these take shape in our political institutions.

Social economy, which is concerned with satisfaction of needs (both individual and collective) and the division of scarce goods. Themes raised here are the concept of scarcity itself and its role in the relationship between people, the debate about growth economy, whether capitalist or socialist, versus the 'economy of sufficiency', and the problem of market economy versus plan economy (*social philosophy*).

One can include in this field Achterhuis' contributions to the readers of 1986 and 1988. In 1986 he discussed Hardin's problem of the 'commons' – which has similarities with the Prisoner's Dilemma – leading to a reinstatement of the idea of commonality, based on Locke, in a future (utopian?) society (thus different to the short term views of Tellegen and Van Asperen). In 1988 he directly challenged the 'basic attitudes approach', arguing that it is not these attitudes towards nature but mainly changes in social relationships which are the key to all troubles, especially the 'mimetic desires' (Girard) which directly lead to scarcity.

Although the economy takes a secondary position in Achterhuis' views, it plays a central role in that of Opschoor's in chapter 14 of this book, and this is a relatively new feature of our environmental philosophy conferences. Opschoor begins with a short historical sketch of market economy developments, in which he discusses the 'tendency towards unsustainability' of this form of economy, and the possibility of altering it by institutional means. Then he discusses the necessity of restricting the market economy on the basis of norms and values agreed upon within society, or in other words, of limiting the belief in growth and progress and allowing the economic process to be partially determined by other ideas about the relationship between humanity and nature. Van der Straaten's and Achterhuis' reactions to Opschoor run remarkably parallel, but they are of more or less opposite tenor. Van der Straaten believes that it is undesirable to enter the field of norms, values and images of humanity too rapidly, because economic theory itself is still faulty as long as it does not fully include the factor 'natural resources' in its models along with the production factors 'work' and 'capital': it is basically faulty economic theory that results in unsustainability. Achterhuis, however, doubts whether traditional economic instruments are able to control the environmental crisis, and finds a radically different direction much more hopeful. This direction is consistent with his articles in the previous readers, especially as regards the importance of social relationships rather than mentality and consciousness, and he believes that one should begin with a thorough analysis of the role that fear of scarcity plays in our society.

For that matter, it may be a good idea to recall Van Dieren's remark on the importance of influencing the business world which he made at the conference in 1986 ('the environmental movement is much more effective than it realizes, as far as the business world is concerned'), as well as his stress on the importance of the environmental-economic scenario developed by Hueting (an economist whose views seem to be less well acknowledged in the Netherlands than abroad). Can this be seen as implicit support *avant la lettre of* Van der Straaten's point of view?

Science. This is not only the basis for the modern worldview, but is also of importance because of its entanglement with all the previous institutions: a public force with a great deal of specific social dynamics and political-economic power (*dynamics of science*).

Modern science has become so important a social institution that it is able to influence almost all of the already mentioned fields: our basic attitudes, the knowledge that we have about nature, and especially also technology and economics. Vermeersch calls this the 'STC complex' (Science, Technology and Capitalism) and Duintjer likewise speaks of the intertwined system of science, technology and economy.[5] However, until now it has not been the subject of study at our environmental philosophy conferences, and it will not be in this book either. This may seem surprising, but on the other hand the subject is indirectly raised in discussions on many other themes. In this connection I refer to Verhoog in the 1984 reader, as well as to the contributions by Tennekes and Chung Lin Kwa in this volume, and to that by Coolen in the 1988 reader and Van der Wal's paper in this book. Both of the latter papers are discussed below.

Technology may be seen in a general anthropological sense as a character-istic feature of humans, or viewed as a social institution which seems to make more of a mark on our culture than anything else. The discussion about technocracy plays a central role here: that is, the choice for all social action becoming subordinate to technical criteria, so that these are converted from a means to an end. On the other hand one can think of 'technology on a human scale', adapted and subordinate to an assessment of needs originating elsewhere, that is to say outside the realm of technology itself (*philosophy of technology*).

In past volumes we have treated technology mainly in a general anthropological sense, especially in the 1988 reader. Van der Wal discusses there the limits to the 'makeability' of reality (and of life in general) and the importance of the so-called unintended, 'additional' phenomena: what happens but cannot be brought about at will, a dimension of humanity that is not technical but most probably more essential. Coolen argues that 'making' or 'producing' and technology do not have to be seen only as negative: technology can also aid self-expression. At the same time a distinction must be made between the technical and the economic aspect of labour, that is between labour through which nature is given a distinct form, and labour performed to satisfy our needs.

In chapter 17 of this book Van der Wal gives a lengthy cultural critique of modern technology, switching from Dessauer's positive to Ellul's nega-tive evaluation of technology. He makes use of the familiar categorization of philosophy into ontology, epistemology and ethics, for both the critical analysis of modern technology and for a 'contra-proposal' opposing the idea of a mechanized and disenchanted reality. For each of these fields of philosophy, he looks at the implications of the 'existing' and the 'possible'. Regarding the two shorter articles in this section, Hilhorst specifically limits himself to the field of ethics. He does not aim to take an alternative image of humanity or nature as his starting point, but instead endeavours to see how ethical reflection can take place within the present framework of technical action in a way that is meaningful and, with respect to nature and the environment, also sensible. Finally Tijmes uses the 'metableticist' Van den Berg's differentiation between the phenomenologically experienced, essen-tially changing reality (reality in its 'first structure') and the reality of science and technology which is directed at objectivity and constancy (reality in its 'second structure'). In our society the latter has obtained the characteristics of a whole new world of its own, on which humanity has become highly dependent and which has a strongly progressing character; this leads to the question as to the relationship between both realities or 'modes of discourse'.

ABOUT THE FUTURE AND THE RELEVANCE OF ENVIRONMENTAL PHILOSOPHY

Naturally review and orientation of environmental philosophy cannot be presented without a perspective on the future, and in the present book this issue is also raised, even though to a somewhat limited extent. I have already said that environmental philosophy is problem directed, but that does not mean that it should lose itself in a tendency to be applicable, or that its relevance should for the most part be measured according to its direct practical use: in fact the same applies to the whole of philosophy. Some time ago a Dutch environmental scientist warned environmental philosophers that they should not concentrate solely on practical applications, and that seems to me to be in accordance with the opinion I mentioned before of another environmental scientist who believes that environmental science can in a certain way be viewed as applied environmental philosophy, thus stressing the applied nature of environmental science, in contrast to environmental philosophy.

That environmental philosophy should not be primarily determined by practical questions does not mean that these questions not should be posed. In fact this is not the first time that we have considered this. A guest speaker at the first conference was Peter Nijhoff, director of the 'Stichting Natuur en Milieu', one of the leading Dutch environmental organizations, and who is more concerned with practical issues than a representative of the environmental movement? (In his lecture he implored us to continue our activities, which were then still totally new in the Netherlands). Furthermore, in the 1986 reader, Kwee described the development of environmental awareness and the environmental movement from a cultural philosophical viewpoint that was also strongly practical: how do we actually design a society that is more favourable to humanity, environment and nature? In Dutch environmental quarters there has always been a lot of interest in environmental philosophy from the very beginning. However I have the strong impression that it was mainly the individual environmentalist and not the 'official' organizations that were interested. As far as I know the latter have never shown much interest in anything deviating from a 'pragmatist perspective': this in contrast to, for example, the situation in the United States. It is well known that the Dutch environmental movement is looking now for new impetus, new zest, maybe because pure pragmatism seems to have reached the end of its possibilities.[6] It seems to me that it would be advisable to look at the more 'theoretical' perspectives offered by environmental philosophy in this respect. As yet Dutch environmental policy has reached no further than the second phase in the history of the analysis of the environmental issue, as distinguished at the beginning of this paper; I think that the same can be said of the 'institutional' Dutch environmental movement. There is still far too little awareness of the fact that there is much more wrong than can be studied from a purely pragmatist perspective only: the situation has barely improved under the ruling regime, and in many fields it has unmistakably worsened. Looked at in this way, there is nothing purely 'theoretical' in environmental philosophy, and the proposals made using this perspective cannot at all be thought of as 'abstract'.[7] I wonder to what extent things will still have to worsen before the insight is gained that the problems are so fundamental that they cannot be solved in any way other than by using just such a 'theoretical' basis. Maybe this is where the 'usefulness' of environmental philosophy lies: it is definitely not a sufficient, but certainly a necessary condition for an approach which, at least in the long term, actually may bear fruit.

The above indicates yet again that it is necessary to pose the question as to the future perspectives of environmental philosophy, in particular as to its possible contribution to a long term solution of the environmental issue. Note that I am now talking about the 'solution' (if one can speak of a solution in the case of such complex and comprehensive issues at all) to a social problem, not a philosophical problem (if it were possible at all to solve philosophical problems). Philosophical analysis can indeed contribute, and I believe make an essential contribution, to the solution of this problem. The final chapter, Vermeersch's essay, discusses this. He broadly sketches the main viewpoints of the environmental-philosophical discussion: ideological versus institutional analysis, and anthropocentrism versus ecocentrism. In both cases he doubts the first alternative and chooses the second, even though his own anthropocentrism is definitely of a moderate flavour. But even those who prefer the other viewpoints would perhaps agree with his conclusion, that environmental philosophy is most probably not only the anthropology of the future, but possibly even the philosophy of the future. But this means that environmental philosophy would still have to live up to these expectations, and in order to do so Vermeersch provides us with a priority list that we can all begin with. It would be a good thing for government and the environmental movement to take a thorough look at this list. I believe that it should be used to call environmental philosophy to account.

NOTES

1. W. Achterberg & W. Zweers (eds.) 1984. *Milieucrisis en filosofie; Westers bewustzijn en vervreemde natuur* (Environmental Crisis and Philosophy: Western

consciousness and alienated nature). Amsterdam, Ekologische Uitgeverij; W. Actherberg & W. Zweers (eds.) 1986. *Milieufilosofie tussen theorie en praktijk; van ecologisch perspectief naar maatschappelijke toepassing* (Environmental Philosophy between Theory and Practice: from ecological perspective towards social practice), Utrecht, Uitgevij Jan van Arkel.

2. J. van Eupen (ed.), 1986. *Milieucrisis en filosofie; verslag van een studie-weekend* (Environmental Crisis and Philosophy: report of a study-weekend), Steunpunt voor Natuur- en Milieueducatie (Institute for Nature and Environmental Education). Amsterdam; W. Achterberg & W. Zweers (eds.), 1987. *Milieufilosofie tussen theorie en praktijk; verslag van een studie-weekend* (Environmental Philosophy between Theory and Practice: report of a study-weekend). Amsterdam, Steunpunt voor Natuur- en Milieueducatie.

3. W. Achterberg (ed.) 1989. *Natuur: uitbuiting of respect; natuurwaarden in discussie* (Nature: Exploitation or Respect? Values of nature under discussion). Kampen, Kok/Agora, 1989.

4. A more thorough treatment can be found in W. Zweers, 'Milieufilosofie' (Environmental Philosophy) in: J.J. Boersema et al. (eds.), 1991, 4th edition. *Basisboek Milieukunde* (Environmental Science Textbook), chapter 18. Meppel, Boom.

5. Duintjer, O.D., 1988. Het belang van nieuwe spiritualiteit in een expansieve maatschappij (The relevance of a new spirituality in an expansive society). In: B. Nagel (ed.), *Maken en breken; over productie en spiritualiteit* (Making and breaking; on production and spirituality), pp. 17-47. Kampen, Kok/Agora.

6. See also Cramer, J., 1989. *De groene golf; geschiedenis en toekomst van de milieubeweging* (The Green Wave: History and future of the environmental movement), pp. 136-9. Utrecht, Uitgevij Jan van Arkel.

7. Cf. 1990 Commissie Lange Termijn Planning Milieubeleid (Commission on Long Term Environmental Policy Planning), Reply of the commission on the contribution by Vermeersch, in: *Het Milieu: denkbeelden voor de 21 e eeuw* (The Environment: Ideas for the 21th Century), p.43. Zeist, Kerckebosch, Zeist.

Chapter 2

FIRST THE JEW BUT ALSO THE GREEK: IN SEARCH OF THE ROOTS OF THE ENVIRONMENTAL PROBLEM IN WESTERN CIVILIZATION

Jan J. Boersema

1. INTRODUCTION

The days when the environmental issue was seen as a technical defect in our social machinery are now in the past. The realization is dawning that we are confronted with a very complex problem, which is closely interwoven with our civilization. Approaching that problem is made no more simple by this realization. Therefore it would seem helpful, if not essential, to carry out an anamnesis, an analysis of the history of the illness. How far back should we delve to expose the roots? Back to the previous century? To the beginning of agricultural civilization? Two things are of importance in answering these questions.

In the first place, a further clarification of the problem is necessary. This involves the translation of an issue determined by society, into a problem which is also scientifically interesting and researchable.[1] The norms and values of the translator will inevitably play an important role during the translation, although this need not always be explicit. Such a translation will give specific direction to the research, the methods and the selection of relevant facts. If the environmental issue is defined in terms of an industrialization that has gone astray, such research would not have to delve back further than the previous century. It is somewhat different if our ideas about the place of humans in nature are regarded as the key problem. An analysis of this would reach much further into the past. Hence a search for the roots of the environmental problem should start with a further specification of the problem. This seems obvious, but in fact it is not. The majority of the historical analyses use terms such as 'the present environmental crisis' or 'our ecological crisis', without explaining these terms. The word 'crisis' especially seems to be in vogue. However, as a rule, it usually becomes apparent further on in the study that the author implicitly holds a particular opinion on the crisis. Hence, I shall briefly indicate the definition of the problem that I have used in my study in the following section.

Secondly, the aim of the anamnesis determines its historical depth. If anamnesis is only important to solve the problem, one does not have to go back further than necessary to that purpose. For example, surgeons are less concerned with their patients' mental histories than psychiatrists. However, if a scientific, causal explanation and analysis are needed as well as a solution, then the cause/effect chain will have to stretch much further into the past. One can speak of a twofold aim as far as the environmental issue is concerned: we are in search of both the solution and the cause. Science is called in to help in both cases. However, its task is not identical in the two, because factors other than just science (for example money, political will etc.) are also of importance in society in solving environmental problems, while science more or less has a monopoly on the analysis of the causes. Thus the solution and cause are not a logical continuation of one another. The presumption that we need to know the cause of a societal problem such as the environmental problem in order to solve it, is more probable than the reverse proposition that we will be able to solve a problem once we know the cause. The relationship of cause and solution is less direct than is often presumed, and the link is most probably not equally strong in both directions. For that matter, if we look to the medical world in search of analogies, we see that the same is true of some illnesses. We will primarily concentrate on an analysis of causes in this chapter, and their relationship with possible solutions will only be discussed briefly.

2. FORMULATION OF THE PROBLEM

Our relationship with our natural environment is intense. This relationship, which is often called metabolic, forms the basis of every society. Naturally it has a strongly materialistic character, although it is not limited to this. Humanity has always used the natural environment to satisfy basic needs, such as food, clothing, shelter, safety and transport. These characteristics do not distinguish us from other organisms. However, using Maslov's terminology, our social and developmental needs also lead to some appropriation of nature. This metabolic relationship with our surroundings has especially influenced the environment. We have drastically altered the 'face of the earth'.[2] Furthermore, we have been rapidly confronted with the negative side effects of our actions: salinification, exhaustion, erosion and desertification. The eradication of species of plants and animals also has a long tradition, which, according to some people, extends back to the Pleistocene. Local pollution of the ground, water and air by toxic substances and substances found in damaging quantities also goes back a long way, even though it is of a later date than the extermination of species. That we speak of a modern problem, despite its long history, is primarily due to the enormous effect which it now has on nature, and also due to our greatly increased knowledge of the problem. However, that is not all. It is equally important that our present-day situation is frequently viewed *as* a problem. The smoking chimney has changed from a symbol of progress and redevelopment to a symbol of environmental pollution, a source of emission which must be cleaned. Vaclav Havel sees the chimney that 'pollutes heaven' as a 'symbol of a civilization which renounces and denounces the natural world and is contemptuous of her imperatives'.[3] This remarkable change cannot be explained by the assumption that people used to be blind to the disadvantages, because as far as the most evident forms of environmental pollution and damage are concerned, protest against them is just as old.[4] The shift in thinking has been mainly brought about by our modern perception of a relationship between all the different environmental problems, which are no longer categorized as avoidable by-products of our social development. Many people perceive environmental problems as inherent in development, and hence it is development itself that should be the topic of discussion. In such discussion, the relationship between environment and society is described in terms of 'sustainability' and 'environmental quality', in which the negative side (unsustainable, lack of quality) is seen as the crux of the problem, and the positive side is seen as the solution, or at least as the aim (sustainable development, see the Brundtland report and the National Environmental Policy Plan, the NMP). This pair of concepts can be concretized in three ways: in time, in space and in relation to those concerned:

— in time, by taking future generations into account when assessing our present relationship with the environment. We can only speak of sustainability if our offspring are left with the same possibilities as those which we were given. It is not yet clear how we should do this, although useful suggestions have been made as far as energy, raw materials and environmental norms are concerned.[5]

— in space, by applying both concepts on a global scale, and not proposing 'solutions' which will lead to a decrease in sustainability and quality elsewhere. This is particularly relevant to developing countries.

— The parties concerned are the ever widening categories to which the concepts can be applied. Besides thinking of future generations and people living elsewhere on earth, we must especially think of nature as an entity in its own right, which should be taken into consideration.

Up to now the concept of quality has not been defined very rigorously. In government documents, it usually applies to specific requirements with which products or environmental components, such as soil, water and air, must comply. Others[6] put the interaction between society and environment into a broader perspective and use the concept of environmental quality, namely that of the quality of human life or wellbeing, and that of the intrinsic (i.e. not instrumental or individual) value of the environment and its different parts. This broader view of environmental quality brings us close to the more general concept of 'quality of life'. Even though I prefer the broader description, this raises the question as to whether the realization or maintenance of environmental quality can always be combined with the other aim: sustainability. The realization of quality, even if it is concerned with things that seem non-material, such as democracy and human rights, is not simple: it will always use finite resources. At the same time we do not believe that sustainability can be achieved by shifting the costs to future generations, to people living elsewhere or to nature. Little insight is required to see that these processes of shifting responsibility are prevalent at present. Sustainability can, however, only be realized by thoroughly reconsidering the entire concept of quality. The environmental problem touches the foundations of our western culture when defined in this way, because the western world has 'qualitatively' turned out to be exceptionally successful. This success is central both to the problem and to its radical nature.

The above description of the environmental crisis is the starting point for this chapter, and I shall now continue by asking what ideas within our culture have contributed to the crisis. I shall begin with a biological/anthropological preamble, and will then focus chiefly on elements of Greek, Jewish and early Christian philosophy. It must be noted that this emphasis on ideas, 'Ideengeschichte', is not meant to be seen as a denial or underestimation of material factors, or the 'Wirkungsgeschichte' of ideas. As far as this is concerned I agree with K. Thomas and E. Vermeersch, who both point out that a cyclic interaction of ideas can both result in, and lead to, altered material situations.[7] Furthermore, the environment does not actually suffer from ideas, but from those actions which accompany them. And the precise relationship between behaviour and ideas is not properly understood in the environmental field either.

3. COSMOLOGY

The fight for survival is one of humanity's most fundamental motives. We are not different from other organisms in this respect. However, quality of life is also important to us. It plays such an important role that a lack of quality has been seen as sufficient reason to end a life, whether one's own or someone else's, from time immemorial. The expression 'rather dead than red' has very ancient roots, and what is applicable to individuals is, to a large extent, also applicable to the society in which they live.[8] Regarded in this light, the two concepts 'sustainability and quality' can be described as an ancient pair, which do not always have to be meshed together.

Early humans needed to be aware of their surroundings and its many dangers to ensure survival. In other words, they were able to interpret and act according to what they experienced. This requires some sort of a view of nature. In order to give meaning to the concept of 'quality', it was also necessary for them to form an image of their own role and significance within their surroundings; in fact a picture of themselves and the meaning of their existence (a self-image). Both 'images' are closely related to one another, and as Zweers mentions elsewhere in this book, they are each other's mirror image.

With this we have reached the field of philosophy, via a biological/anthropological description, since the term cosmology seems to be very appropriate for this mirror image.[9] Cosmologies can thus be seen as cognitive and mental impressions, whereby people (and cultures) succeed in surviving and giving life some meaning, to a certain extent. It is conceivable that these cosmologies may be recognized and described by someone other than the subject himself. The term describes all those ideas on reality, the forces which are at work, and one's own role as a person within reality. Löwith, followed by Wildiers, believes that three quantities are of essential importance, namely God, humans and the world.[10] They call this the metaphysical trinity (see Figure 2.1). These great powers constitute the triangle forming the scope for the interpretation of reality. Zweers therefore speaks of a triangle of meaning.

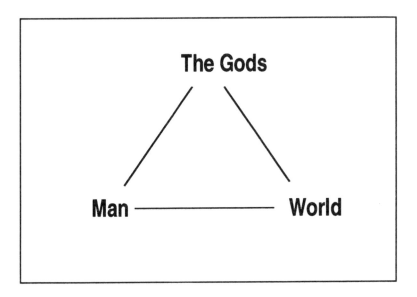

Figure 2.1. The Triangle of Meaning

An interesting observation made by cultural anthropologists is that these great powers, the actors in the triangle, can be found in almost all cultures, although there are great differences in the way in which they are presumed to work, and in the underlying relations between them. There are differences of opinion concerning the latter both between and within cultures.[11] The links are close and the actors are strongly related to one another in so-called primitive societies and in animistic societies. The whole world is full of gods, mystical forces and holy sites. The dividing line between humanity and the rest of the world is not sharp, but should be seen as a differentiation without division. Gods and humans partly coincide, for example in our ancestors. According to many researchers there is a fundamental idea about order and the meaning of existence in these societies. However this order is known to a limited extent and meaning is certainly not arrived at by linear means. Cyclic views on time dominate. The concept of reality and the grasp of reality resulting from it are seen to be of little importance. Uncertainty and dependence play a dominant part. In one aspect, the relationship with nature is one of respect and alliance, and in another it is one of fear.

It is important to note that societies with such cosmologies are, on the one hand, capable of having a sustainable (continuable for centuries) relationship with the environment. On the other hand, however, the 'quality of existence' is fairly static. Furthermore, we are inclined to define this quality as being negative, stunted and 'primitive'. This stimulates our curiosity about the cosmologies of the cultures which have influenced western civilization. Although it may be possible to distinguish animistic characteristics in our society, we tend to turn to Jewish and Greek culture.[12] The general opinion is that Jewish beliefs have had a major influence on our society via Christianity, while Greek beliefs have been of influence via Rome, the Renaissance and humanism. Without wishing to contend with this general image, the following sections will aim to demonstrate that our present ideas concerning the environment can more realistically be called Graeco-Christian than Judaeo-Christian in some salient features. This refers to the suggestions made by Passmore, who disagrees with White.[13] For clarity, both roots will be dealt with separately in the following sections. We will begin with the Greeks.

4. THE DOMINANT GREEK COSMOLOGIES

The millenium of Greek philosophy, a period which officially ended in 529, when the emperor Justinian closed the last ancient philosophical schools in Athens, is supposed to begin with Thales of Miletus, the oldest of the so-called Ionic nature philosophers (sixth century BC). Thales and the other nature philosophers also marked the beginning of a western scientific culture, which can be seen as a break with the past. Their thought and practice may be summarized as follows:[14]

— They gradually abandoned mythical presumptions and developed fundamental criticism of the priests' cults. They began to study 'this' world.

— They started wondering about the world, looked for coherence and tried to reduce everything to one explicative principle, the first cause (the *arche*, a word which means origin as well as dominion). Control lies in understanding and in explanation.

— They saw the *logos* (reason, the word) and logical argumentation, language and mathematics as outstanding human characteristics.

— They based their arguments on observation and even more so on thought. Knowledge is acquired by the exercise of reason. Revelation and old traditions lost ground as sources of knowledge; they sought a rational explanation for the whole cohesion of things.

Compared with the 'primitive' culture of the previous section, it is noticeable that under this new dispensation reality was now thought to be intelligible and recognizable, and that it was believed that man, with his reason, is perfectly capable of understanding reality. The Greeks expanded their philosophical systems on this philosophical-scientific basis, the most important for our purpose being the Academy (Plato), the Lyceum (Aristotle) and the Stoa.

Before looking any further at the above I would like to make a few linguistic comments on the two central concepts: *cosmos* and nature. There are two basic meanings to the word *cosmos*: (i) order, something ordered and harmonious; (ii) ornament, decoration. Both meanings can be found in the later philosophical use of the word nature (*phusis*), the basic meaning of which is 'the being', according to some philologists.[15] The root *phu* can be found in the Latin *fui* (I have been). The medio-passive *phuesthai* means 'to grow' and may be characterized as an ingressive: 'beginning to be'. The active *phuein* is causative: cause to grow, stem from. The primary meaning of *phusis* can thus be subsumed in: that which stems from, the true nature, nature. The later meaning of pre-existing nature, living reality, does not appear until approximately 450 BC. This ambivalence of the notion will recur in this study.

Plato (427-347) believes that the cosmos is a whole and complete entity, ordered by the great artisan (the Demiurge), even though the real world, the ideal image, is hidden behind its mirror image, within which we live. The theme of order – derived from, and the opposite of, chaos – is especially important in the *Timaeus*, where he expounds his cosmology. Plato was uneasy about the concept of nature, which smacked of powers of chaos and which did not correspond with his ideas on the perfect cosmos. The statement 'nature cannot teach me anything', which he attributes to Socrates, most probably originates here. In the *Phaedrus* he writes: 'You can learn from man but not from trees.' This fixation on man is not only characteristic of Plato. All Greek philosophy can justly be called humanistic in the broader traditional meaning of the word,[16] though one cannot find a narrow preoccupation with man and disdain for the other actors in the 'triangle of meaning'. In *Timaeus* we read that we are heavenly creatures; man is the only creature that walks upright, and hence the head (seat of reason) links our divine part (the immortal soul) with heaven.

In spite of Plato's orientation towards transcendental realism, the world of ideas, he had a keen eye for, and had definite opinions on 'this' world. This appears, for example, from his accurate description in the *Critias* of the function of timber and soil on slopes in the drainage of low lying areas. It is even more apparent in his view of society as described in the *Republic* and the *Laws*. In both works Plato deals with the Greek *polis*, the city state and the way in which it should be governed. Democracy does not get off lightly and he shows himself to be an advocate of aristocracy and meritocracy. However, more can be discovered in these books. In both he proves himself to be knowledgeable about several crucial parameters in the relationship between humanity and the environment, namely population size, scarcity of natural resources and the amount of arable land. Plato recommends sobriety, because wealth and abundance are obstacles to man's true happiness, the latter being purely spiritual. He does not shrink from proposing crass measures. Wise men should control the size of the population, by measures regulating sexual intercourse, and by abortion and infanticide. He is opposed to the commercial, materialistic city democracy in Athens. In his view the ideal society has an agricultural, small-scale, traditional economy.[17] In such a society nature is to Plato's liking: orderly and beneficial to man.

We find both meanings of the concept of nature in Aristotle's (384-322) cosmology. He is fascinated by phenomena such as growth and movement, and these play a central part in his philosophy. Movement is the explanatory principle, the first cause of this reality. This is why he calls the deity, who is at the origin of everything and has started everything, the 'Prime unmoving mover'. In nature, growth is a very special form of movement. Organisms develop through growth, they grow towards their destination, towards 'what was already there but had yet to emerge'. He uses the term *entelechie* to describe this (i.e. carrying its aim within itself). The aim (*telos*) of an organism, is therefore also the driving and determining force of growth. Nature has an aim which is realized by virtue of her nature, her character.

Aristotle was just as convinced of order in the cosmos as was Plato. However, he concentrated rather more on nature itself and less on the deity, its origin. Nature itself works in the same way as Plato's 'great artisan' who established order. He believes that growth, movement and change result, not in something unpredictable, but rather in a functional, hierarchical, ordered whole, in which everything has its own fixed place, purpose and meaning. 'Nature does nothing in vain' is a characteristic phrase of both Aristotle and his student Theophrastus (a landscape ecologist *avant la lettre*).[18] Organisms and events that fit badly into his scheme of natural order and systematics are highly intriguing to Aristotle. He devotes a full size passage to the ostrich, definitely a bird, but displaying a few characteristics that are unbirdlike.[19]

Aristotle and Theophrastus are very clear about purpose and hierarchy in nature. The purpose of the plant is reproduction and the production of fruit. Wild fruit trees fail to a certain extent, because their fruit is hardly edible.[20] This indicates the order in the hierarchy: plants serve man, either directly, or indirectly through animals. Man is the ultimate purpose of the whole. Even Aristotle, who in comparison with Plato was highly knowledgeable about nature, especially wild fauna, does not mention nature's 'intrinsic value' independent of man. On the contrary, in a piece of work attributed to him, we find the following passage: 'Whenever the nature of animals reaches completeness, it becomes tame. Things that are totally complete are always tame and not wild.'[21] This is a remarkable thought, and although it cannot be found in this form in his classical biological works, it should not therefore be thought of as unaristotelian.

Aristotle's system is not limited to the animal world. People are also hierarchically ranked in the *scala naturae*, with the Greek philosophers at the top and the slaves and barbarians somewhere right at the bottom. Aristotle believes that slaves are naturally meant to carry heavy loads. This is why nature has equipped them with broad and strong shoulders. This is why we are not only *allowed* to treat them as slaves, but in fact *should* treat them as such, to allow them to achieve their own *telos*, their natural destination.[22] This is the first time that we see nature introduced as a norm for ethics, a notion that was to be developed into the principal proposition of the philosophers of the Stoa.

The philosophers of the Stoa derive their name from the arcade in which they used to meet and teach. It is customary to distinguish three groups in chronological order:

— The older Stoa (approximately 300-150 BC), including Zeno, Cleanthes and Chrysippus.

— The middle Stoa (150-50 BC), including Panaetius, Posidonius and Cicero.

— The Late or Roman Stoa (25 BC to approximately 180 AD), including Seneca, Epictetus and Marcus Aurelius.

The typically stoic drift of thought is one that was fed from different sources, given the long period of time and the number of thinkers involved. Zeno, the founder, and Chrysippus were the most original thinkers, but it is mainly Cicero who shaped and disseminated their ideas. Stoic philosophy has been of great importance, even though authors have varying opinions on this matter. Hahm is the most outspoken: 'for half a millennium Stoicism was very likely the most widely accepted worldview in the western world... it appealed to all classes... it left its mark on Christianity'. Green is more diffident in his estimation of the influence of the Stoics.[23]

The philosophers of the Stoa saw the world as an orderly and logical entity. The *logos* plays a key role in their cosmology and has religious characteristics. Because man also has a *logos*, he is able to get through to the divine, the *logos* which controls the cosmos. With his *logos* he may actually collaborate with the divine *logos*, but at the same time the *logos* is the unique instrument for increasing one's knowledge of the divine. Like all philosophers, the Stoics asked themselves what the relationship was between 'good' and 'nature', and they phrased a clearcut answer to this question: a good life is life in accordance with nature. Cosmos, good and nature merge in their philosophy. However, when considering 'life in accordance with nature' nature must also be read emphatically as humanity's own nature. According to their teaching, people are primarily driven by the urge towards self-preservation, and therefore attach most importance to that which is most familiar and most related (*oikeion*). The question of the relationship between people and also that between humans, animals and plants – a question that Aristotle and others also concentrated on – was given moral status by them. Aristotle and Theophrastus saw many similarities between the different forms of life and also between humans and animals. Of course, people were logical beings that could easily be distinguished from the *a-loga*, the irrational beings, and the hierarchy within nature was clear, but these philosophers did not enter these findings into a closed ethical system. The philosophers of the Stoa did just that. Objective, biological data of relatedness (the *oikeiotes*) are differentiated from the perception, the feeling of relatedness (the *oikeiosis*). The latter extends to everyone via those nearest to you, your own body, your offspring and family. It is this principle that determines the ethical boundaries. No *oikeiosis* exists with animals as irrational beings, and this is why animals fall outside the moral community.[24] Thinking in terms of moral circles has its roots in the Stoic doctrine of relatedness, even though they can be said to have a very clear system: a sharp division between human and non-human, but moral equality among people. They had a full human circle, including women, slaves and barbarians, a remarkable phenomenon in that world, even though it was of little practical consequence. They were primarily interested in man; they had a 'philosophy of humanity' but no 'philosophy of nature', although nature is a recurring theme. The Stoic doctrine that the cosmos is meant for humanity, is in total agreement with this.[25] Their belief was shared by almost all the philosophical schools and led to fierce debates about the use (to humans) of the fly. The lower orders derived their right to exist from their function for the higher. Anything present on earth, of necessity, had to be useful for something, eventually for humans. Nature does nothing in vain, without a purpose.[26]

The most important characteristics of the cosmologies discussed here are given in Figure 2.2.

5. JEWISH COSMOLOGY

The heading of this section immediately poses several questions. Jewish cosmology? Who are these Jews? If we take them to be the writers and characters of the Old Testament,[27] the second question to arise is: did they have a cosmology? The word cosmos does not even occur in Hebrew, and philosophical reflections on such an abstract concept are definitely not Jewish. The Old Testament (OT) speaks in terms of concrete objects such as the sun, moon and stars but the general word 'nature' is not even found. The world is described as a creation and the Creator is spoken of as a person. Hence 'the Old Testament view on creation', might have been a more appropriate heading. However, I have chosen the term Jewish cosmology, firstly because the word Jewish keeps cropping up in later literature in combinations such as Judaeo-Christian; a second and more important reason is that it is possible to find a cosmology in the OT in as far as it is possible to find a coherent image of the three great actors in the triangle of meaning. A few aspects will be elaborated on in the following.

a. The world as God's creation. One of the central themes of the story of creation in Genesis 1 is that of order and chaos. God orders the chaos with his works of creation and drives back the powers of chaos. Everything is given its own purpose at a fixed time, in a clear sequence. The second story of creation (Gen. 2,4-2,25) depicts man and his 'helpmate suitable for him' living in harmony with creation, as cultivator and keeper of the Garden.

b. This belief in creation marks a clear break from the animism of the nations surrounding the Jews. The world has been made by God, but the world itself is not divine. For man this means that nature or natural objects should not be worshipped, and that everything should be seen as the result of God's creative power.[28] The belief in creation also contrasted with the Greek belief in that there is a very personal image of God and because of the distinction between God and creation. Greeks, such as Proclus and Plotinus, thought in terms of an 'emanation', an outpouring of the divinity into his handiwork. To the Jews nothing is inherently holy, neither sun, tree, nor person, but everything is related to the holy, or rather, the Holy One. Everything created by God is morally relevant, although not always to the same extent, as we will see below.

c. The image of the world is theocentric rather than anthropocentric. The belief that the world has been created for humanity, and that the use and value of all things is vested in use and value to humans, does not agree with the OT. The week of creation does not end in man, but in the sabbath. In the OT there is evidently a relationship between God and non-human creation. A well-known example is the so-called rainbow covenant in Genesis 9, where it says that God enters into a pact not only with Noah, but with 'all that lives, every living soul'. In the Psalms creation sings God's praise. It also happens the other way round: God enjoys seeing his creation and playing about with it. These are all relationships in which humans have no role, or which have no direct bearing on them. They seem to be independent links in the triangle of meaning, which is now beginning to look more truly like a triangle.

d. Man is a unique creation, who has been given a separate position which is in many respects above the other creatures. The fact that man has been created in 'God's image', is not only of imaginable, but also moral importance. It will be far from easy to find in the OT the notion that man is simply 'an organism', one in a long line of evolution.

e. The God of creation is a God of history. This is a continuing history and not one of ever recurring cycles. This view of linear history implies the idea of development and progress: the expectation of a better world is pervasive. This is related to the following point:

f. Creation was originally good and complete. However in the eyes of the author of Genesis 3, the original harmony of creation is disrupted by the Fall. This disruption is not lasting, and it is promised that the rift will be closed. In the end harmony will be restored in an act of re-creation.

I believe that the complex and pluriform ideas about humanity and nature found in the Hebrew bible can be understood using the perspective of threefold creation. This can be imagined as a triptych. The depiction in the story of Genesis of the creation before the fall forms the left side, and the prophetic, eschatological images of the re-creation form the right side. The people of Israel in the OT, the world as we know it, is found on a significantly larger panel in the middle.

It is unmistakable that the bible attributes far-reaching consequences to the Fall as far as the relationship between humans and nature is concerned. The partners are at odds with each other, hostility increases and death and chaos emerge. The world becomes a savage place. Harmony has disappeared and the few passages dealing with re-creation concentrate on the non-harmonious aspects of the human-animal and the animal-animal (!) relationship.[29] Essential elements of the lost order in paradise return in the image of re-creation. There is no return to paradise itself – what else is the origin and meaning of the image of the new city, the city of God? – but there is a restoration of the relationships, of the wholeness of creation. Apart from the difficult question as to how creation actually took place, or will take place, it is beyond doubt that this triple perspective of creation was present in the minds of the bible writers, and that they wrote and acted in accordance with this image.

To make this clearer, we shall need to look more closely at the rules governing the relation with God, with one's fellow men and with creation. These rules are found in Jewish ethics, the torah, or the Law. They depict 'dualism': they rule for the present, although they refer to God's intentions for this world on a higher level; they function in a world where chaos and death seem to prevail. They do this firstly by keeping society 'livable', and secondly by emphasizing that chaos and death do not and ought not to form the basic pattern in creation. This is why there is a 'Sabbath rhythm' in OT legislation. Legislation made it possible to recover from exhaustion in life, in the social order and in the relationships that have gone awry, after a period of '6 + 1'. This is the case after 6 days on the normal Sabbath of everyday activities, after 6 years in the Sabbatical year for all that happens on the land, and after 6 + 1 Sabbatical years, the fiftieth year is a jubilee year in which social order is restored. This Sabbath rhythm is not so much concerned with peace, as with the consecrated restoration of relationships, and with wholeness. It is remarkable that agricultural and domesticated animals are emphatically included in this Sabbath rhythm. However, this was to be expected: in those times surrounding nature and the forces of nature might turn into fatal powers. The desert and drought were not just geographical phenomena, but were regarded as forces of chaos. Against this background it is not difficult to appreciate the importance of livestock for the pastoral patriarchs, and the importance of fruit trees and crops for the sedentary Israelites. It will also be evident that generally, domesticated nature and 'wild' nature are looked at in different lights. This is a difference with moral overtones, or more precisely a difference arising from the religious view of creation. Furthermore, a prevailing idea is that domestication is closer to the real meaning of creation than wildness.

M. Jacobs has attempted to categorize the many – 702, according to him – biblical references to animals. He indicates significant differences in the appreciation of domesticated and 'wild' animals. For example, the former appear to be mentioned more often in relation to wealth, whereas wild animals tend to figure as metaphors. In his study *World and Counterworld* Houtman also emphasizes that to the Israelites domesticated 'nature' has a totally different moral charge from nature that has not been cultivated. He uses the phrase 'Janus face' for 'wild' nature: sometimes mentioned in a positive, lyrical sense and sometimes in a very negative and shocking sense, as a curse threatening chaos.

In her study *Purity and Danger* the anthropologist Mary Douglas has linked the concepts of 'pure' and 'impure or polluted' to this theme of order and chaos.[30] She gives a novel and plausible interpretation of the food laws found in Leviticus 11 and Deuteronomy 14. In these chapters the animals are distinguished into clean and unclean, and sometimes criteria are given concerning the grounds on which the classification should be made. However in the majority of the cases the criteria are either lacking, or not very logical. Especially the long list of unclean animals which must not be eaten has long been a puzzle for interpreters of the bible, since they could not make sense of such an arbitrary enumeration.

A central element in Mary Douglas's explanation is the term 'holy', which often appears as a 'reason' (do this ... *because I am holy*) in the chapters mentioned. Holy is that which is in the greatest possible agreement with God's intentions, because he is the personification of holiness. It refers to wholeness, completeness and 'unadulterated', purity. The 'order of creation' is derived from this notion. The criteria used to categorize the animals, reflect the fundamental order of creation, and the story of creation. They concern:

— Killing or not killing of (other) animals. This important criterion is tested twice by looking at rumination (a proof of vegetarian food habits) and at cloven hooves (uncloven hooves supposed be a possible weapon in intraspecies fights).

— Being adequately equipped for the domain in which one feels at home. Wings for the air, fins and scales in the water and feet for land. All this ensures proper movement: flying, swimming and walking or jumping.

— Being 'whole' and without faults.

Everything that smacks of being mixed, of thwarting the 'barriers of the system', is unclean. It can even be an abomination, because there is further subdivision within the categories of both clean and unclean, a sort of moral order. For example, sacrificial animals must meet the strictest requirements, because they come closest to the most holy. This is in sharp contrast with the dead, to be regarded as the most unholy. This regulation of a ritual in which animals are killed clearly demonstrates the dualistic nature of the torah. The dietary laws and the purity laws continually remind Jews of the more profound dimensions of the relationship between man and nature.

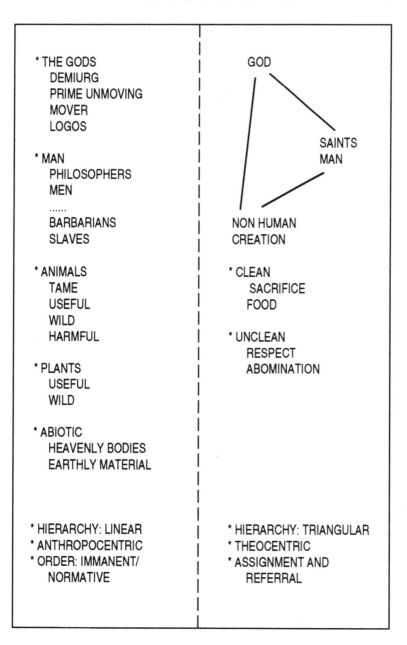

Figure 2.2. Left: Greek Cosmology; Right: Jewish Cosmology

Another interesting aspect of man's understanding of nature can be found in the OT wisdom literature, especially in the book of Job. Job struggles with the question of his suffering, which he thinks he is having to undergo for no good reason. His friends each have their explanations, but these do not convince Job. Finally God appears, speaking in a whirlwind or tempest, and chapters 38-41 offer a theology of creation in poetical images of unprecedented splendour. Nature in its entirety is reviewed, beginning with abiotic phenomena, and Job is continually asked: Can you do this? Have you made that? Do you understand how that works? The implicit answer seems to be: no, this is far beyond the wisdom of Job. Only the Creator understands this, and now and then it would seem that even he himself has difficulty understanding everything. The problem of human suffering seems to be related to the question of who rules, but not in the way that Job's friends think. Their logic was relentless: Job must have sinned, or else God would not have tolerated his suffering; if Job had not sinned God would definitely have been able to prevent the suffering. Is God not almighty after all? Chapters 38-41 suggest that the real answer to that dilemma appears to lie in nature, of which man has such inadequate knowledge, and in which forces are at work which man does not understand at all. The beauty of creation, its harmony and coherence, and on the other hand its mysteries and its sheer power, seem to conceal the answer to Job's questions, questions to which his friends could only offer the wrong answers.

Comparing these considerations with the Greek ideas, we can make the following comments on Jewish cosmology (see Figure 2.2). The Jews see creation as an ordered whole, which humanity has disrupted. In the end, creation is not there for our sake but for the Creator. One can speak of a definite hierarchy within the triangle of meaning, but it is a real triangle since not everything revolves around humanity. Humans do play a very special part and are made aware of their responsibility. The order of creation is not a static piece of information, but an assignment telling everyone to strive after a better, re–created order. Forces of chaos will not figure in this re-created new world.

6. EARLY CHRISTIAN COSMOLOGIES

Christianity developed from Judaism in a Greek climate. The first and most exemplary source is the New Testament (NT), which along with the OT forms the dogma, the Holy Scriptures of the Christian church.[31] This section firstly deals with a few details from the NT, in which we note different emphases in the gospels on the one hand and the letters of Paul on the other.

The early Christian explanations of the OT as given by the Church Fathers will then be considered.

The New Testament

In the NT we read relatively little about nature and the relationship between humanity and nature. This is not so very surprising. The NT is about the life and teachings of one man, Jesus of Nazareth, and not about the history of a nation on their way to the Promised Land, which we find in the OT. The time span in which the books of the NT were written is much shorter than that of the OT, only a few decades. The following points are important in our argument.

In comparison with the somewhat legalistic ideas of the Jewish clergy of his time, especially those of the Pharisees and scribes, Jesus recalls the original meaning of the law, the torah and the prophets. He does not disregard the law, and instead wants to fulfil it, to complete it. The law finds its fulfilment in his person, because he wants to reconcile the fallen world to God the father. Re-creation is thus made possible by him. His liberating work contrasts sharply with the restrictive literal regime of the law which the moral leaders of the Israelites had imposed. This is exemplified by Jesus's attitude towards, and his preaching about the Sabbath. Picking food to fend off hunger,[32] saving an animal and healing the sick,[33] are activities which in his eyes belong to the Sabbath, more so than the minute measures of the Pharisees. 'The Sabbath was made for man and not man for the Sabbath', says Jesus in the Gospel according to St. Mark.[34] This sounds as if it focuses on man, and so it does in as far as laws are subservient to humanity. However the phrase is not anthropocentric relegating and excluding the rest of creation. Jesus's words and deeds really resonate with the order of creation in which every organism counts –including the sparrow on the roof– but man especially so.

At the beginning of the Gospel according to St. Mark,[35] there is the story that Jesus, baptized by John, is subsequently visited by the devil in the desert for forty days. Mark ends the passage with the words: 'He was with the wild animals and the angels served him.' This preparation for his earthly activities is also characteristic of the other two great prophets, Moses and Elijah. They also spent time in the desert and were given their assignments to lead the Israelites through the desert against their own wishes.[36] The great leaders of the Israelites – Moses representing the law and Elijah the prophets and together thus representing the OT in its entirety – both act as masters of the desert to a certain extent. The desert, symbol of those forces of creation that are hostile to humanity, the habitat of devils and demons, is defied by all three. In a way they bring about a personal reconciliation with the forces of chaos in 'wild' nature and they anticipate re-creation. This is why they do not die normal deaths, they have also mastered death. Moses and Elijah are 'taken up', and Jesus 'defeats' death in the wording of the NT. Partly because of this he is able to complete the unfinished work of his two predecessors. In my opinion this analogy is a major symbol, which I shall call 'the motif of saints', because it often reappears, especially in the lives of the later saints. Very often they live in the desert and seem to have partially 'restored' the relationship with 'wild' nature. Therefore the avoidance of the world and asceticism, which are generally given as the reasons for living secluded lives, are not necessarily related to avoiding nature, let alone contempt of nature. It is worth noting that in the saints' lives the threat of 'wild' nature is lessened or is completely absent. In fact it appears that there is a re-establishment of man's moral authority over nature. Animals are blessed, but are also reprimanded and even cursed if they commit outrages against humans or other creatures.[37] This typical and peculiar saints' motif is completely different from the Stoic doctrine.[38]

If we move away from the prophets and Jesus to the rest of the NT, we appear to find more analogies with Greek doctrine. This is hardly surprising because the apostles spread the gospel in a Greek world. The Romans possessed the military power, but the spiritual climate was dominated by the Greeks, particularly by the Stoic philosophers, the neoplatonists and, to a lesser extent, the Epicureans. The apostles had to defend their new teachings against both Jewish and Greek ideas. The break with the Jews must have been both sharp and socially drastic. Thus, Peter makes it perfectly clear that he no longer observes the separation between clean and unclean animals and the eating practices and offerings related to this, after Christ's conclusive offering and the descent of the Holy Ghost at Pentecost.[39] This opened new possibilities to the uncircumcized, but caused a split between Christians and Jews in everyday life. It had become embarrassing to have meals together.

Nature is mentioned only very occasionally in the letters of St. Paul. Without regarding worldly life as low, St. Paul appears to have been attracted by the spiritual life. His opinion of marriage differs markedly from those of the Old Testament, for example in the wisdom literature and the Song of Songs. Paul was not unfamiliar with the Greek philosophies. He openly debates with Stoic and Epicurian philosophers and defends a personal God who has made the world, guides this world by His providence and will judge her by His resurrected son, Jesus Christ.[40] The eschatological notion, which was of great importance to Paul and in which he encompasses 'the entire creation in all her parts'[41] places him in the authentic Judaeo-Christian line.

Passmore on the other hand, and other authors, quote certain passages in the Pauline letters to prove that Paul, and thus the NT, began the hellenization of early Christian thinking.[42]

The Church Fathers

The hellenization mentioned above is evident in the interpretation of the Old Testament given by the Church Fathers from the second century onwards. In reaction to gnosticism and the Manichees, who discard the allegedly bad and immoral God of the OT, the Church Fathers begin theological reflection on the OT and particularly on creation. I believe that this led to important changes and sowed the seeds for a Graeco-Christian way of thinking about the relationship between humanity and nature, which diverged from the Old Testament way of thinking in various respects. Almost all the ideas mentioned in section 4 can be traced back to the Church Fathers, but rarely in an unadulterated form. Many notions are mixed and some are confused due to a lack of knowledge and scarcity of texts. This affected various Greek views, as well as Greek and Christian views. Hence Marcia Colish,[43] in a thorough study on the influence of Greek and especially Stoic philosophy on western tradition, warns against premature conclusions on influence. There may be all sorts of reasons for similarities in definitions and ideas, or a specific use of words, and these cannot be used as conclusive evidence of a line of influence without further evidence. Nevertheless there is reasonable agreement about the shifting of accents in early Christian views about the relationship between man and nature under the influence of Hellenism.

Thus neoplatonic ideas about nature and the supernatural, body and soul, begin to play an important part in the explanation and appreciation of sublunary, earthly reality. The overestimation of the spiritual also leads to allegorical interpretations of the bible and especially of the 'nature passages'. It is here that we find some roots of the belief that creation should be read and interpreted as a book, and of that particular hermeneutic tradition. Colish believes that both Augustine (354-430) and Ambrose (339-397) are particularly important links between Plato and the Christian views of later years.

Philo of Alexandria (approx. 25 BC to 50 AD) was a major force in the 'hellenizing' process of the Jewish inheritance in the early Christian tradition. The works of this hellenized Jew were a profound influence on Church Fathers such as Origen, Clemens etc. Plato's *Timaeus* is found to have a strong influence on Philo's work, especially in his interpretation of the Pentateuch, the five books of Moses, the torah. Philo has adopted the most important principles of Platonic cosmology (its rational structure, its comprehensiveness etc.).[44]

In *De Animalibus*, Philo deals with the 'great chain of being', the cosmological hierarchy and the position of animals in relation to humans. The *logos* is essential to Philo and he consequently comes up with the classical question: do animals have *logos*? Against his cousin Alexander, Philo argues that man is the only organism gifted with a *logos*, a rational spirit, a fact implying man's superiority over animals.[45] As man has been created 'in God's image', he believes that the human *logos* is comparable with the divine *logos*. Since animals are not gifted with a *logos*, there can be no virtue or absence of virtue. Ethical categories do not apply here. We clearly descry some stoical influence here. This is more evident still when Philo discusses the hierarchy in creation, the The irrational exists for the sake of the rational, and in the end everything is made to serve man.[46] A great many Church Fathers hold this belief. I think that this is an important difference between the OT and the way in which the Church Fathers read it, influenced as they were by Greek philosophy. God has created the world and all that it contains for the sake of man, man is the purpose and centre of creation. This is how the Church Fathers viewed and read the OT, and by doing so they moved, probably unwittingly, closer to the dominant Greek cosmologies, not only in their point of view but also in their line of reasoning. The church father Origen illustrates this beautifully in his defence of the writings of the heretic philosopher Celsus.[47] The latter had posed the question: 'If the world was made for man, then why is earth more hospitable to animals?' Origen says that this was all in the game, so that man should use his intellectual techniques to discover agriculture and the art of forging, and use these to provide his essential needs in life.

An important issue on which the Church Fathers are not really in concord was the question as to whether nature and the natural order might serve as a norm for human behaviour, and how this was to be related to God's order. The philosophers of the Stoa were crystal clear as regards this issue. In general the Church Fathers all took nature as a norm, but they applied it in different ways. This difference may be observed in what is usually known as the *theology of cosmetics*. The following questions arose: May a man have long hair, is that natural? May we dye clothes? If God had meant us to wear blue clothes, would He not have given sheep blue wool? etc. In actual fact this debate was never resolved, and the use of nature as a norm reappears, as we shall see below.

St. Augustine was probably the most important Church Father of the first few centuries. He believed that humanity occupies a central position in creation, albeit of limited power. St. Augustine's epistemological position is different from the Stoics, because for him 'love is the *a priori* of knowledge'.[48] Augustine's ideas of agriculture are similar to those of Plato, because he believes that agricultural man does best by taking up a dialogue with nature.[49] He believes that there is a moral aspect to the relationship with animals. This applies especially in the case of tame animals, since these live under the supervision of man. Augustine did not lack insight into human nature and reality, which we can see in the following quotation: 'Sometimes we do not know the place of animals in this world: sometimes we do, but then we value our own interests more.'[50]

Table 2.1 gives a summary of the views discussed in the previous paragraphs. Its aim is merely to visualize a few of the ideas and shifts in ideas.

7. DISCUSSION

Whenever we approach a certain question from a historical point of view, the danger exists that ancient texts and facts are imposed on our presentation of the question, and that they worm their way into our train of thought. This may be quite troublesome when problems and concepts are discussed which were never actually experienced as such, or in a different way altogether.[51]

An entirely ahistorical approach, however is possibly more dangerous. An example of this approach is the opinion that the environmental crisis is so modern a phenomenon, that history is irrelevant to its solution. Another example is the idea that there must be a total break with western culture if this world is to have a future. Both positions underestimate the factor of cultural continuity. This is why it is quite relevant to comment on the status of the cosmologies discussed here and their role in our cultural history, before discussing their relevance to the current environmental debate.

a. The colour and wealth of shades to be found in the roots of our civilization are not done sufficient justice by just mentioning a few key Greek philosophical ideas, by indicating the main drift of Jewish doctrine and by sketching the views which the early Christians may have derived from Greek philosophy, as was done in sections 4, 5 and 6. As far as the OT is concerned, I would refer to passages in the wisdom literature (especially the book of Job and also Ecclesiastes), for a view that differs from that in the *torah*. Much had to be left undiscussed. However, I believe that the main point, as sketched in the summary, remains upheld.

The Greeks held a great variety of opinions,[52] but they were not all equally influential. 'Animal friendly' authors such as Porphyry and Plutarch[53] had remarkably little influence, let alone the poet Bion and the rather obscure Xenocrates. As far as our subject is concerned, it is important that there was a certain amount of agreement among the most important schools concerning the relevant points.

Ideas/ views	Primitive cultures/ Animism	Plato	Aristotle	Stoics	OT	NT	Church Fathers
Cosmos well-ordered and good	±	+	+	+	±	±	±
Order is immanent	++	+	+	+	−	− −	±
Order intelligible and logical	−	+	+	++	±	±	±
Order hierarchical							
Man takes first position	±	+	++	+	+	+	++
Man is the purpose of the cosmos	?	+	+	++	−	−	±
Cosmos/ nature as a norm	+	+	+	++	−	−	±
Differenti-ation nature/ super-natural	−	++	±	±	−	±	±
Allegorical explanation of nature	±	+	−	−	±	±	±
Moral bonds between man and animal	+	−	−	−	+	+	±
Domesticated animals in different moral category	+	+	+	±	++	+	±
Linear interpretation of history	−	±	−	−	+	+	+

++ = the idea is of great importance
± = the idea does not play an important part/ author(s) is (are) not univocal
— = the idea is explicitly opposed

Table 2.1. Schematic survey of several ideas and their importance for each of the cosmologies discussed in the text

Van Bavel[54] has recently shown that there were more nuances in the ideas of the early Church Fathers, than had previously been believed. The value of this type of study is that it also indicates why certain viewpoints were taken, and what the context of certain statements is. Unlike the Greek philosophers, the Church Fathers were not primarily concerned with animals, or the relationship between man and animals. They dealt with the question of the goodness of creation and the place of evil, with man's free will under Providence, and in general with the position of man in relation to God and the cosmos.[55] The extinction of the lion in the Middle East, for example, was part of the historical background of their discussions and writings, but is not reflected in their considerations. The fact that early Christianity was strongly linked to, and flourished in, urban surroundings, is certainly significant.[56] All this does not disprove the fact that the specific view of the position of man's relation to nature, and of the use of Old Testament texts in Christian doctrine was influenced by the Church Fathers

b. Western culture has been marked and influenced by Christianity to a large extent, especially in the dominant cosmologies of the culture. In section 6 above it was proposed that, at a very early stage, Christianity was influenced by Greek philosophers. In this first process of hellenization, certain OT (Jewish) elements were moved to the background. However later Jewish traditions did not exert much influence either. The emancipation of Christianity from Jewish traditions was accompanied with strongly anti-Judaistic feelings. The fact that Jewish traditions lost their influence is also indicated by the fact that the Talmud and Misjnah have also left very little trace in western ideas. This loss is, to a certain extent, regrettable. A broad exchange of ideas would most probably have led to a balanced interpretation of the law and the prophets. Furthermore, Jewish tradition itself has also drifted away from the Old Testament in some aspects, making its teachings exclusively concerned with humanity.[57] Recent Jewish authors have connected this with the loss of a Jewish homeland and the unavoidable abandonment of an agricultural lifestyle. Emphasis changed, and people had to concentrate on survival.[58] In the last few decades a reorientation on these traditions has been going on.[59]

The classical authors came to the fore again in the late Middle Ages and the Renaissance. Their works were translated from Greek and Arabic into Latin and were studied in Western intellectual centres. This second hellenization process was as far-reaching as the first, because it was now connected with a science that had moved in an experimental, technological direction. Intellectual speculations could now have direct, practical consequences. This is not the context to study this phenomenon,[60] but I would like to mention one characteristic example. It is the famous/infamous debate in

Valladolid in 1550 between Las Casas and Sepulveda concerning the submission of the Indians. The common ground of the debate was the hierarchical rank of people, and the crucial question was where the Indians fitted in this christianized Aristotelian scheme and how they should be treated accordingly. Sepulveda thought they were barbarians, slaves by nature, and asked for their submission. Las Casas did not disagree with the scheme itself, but he ranked the Indians higher on the scale than his opponent did. He found the Indians to be intelligent, good-natured and definitely suitable for conversion to Christianity. The dramatic outcome of this history for the Indians is known only too well.[61]

c. In spite of various diverging and interesting undercurrents, a cosmology has developed since the late Middle Ages which may be said to be characteristic of western culture. Dijksterhuis has described this development under the very apt title: *The mechanization of the world image*. This world image may be characterized as follows:

— The world is a regulated, orderly, whole.

— The very nature of this world order is hierarchical.

— This order works mechanically and is intelligible (knowable).

— Humanity is ranked at the top of the *scala naturae*.

Science and especially natural science begins to play a more important part in the interpretation of reality. However, at that time, it is only an instrument in the search for an ultimate meaning of the cosmos. By far the majority of natural scientists believed that the study of nature and natural laws would provide us with knowledge concerning the Creator of everything. This remained the generally accepted motive for carrying out scientific studies up to the beginning of the nineteenth century. In general, the responsibility that some people felt towards a higher power ensured a certain element of prudence in interfering with creation. Despite the damage to nature, especially wild nature, occurring universally, and despite the dominant Cartesian view, this responsibility formed an ideological restraint on such despotic behaviour. Passmore shows that the image of man as the steward emerged again in this climate and is explicitly found in the seventeenth century.[62] Again, because the image of man as the 'keeper of the garden' has always been present in the interpretation of the second story of creation, which is therefore called the garden story.

The Enlightenment and the growth of secularization in the previous century, changed the climate. Man's christian belief dwindled, which left only belief in man. This paved the way ideologically towards a relationship between humanity and nature in which ultimately western man came to be all powerful, with domestic, wild and other organisms and abiotic nature on a level far inferior to him.[63] The theory of evolution did not actually affect this view: on the contrary, it seems to have given scientific backing to this attitude, despite its emphasis on the similarities between humans and all other organisms.

Peter Singer, discussing western traditions in his book *Animal Liberation*, suggests that cosmology was not discussed seriously prior to the nineteenth century. Even Francis of Assisi remained within this framework.[64] However Singer claims that there was an important breakthrough in the nineteenth century, which led to gradually altering attitudes concerning animals. His theory interprets this change as 'an extension of moral rights to animals'; the animals were admitted to the moral circle from which they had been excluded for centuries, in accordance with Stoic philosophy. Passmore[65] assesses this change somewhat differently: he interprets it 'as a restriction of human rights with regard to animals'. He means that there is growing awareness that the previously unlimited rights of man concerning animals must now be restricted. The *scala naturae* as such was not at stake, but it was believed that civilized people should treat slaves and certain animals humanely. I believe that Passmore is more realistic here. Many studies, mainly dealing with developments in England, indicate that the positive changes in the nineteenth century did not affect animals in general, but rather a special selection of animals. Keith Thomas attributes this selection to the industrial revolution, which made people less dependent on animals such as horses and dogs. This independence allowed them to feel affection which had never before had the chance to arise.[66] Other authors have also pointed out the anthropocentric, economic and selective elements of this developing love of animals: it was chiefly felt for horse and dog, and was excellently compatible with foxhunting and big game hunting in the colonies.[67] Reasonable treatment of certain domestic or pet animals is seen as an indication of civilization,[68] while the slaughter of big game in the colonies is also regarded as humane action.[69] Thus these nineteenth century developments can hardly be said to have led to real change or improvement. On the one hand people's ability to alter nature according to their wishes greatly increases and there is supposed to be a justification for submission, especially as far as wild animals are concerned. On the other hand however, we see a development tending to a humanization of relations with certain species of a domesticated nature. This development was operative within the framework of the dominant cosmology: I do not believe that there has been a fundamental change in this respect.

d. Finally, in the twentieth century three developments have taken place which call for a thorough rethinking of the dominant 'mechanistic' cosmology:

— In the first place, the belief in progress and the optimism about the basic goodness of humanity was dealt a heavy blow by the two world wars and especially by the way western civilized nations took part in them.

— Secondly, modern physics has undermined the classical ideas about the observer-independent 'facts' and the knowledge of reality,[70] while the mathematical chaos theory has shown that even deterministic complex systems may have a basically unpredictable character.[71]

— Finally, the present extent of the environmental crisis has once more drawn our attention to the disturbed relationship between humanity and nature, and to the necessity of finding new bearings in this respect.

Although it is widely recognized that these three developments imply the intellectual and moral collapse of the dominant cosmology, it is hard to say what the consequences for a new cosmology will be. The central questions which then arise are: will there be a completely new cosmology, and linked to this: how radical should the departure from tradition be? Three different approaches may be distinguished in the current thought.

The first and most radical is the idea that the new cosmology should be looked for and will be found completely outside the western tradition. Attention is mainly focused on the Far East. This seems to me to be a rather poorly considered suggestion. There are certainly many attractive elements in oriental thinking,[72] but I believe that adopting a cosmology from a tradition which has developed separately from ours in the course of several thousands of years is virtually impossible. A cosmology cannot be compared with a coat which can be put on and taken off just like that.

The second trend is that of the radical ecophilosophers. The 'Land Ethic'[73] and the 'Deep Ecology' movement[74] which developed from it, are the most important representatives. They concentrate not so much on other cultures and not explicitly on the past, but are seriously trying to develop a new type of cosmology. They feel that a fundamental change of direction away from the past is necessary. It appears to be an environmental philosophy which breaks new ground.[75] The most remarkable break with the past concerns the position of humanity. An appeal is made for equality of all life, favouring one species above another is called 'speciesism', comparable with other reprehensible '*isms*'. This is a new idea within our society. Our insignificance, our supposed modesty, are ideas that one can find alongside notions in which humanity is seen as almost godlike, for some reason or other; however, the idea that we are not different from non-human beings is definitely new, and is in distinct contrast to prevailing opinions in our culture. The Deep Ecology movement also calls for a different concept of science, with a synthesis between physics and metaphysics. It finds this synthesis in ecology, and transforms it into a kind of world view. The laws and concepts found in the science of ecology assume a moral dimension in this approach: they are regarded as important for society. Difficult choices can be made by using concepts such as wholeness and diversity. This may be seen as a partial repetition, or rather expansion, of the discussion on the hidden prescriptive character of ecological concepts which took place in the Netherlands in the 1970s. The fundamental criticism then was that factual descriptions are often mixed with normative statements. This often happens unwittingly. The slogan that human behaviour should 'fit in ecologically' is a relic of that period. This expression has now been replaced by the aspiration to 'sustainable development' in Dutch governmental policy.

However, the break with the past is less complete than is sometimes suggested.[76] Radical ecologists also include traditional themes in their approach, even though they do not do this explicitly and are most probably not always aware of the fact. Thus the Aristotelian concept of *entelechy* is found in their concept of 'self-realization'. Whereas Aristotle used this concept to describe what appeared to him to be the true power of nature and used it only partially as a norm for human behaviour, the opposite is true of the radical environmental philosophers. The Stoa also used nature as a norm, but in an adapted form. The philosophers of the Stoa believed that 'life in accordance with nature' was a life in accordance with 'the human belief and ideas of how nature is working and in harmony with itself'. The deep ecologists, however, believe that 'nature knows best' and that ecology reveals to us what nature demands of us. I have used the word 'reveal' to stress the fact that ecology takes on religious importance. The definition and use of the term 'intrinsic value' in the writings of radical ecologists reminds us of a religious approach to nature. It is a revival of animism which has always been with us to some degree or another. In it, the intrinsic value of nature is a godlike greatness found in nature and in natural phenomena. It would seem to me that one of the conditions for a fruitful environmental philosophical debate is recognizing this religious character. Apparently there is felt to be a gap in the corner of the triangle of meaning, within cosmology, where God used to be. In the company of radical environmental philosophers we witness the development of a cosmology that is an unlikely combination of animism and stoic ideas. It is remarkable because Greek ideas about nature are used as norms, which are then mixed with a completely different concept of humanity. In my view, humans and their special responsibility, especially for this world, are not always recognizable in that combination. It is significant that extreme advocates of bioegalitarianism in North America have been accused of 'ecofascism'.[77] Even though I find this accusation far too strong, there is undeniably tension between a strictly ecocentric view, and upholding and protecting certain human values. Besides that it is certainly questionable whether a cosmology that relies heavily on an animistic and fairly static view of natural order has sufficient vitality and is capable of giving satisfactory answers to the questions we face if we attempt to give meaning to the concept of quality in its broadest sense.

In the third school reorientation takes place on the basis of an explicit, specific search into the past. The researchers will inevitably have taken individual and partly subjective positions, but this is not an obstacle to public discussion. Various attempts have already been made.[78] I believe that the use of valuable elements of Jewish cosmology as mentioned above could be fruitful for this reorientation. I would present by way of example the recognition of the 'intrinsic value' of creation, of the rhythm of Sabbath for the quality of life and the differentiation of the concept of 'nature'; all these elements may be used as a basis of an environmental ethic.[79] I would also mention the immanent, referential character of the present order of creation, an order which invites admiration and study, but which may never have the final say. Responsibility and hope are important here. Anyone who rereads the philosophical literature, equipped with a modern physicist's stock-in-trade will admit that there is less new insight to be gained than we used to believe: the fundamental limits to human knowledge were already known to Job. And not only to Job: this knowledge can also be found in ancient philosophy.[80] The most important lesson which our historical survey may produce will most probably be modesty, a modesty which humanity will badly need in dealing with the environmental crisis.

NOTES

1. For a more detailed explanation of the concepts social and scientific in relation to environmental problems see: Boersema et al.(1991:section 1).
2. For good reviews see: W.L. Thomas (1956) and Simmons (1990).
3. Havel (1990: p..89).
4. Van Zon (1991).

5. Opschoor & Van der Ploeg (1990); Reijnders (1990).

6. Opschoor, in: CLTM (1990: pp.101-103); NWO research program *Sustainability and Environmental Quality.*

7. K. Thomas (1983: p. 301); Vermeersch (1990: p. 17)

8. To a certain extent, because the environmental crisis has also confronted us with the fundamental differences between individual and collective action. We will not go into this in this chapter.

9. I use the word 'cosmology' because of the meaning of the Greek words from which it was derived and furthermore because I find the term 'world image' to be too superficial, and the terms 'religion' and 'metaphysics' carry too many overtones.

10. Löwith (1967); Wildiers (1988).

11. Glacken (1967).

12. I use the term Jewish with reference to the modern English-language environmental literature in which Jewish thought, Jewish tradition etc is spoken of. A generally accepted and relevant differentiation between Ancient Hebrew and Jewish is beyond the scope of this chapter. The word 'culture' is used to refer to written cultural expressions, i.e. the philosophical and religious literature.

13. Passmore (1974: p. 17); White (1967).

14. The following authors on Greek philosophy are used in this compilation: Armstrong (1947); De Vogel (1967); Guthrie (1965); Bos (1991); and Diogenes Laertius.

15. I am indebted to professors Holwerda and Radt who drew my attention to this development in meaning. A comprehensive discussion of the word *phusis* can be found in Holwerda's thesis (D.Holwerda, diss. RUG, Groningen, 1955).

16. Greek anthropocentrism and humanism were often full of religious meaning and of responsibility for one's fellowmen and for the world. Hence the sophist Protagoras' ('man is the measure of all things') fate: his books were burnt since they were thought to be irreligious.

17. Koolschijn (1990) characterizes Plato's opinions about the ideal society using the term 'green dictator': this sounds like a surprisingly topical description. The question remains as to whether Plato is not strait-jacketed into a modern position.

18. Theophrastus, *De Causis Plantarum,* II, 1, 1.

19. Aristotle, *De Part. Anim,* IV, I3, 14.

20. Theophrastus, *De Causis Plantarum,* IV, 4, 2

21. Filius (1989:165).

22. Aristotle, *Politics,* I, 1254b-1255a.

23. Hahm (1977: introduction p xiii); Green (1990: chapter 36).

24. Cicero, *De Finibus,* III, 20, 67; see also Brink (1956).

25. Cicero, *De Natura Deorum,* II, 133.

26. Aristotle, *De Caelo,* I, 4, 271a33.

27. Obviously the Old Testament cannot be seen as a uniform source. Each book has a specific character but there is a general division into torah (the five books of Moses, also known as the law) prophets and the writings.

28. A very good example of this can be found in Psalm 19,2 which says: 'The heavens declare the glory of God.'

29. The most distinct passage is: Isaiah 11, 1-10.

30. Douglas (1966) and in more detail: Douglas (1972).

31. A canon fixed and accepted in the first few centuries. The OT at the end of the first century, the NT on the Councils of Hippo (393) and Carthage (419).

32. Matth., 12,1-8.

33. Luke 6,6-11 and 13,10-17: Mark 3,1-6.

34. Mark 2,23-28.

35. Mark 1,9-13.

36. Moses: In both stories the mountain of God, Horeb, is mentioned and in the story of Elijah, the period of forty days and forty nights compares with the account of St. Mark.

37. A.o. Helène Nolthenius (1988: p.139,167 c.f.)

38. Traditionally, the idea that the harmony between man and animal might be re-established has always been present, for example with the Church Fathers (e.g. Irenaeus, Adv Haer V 33, 3-4, who refers to Papias in his description of re-creation) and with Luther (see Pelikan 1961).

39. Acts 11,1-18.

40. Acts 17,15-34.

41. Romans 8,18-30.

42. A.o. by Passmore (1974: p.16 and note 44).

43. Colish (1985).

44. Runia (1983).

45. Runia (1983) calls this idea 'in line with Biblical and Judaic views', but feels that Philo defends himself with arguments derived from the Stoics. I myself am not so sure whether having a logos and obtaining 'dominion' are in fact biblical. The relationship between logos and the image of God is possibly even more dubious. I believe that Philo rightly falls back on the 'real' source.

46. Terian (1981: p. 45) and SVF II 1152-1167.

47. Origen, Contra Celsum IV, 76. It is not inconceivable that Celsius has borrowed the question from Cicero, who allows Velleius to define it (*De Natura Deorum,* I,9,23).

48. An idea which was launched again quite recently by for example Scheler; see also Kockelkoren's contribution to the present study.

49. St. Augustine, *De Gen. ad Litt.,* III, 18, 27-28.

50. *De Civitate Dei,* XI, 16 and XII, 4; On the Church Fathers also: Van Bavel (1990).

51. Phrases like 'The bible is loaded with ecology' (Hans Bouma) and 'The bible is a green book' (Roel van Duyn) are suspect for this very reason. Francis of Assisi has also been 'ecologized' in such a way that little remains of the medieval mystic and saint. See Nolthenius (1988) and especially Sorrell (1988) for a far better view on him.

52. A Russian author once gave the following advice: 'Start your lecture with the Greeks and you will be able to keep it short.'

53. Plutarch is the most original. Especially his *Moralia* containing essays on the cleverness of animals and the consumption of meat are well worth reading. These works are within the Greek humanist tradition. Montaigne was strongly influenced by Plutarch. Perhaps Pythagoras was the only real dissident. Unfortunately none of

his writings survived.

54. Van Bavel (1990).

55. And not only the Church Fathers, it also seems to be the case in the *Corpus Hermeticum*, a gnostic religious paper which was most probably written in Alexandria in the first century, and in which Jewish, Greek and Egyptian influences can be recognized. See ibid. (1991: Introduction, pp. 13-27).

56. For a historical sketch of the world in which Christianity originated see: R. Lane Fox.

57. For this point see: Schwarzschild (1984)

58. Freudenstein in: Konvitz (1972): he now believes the time is ripe for a 'deeper understanding and acceptance of the concern for the environment evinced by the Jewish tradition', p. 274.

59. Landmann (1959); Cohen (1959); Konvitz (1972); Stein (1980); Ehrenfeld and Bentley (1985).

60. I refer to Van Dijk, (see this book) and to Van der Pot (1985); Glacken (1967); Dijksterhuis (1950) and Thomas (1983).

61. For a detailed account of this debate and its historical context see: Lemaire (1986: p. 77).

62. Passmore speaks of a persistent but never very strong line in western tradition which may date back to the works of the neoplatonist Iamblichus (Passmore (1974: p. 28).

63. Marx believes, for example, that as a result of the decline in religious belief in society, nature 'simply becomes an object for mankind, purely a matter of utility', Marx's Grundrisse, published by D. McLellan (ed), (London 1971: p. 94).

64. Singer (1975, revised edition 1990, p.198).

65. Passmore (1975: p. 217).

66. This is a paradox which we can still recognize. Today it also appears that the love of nature tends to increase the more nature is endangered, and the less it is seen as a serious factor in economic policy.

67. See a.o. Harwood (1928); Pollock (1968); Harrison (1973); Thomas (1983); Ryder (1989) and Ritvo (1990).

68. Darwin also writes in this vein. In *The Descent of Man* he says that humans have only recently acquired a sense of humanity for animals, since savages do not as yet have this characteristic. (2nd ed. 1889, part 1, chapter IV, p.123). He refers to the North and South American Indians, who are thought to have lived in such harmony with nature.

69. Besides the *Saint motif* which has been discussed above, there is a so-called *Herculean motif* here. The Greek hero Hercules had to carry out ten nearly impossible labours. In some of these he beat mythical wild animals that were thought to be invincible. Although the original story was strongly mythical, it was used to justify the extermination of presumably dangerous predators in later ages. According to Carcopino (1955), the slaughter that went on during the ancient circuses disgust us now, but they had one use: the emperors cleared their territory of wild animals. The lion disappeared from Mesopotamia, the tiger from Hyrcania and the elephant from North Africa. Carcopino concludes: 'The Roman empire has passed on the benefac-

tions of Hercules to civilization, via the *venationes* and the amphitheatre' (vol.II p.126).

70. Prigogine and Stengers (1985)

71. Gleick (1988); see also Tennekes' contribution in this volume.

72. See for example, Dwivedi and Tiwari (1987) for a summary of Hindu opinions.

73. The name was coined by Aldo Leopold in his classic work of 1949.

74. This is definitely the most influential school, especially in English speaking countries; see Naess (1973); Devall & Sessions (1985) and especially Goldsmith (1988).

75. Taylor (1984: p. 160) for example speaks of 'nothing less than a revolution in our ordinary ethical vision'.

76. Zweers consciously follows this double track, in his contribution to this book, but it shows a radical break with present day ideas.

77. See Nash (1989: p. 155) for an evaluation of this controversy.

78. Reijnders (1984: chapter 10); Opschoor (1989).

79. Such ethical ideas are very similar to Stone's (1988) 'Moral Pluralism'.

80. For example the Roman humanist Seneca: 'We do not know everything, because the greater part of the universe, God, remains hidden to us'; *Naturales Questiones* VII, 30,4.

REFERENCES

References throughout the text and notes to classical authors are to the editions in the Loeb Classical Library, W. Heinemannn Ltd., London/Harvard University Press, Cambridge Mass, unless indicated otherwise.

Armstrong, A.H. 1947/1981. *An Introduction to Ancient Philosophy*. University Paperback reprint 1981, London, Methuen & Co. Ltd..

Arnim, Ioannes Ab. 1903. *Stoicorum Veterum Fragmenta* (4 volumina). Lipsiae in Aedibus B.G. Teubneri MCM III.

Bavel, T.J. van 1990. 'De Kerkvaders over de Schepping', *Tijdschrift voor Theologie*, jrg. **30**, 1: 18-34.

Boersema, J.J.et al.(eds.) 1991 *Basisboek Milieukunde* 4e druk. Meppel, Boom.

Bos, A.P. 1991. *In de greep van de Titanen Inleiding tot een hoofdstroming van de Griekse filosofie*. Amsterdam, Buijten & Schipperheijn.

Brink, C.O. 1956. Oikeiosis and oikeiotes: 'Theophrastus and Zeno on Nature in Moral Theology', *Phronesis*, 1: 123-145.

Carcopino, J. 1955. *Het dagelijks leven in het oude Rome*. 2dln. Utrecht/Antwerpen, Prisma boeken Spectrum.

Cicero, *De Natura Deorum*

Cicero, *De Finibus*

CLTM, 1990. *Het Milieu: denkbeelden voor de 21ste eeuw*. Commissie Lange Termijn Milieubeleid. Zeist, Kerckebosch BV

Cohen, N.J. 1959. *Tsa'ar Ba'ale Hayim - The Prevention of Cruelty to Animals: Its Bases, Development and Legislation in Hebrew Literature*. diss. Cath. Univ. of

America. Washington D.C., The Catholic University of America Press.

Colish, M.L. 1985. *The Stoic tradition from antiquity to the early middle ages.* two volumes. Leiden, E.J. Brill.

Corpus Hermeticum, 1991. Ingeleid, vertaald en toegelicht door R. van den Brink en G. Quispel, derde herziene druk. Amsterdam, Pelikaan; Baarn, Ambo.

Darwin, Charles, 1889. *The Descent of Man, and selection in relation to sex.* second edition, revised and augmented. London, John Murray, Albemarle Street.

Deval, Bill and G. Sessions (eds.) 1985. *Deep Ecology.* Salt Lake City, Peregrine Smith Books.

Dijksterhuis, E.J. 1950. *De Mechanisering van het wereldbeeld.* Amsterdam, J.M.Meulenhof.

Diogenes Laërtius 1989. *Leven en leer van beroemde filosofen.* vertaling R. Ferwerda en J. Eykman. Baarn, Ambo.

Douglas, M. 1966. *Purity and Danger: An analysis of concepts of pollution and taboo.* London, Routledge & Kegan Paul.

Douglas, M. 1972. 'Deciphering a meal', *Daedalus,* 61-82.

Dwivedi, O.P. and Tiwari, B.N. 1987. *Environmental Crisis and Hindu Religion.* New Delhi, Gitanjali Publishing House.

Ehrenfeld, D. and Bentley, P.J. 1985. 'Judaism and the practice of stewardship', *Judaism,* **34**: 301-311

Filius, L.S. 1989. *Problemata Physica Arabica.* (2 dln) Dissertatie, Vrije Universiteit Amsterdam.

Freudenstein, E.G. 1972. 'Ecology and the Jewish Tradition'. In Konvitz, M.R. (ed.) *Judaism and Human Rights,* pp.265-75. New York, W.W. Norton & Company inc.

Fox, R.L. 1986/1989. *De droom van Constantijn. Heidenen en christenen in het Romeinse Rijk 150 AD-350 AD.* vert. Anki Klootwijk, Amsterdam, AGON BV.

Glacken, C.J. 1967. *Traces on the Rhodian Shore: Nature and Culture in Western Thought from Ancient Times to the End of the Eighteenth Century.* Berkeley/Los Angeles, Univ. of California Press.

Gleick, J.1988. *Chaos, de derde wetenschappelijke revolutie.* Amsterdam, Contact.

Goldsmith, E. 1988. 'The Way: An Ecological World-view'. *The Ecologist,* **18**, Nos 4/5: 160-185

Green, P. 1990. *Alexander to Actium.* London, Thames and Hudson.

Guthrie, W.K.C. 1965. *A History of Greek Philosophy.* 4 vols. Cambridge, Cambridge Univ. Press.

Hahm, David E. 1977. *The Origins of Stoic Cosmology.* Ohio, Ohio State University Press.

Harrison, Brian 1973. 'Animals and the State in nineteenth-century England', *Engl. Hist. Rev.* **88**(349): 786-821.

Harwood, Dix. 1928. *Love for Animals, and how it Developed in Great Britain.* diss. Columbia Univ., New York.

Havel, Václav 1990. *Naar alle windstreken,* Baarn, de Prom.

Jacobs, Milton 1977. 'Animals and God-Man-Nature in the Old Testament', *Jewish Journal of Sociology,* **18**, 2: 141-154.

Konvitz, M.R. (ed.) 1972. *Judaism and Human Rights*, New York, W.W. Norton & Co Inc.

Koolschijn, G. 1990. *Het democratische beest. Plato's tegenstander.* Amsterdam, Bert Bakker.

Landmann, Michael 1959. *Das Tier in der jüdischen Weisung.* Heidelberg, Verlag Lambert Schneider.

Lemaire, T. 1986. *De Indiaan in ons bewustzijn: de ontmoeting van de Oude met de Nieuwe Wereld.* Baarn, Ambo.

Leopold, Aldo 1949. *A Sand County Almanac.* Oxford/New York, Oxford Univ. Press.

Löwith, K. 1967. *Gott, Mensch und Welt in der Metaphysik von Descartes bis zu Nietzsche.* Göttingen.

Marx, K. *Grundrisse*, D. McLellan (ed.), 1971 London.

Naess, A. 1973. 'The shallow and the deep, long-range ecology movement', *Inquiry* **16**: 95-100

Nash, Roderick Frazier 1989. *The Rights of Nature. A History of Environmental Ethics.* Wisconsin/London, University of Wisconsin Press.

Nolthenius, Helene 1988. *Een man uit het dal van Spoleto. Franciscus tussen zijn tijdgenoten.* Amsterdam, Querido.

NWO, 1991. *Duurzaamheid en Milieukwaliteit, voorstel voor een NWO prioriteitsprogramma.* Den Haag.

Opschoor, Hans 1989. *Na ons geen zondvloed, voorwaarden voor duurzaam milieugebruik*, Kampen, Kok Agora.

Opschoor, J.B. & van der Ploeg, S.W.F. In: CLTM, 1990, 81-124.

Origen, *Contra Celsum*

Passmore, J. 1974, *Man's Responsibility for Nature. Ecological Problems and Western Traditions.* London, Duckworth. 2nd ed. (1980).

Passmore, J. 1975. 'The Treatment of Animals', *Journal of the History of Ideas*, **36**: 195-218.

Pelikan, J. 1961. 'Cosmos and Creation: Science and Technology in Reformation Thought', *Proceedings of the American Philosophical Society,* **105**, no. 5, Philadelphia.

Plato, *Timaeus and Critias.* Transl. Desmond Lee. Harmondsworth, Penguin.

Plutarchus, *Moralia,* XII.

Pollock, N.H. 1968. *The English Game Laws in the Nineteenth Century.* diss. Johns Hopkins Univ., Baltimore, Maryland.

Pot, J.H.J. van der 1985. *Die Bewertung des technischen Fortschritts, eine systematische Uebersicht der Theorieën.* 2 Bände, Assen/Maastricht, Van Gorcum.

Prigogine, I. & Stengers, I. 1985. *Orde uit Chaos, de nieuwe dialoog tussen de mens en de natuur.* vertaling M. Franssen en M Morreau Amsterdam, Bert Bakker.

Reijnders, L. 1984. *Pleidooi voor een duurzame relatie met het milieu.* Amsterdam, Van Gennep.

Reijnders, L. 1990. 'Normen voor milieuvervuiling met het oog op duurzaamheid', *Milieu* **5**,1990/5: 138-140

Ritvo, H. 1987/1990. *The Animal Estate, The English and Other Creatures in the Victorian Age.* Harvard, Harvard University Press/Harmondsworth, Penguin.

Runia, D.T. 1983. *Philo of Alexandria and the Timaeus of Plato*. Dissertatie, V.U. Amsterdam.

Ryder, R.D. 1989. *Animal Revolution*. *Changing Attitudes Towards Speciesism*. Oxford, Basil Blackwell.

Schwarzschild, S.S. 1984. 'The Unnatural Jew', *Environmental Ethics*, **6**, no. 4: 347-362.

Simmons, I.G. 1990. *Changing the Face of the Earth, Culture, Environment, History*. Oxford, Basil Blackwell.

Singer, P 1975. *Animal Liberation A new Ethics for our Treatment of Animals*. New York, Random House. (second edition, 1990)

Sofisten 1986. *De mens, maat van alle dingen, fragmenten uit de Griekse Sofistiek*. Ingeleid en vertaald uit het Grieks door R.Bakker. Kampen, Agora editie, Kok.

Sorrell, R.D. 1988. *St. Francis of Assisi and Nature*. *Tradition and Innovation in Western Christian Attitudes toward the Environment*. Oxford, Oxford University Press.

Stein, G. 1980. 'Das Tier in der Bibel: Der jüdische Mensch und sein Verhältnis zum Tier', *Judaica* **36**: 14-26 and 57-72.

Stone, C.D. 1988. 'Moral Pluralism and the course of Environmental Ethics'. *Environmental Ethics*, **10**: 139-154.

Stone, C.D. 1987. *Earth and other Ethics: The case for Moral Pluralism*. New York, Harper & Row.

SVF: see: Arnim

Taylor, P.W. 1984. 'Are Humans Superior to Animals and Plants?' *Environmental Ethics*, **6**: 149-160.

Terian, A. 1981. *Philonis Alexandrini De Animalibus: The Armenian text with an introduction, translation and commentary*. Chico, California,Scholars Press.

Theophrastus, *De Causis Plantarum*.

Theophrastus, *Historia Plantarum*.

Thomas, W.L. Jr. (ed.) 1956. *Man's Role in changing the Face of the Earth*. Chicago, University of Chicago Press.

Thomas, K. 1983. *Man and the Natural World, changing attitudes in England 1500-1800*. London, Allen Lane.

Vermeersch, E. in: CLTM, 1990 17-40.

Vogel, C.J. de 1959. *Greek Philosophy: A Collection of Texts with Notes and Explanations*, 3 Volumes, Leiden, E.J. Brill.

Vogel, C.J. de 1967. *Theoria, studies over de griekse wijsbegeerte*, Assen, Van Gorcum & Comp. NV.

Vogel, C.J. de 1968. *Het Humanisme en zijn historische achtergrond*. Assen, Van Gorcum & Comp. NV

Wildiers, M. 1988. *Kosmologie in de Westerse cultuur*. Kapellen, DNB/Uitgeverij Pelckmans/Kampen, J.H.Kok.

White, L. 1967 'The Historical Roots of our Ecologic Crisis'. *Science*, **155**: 1203-1207.

Zon, H. van 1991. 'Milieugeschiedenis', Hoofdstuk 6 in: Boersema, J.J. et al.(eds.) 1991.

Chapter 3

THEOLOGICAL-ANTHROPOLOGICAL REFLECTIONS ON THE ENVIRONMENTAL ISSUE

Paul van Dijk

1. INTRODUCTION

Up until recently the complex of environmental problems was seen as a mainly scientific-technical problem which could be solved using scientific-technical solutions. However it is now recognized that the environmental issue can be categorized using at least three interwoven levels:

a. the scientific-technical level;

b. the political-social-economic level;

c. the level of collective and individual human consciousness.

It is becoming increasingly more apparent that we cannot keep abreast of the high speed of environmental destruction by healing symptoms as they occur ('kurieren am Symptom'). Besides all the necessary technical, economical and political measures, and regarding just these, it is of great importance to ask ourselves something about human nature. Hence the anthropological and ethical question, what is our experience of ourselves facing the reality surrounding us, and what are the basic motives for our activities? Many of these elementary basic attitudes are determined by religion; in our context they are closely related to the cultural tradition of European Christianity.

In order to understand the present life-threatening crisis which we face, we should become aware of the route which has led us into this crisis. A cultural-historical analysis of the hidden and often suppressed factors which have played a role in the development of our attitude toward surrounding reality may be of use.

2. BIBLICAL ROOTS

It is impossible to avoid involving Church and theology in this relationship, because the fundamental attitudes that have contributed to the ecological crisis have biblical roots: the paradigm of man as 'master of nature' (the so-called 'dominium terrae') originates from a biblical line of thought as in Psalm 8:7 and Genesis 1:26 where God commands man to 'rule'.

The historian Lynn White Jr.[1] believes there to be a direct relationship between the ecological crisis and the Christian attitude towards nature. He sees Christianity as the most anthropocentric religion in the world, especially in its western form. In contrast with ancient paganism and the Asian religions, it has not only introduced dualism between humanity and nature, but has also emphasized that God's will is done when humans exploit nature for their own purposes.

If one allows the biblical information[2] to sink in, it must be concluded that nature in Israel is indeed made available to be used as the field of human activity in imitation of the creator. In contrast to the original mythical understanding of life, in which nature as a totality of divine forces and powers was feared and honoured, in biblical thinking it is stripped of its sacred and demonic powers and is made available for humans and their life on earth. It is exactly in this availability that nature should be respected as God's creation and should be hallowed and guided towards its destiny by man as partner and bearer of God's image.

3. THE DE-DEIFICATION AND DESACRALIZATION OF NATURE

It is often pointed out that western science and technology would have been unthinkable without this de-deification of nature[3]; nature is admirable but not venerable. Even though other factors play a role, it is not going too far to state that the Christian belief has helped to develop the religious conditions for humanity's continually increasing control of nature.

However, the *dominium terrae* makes humans responsible for the non-human creation; it does not provide them with unlimited power of disposal. The modern creed that the world is merely material for human activity is not biblically founded. Moreover a dominion which consists merely in the ruler taking pleasure from and making use of his subjects, is unthinkable in the bible. 'Ruling over' always has the added meanings, 'being available for', 'being concerned about'.[4]

Finally the biblical belief in creation does not mean only a distinction between God and the world and between humanity and nature. It also means solidarity between God and the world, and partnership between humans and their fellow creatures. For example, the perspective in Genesis 2 can more readily be seen as geocentric than as anthropocentric: man as the 'servant and guard' of the garden of earth, in order to let it be 'eden' (i.e. sweet). In this context it must be noted that in a culture in which nature is experienced as being almighty and threatening, the orders to 'subject the earth' and to 'control the animals' can be seen as emancipating appeals. Now that the balance of power is reversed and nature has been domesticated and has almost collapsed under human rule, a continual repetition of these commands will not do. Considering that the present age, including its problems (in this case, ecological problems), forms the hermeneutic horizon within which texts are read, all the emphasis should now be put on the other side of the coin: the relative independence and value of nature.

The above process could actually be called a desacralization of reality. This desacralization is different from sacrilege; biblical belief does not put an end to all holiness. God's holiness not only has a desacralizing effect on what we believe to be holy, it also has a sacralizing effect on what we see as freely available property. It is noticeable that in the Old Testament things, places, people and the nation itself, etc., participate in the holiness of their Creator and are therefore also seen as holy: they are sacred. They are holy, not because they contain special qualities for which they deserve adoration, but because they are devoted to God: He has given them a special status, reserving them for special service and testimony. Humans must not violate things which are dedicated to God.

These 'holy' places, times, things and people serve as models for the whole. The special manner in which we have to deal with the things dedicated to God is meant to act as a model for our whole way of life and our interaction with reality. Nothing is holy in itself, sacrosanct, forcing us to our knees, but everything is related to sanctification, so that we are answerable for our dealing with things and people.

In conclusion one could say that from a biblical point of view, we should not propagate a romantic attitude towards nature (and its conservation) as a standard for all human activities: nature is not a law for us. Quite the opposite: cultural work and human technology belong to our assignment regarding nature, because of God's justice and the expectation of the Kingdom of God, which embraces all creatures. With this end in view, humanity has been appointed as steward and manager.

'Cultivating and guarding' (Genesis 2:15) which can also be translated by 'serving and watching', defines the barriers on two sides: both on the side of an ahistorical and irresponsible romantic attitude towards nature and on the side of overweening human pride through which we abuse our God-given freedom by misunderstanding nature's integrity as God's creation and by sacrificing it for our own dubious self interest.

4. Historical Anamnesis

In the historical anamnesis one can distinguish according to Liedke[5] and Howe[6] between the following stages (incomplete and therefore not quite fair to the historical complexity):

The old church, which, through its neoplatonic/stoic concentration on the individual, weakens the power of the biblical *dominium terrae* by interpreting Genesis 1:26 mainly as the domination of reason over affects (symbolized by animals) and the body (symbolized by the earth). This ascetic-monarchic tradition suppressed for the following thousand years the possible consequences which lay in the biblical 'desacralization' of humanity and the world.

Late medieval nominalism. At this time fundamental decisions were taken of which the consequences still affect us. Greek science was activated by its synthesis with the christian belief in creation in the direction of changing the concrete material world. From now on logic and mathematics were used in striving not only towards 'pure knowledge', but towards control of the world. According to Howe[7] theology paved the way for this decisive change in direction. A concept of God was created by late medieval nominalism in which the absolute freedom of divine will and, related to this, a divine arbitrariness bound by no law, obtained the last word. This image of God rapidly provokes an analogous understanding of man, who now develops the wish to freely dominate the world and tries to realize his arbitrariness as an ultimate law. Howe's fundamental hypothesis states that from generation to generation man grows towards the image of God or a surrogate god whom he worships. Human explanations of the world often unconsciously confer expression on this image.

Francis Bacon, in a typical reversal of the biblical sequence (firstly recovery of God's image in man and then of *dominium terrae*) sees the knowledge of nature as a challenge to try and win back the domination over the world which was lost through the Fall, using the instruments of scientific knowledge ('knowledge is power').

Descartes. His definition of men as 'maîtres et possesseurs de la nature' indicates the similarity in thinking between modern science and the scheme of early capitalism: the controllers of nature must also be its owners.

Here the objectivation of nature is complete: the total separation of the two substances, *res cogitans*, the thinking man, and *res extensa*, the rest of the world The result: separation of subject and object. This leads to a loss of reality, a one-dimensional experience of reality, which shifts multidimensional experiences to the sidelines.[8]

Marx can be interpreted as having greater insight into the exploitative relationship between humanity and nature: human work is the category which mediates the 'metabolism' between humanity and environment. In this way the rigid dualism between humanity and nature can be overcome, humanization of nature and naturalization of humanity go hand in hand. Exploitation of nature can be interpreted as a sign of alienation. However, there are still grounds for maintaining that Marx did not manage to break effectively through the overruling western rational-empirical basic attitude.[9]

The neomarxist **Ernst Bloch**[10], who takes up the themes of the young Marx and works them out further, opposes the purely mechanical view of nature in which qualitative values have disappeared. In contrast with the 'Stotz-und-Klotz-materie' view of mechanistic natural science (which sees nature purely as dead material, consisting of particles which bump into each other or cluster together) he speaks of nature as a subject.

Others[11] emphasize the utilitarian nature of our culture: we do not assess reality according to its intrinsic value but according to utility and efficiency. Compared with the general autocentric perception in which everything is viewed according to its expected usefulness, J. Weima proposes the allocentric perception, in which the intrinsic value and quality of the object is honoured.

5. PARTICIPATION AND CO-OPERATION

In relation to the above and especially to Howe's initiative, it is interesting to draw attention to Moltmann's recent analysis in his ecological doctrine of creation,[12] where he links the social trinity doctrine to an ecological creation doctrine. As long as God is considered to be the absolute subject, the world must be seen as the object of his creation, maintenance and salvation. The more transcendent God is considered to be, the more the world should be understood as being immanent. Because of the monotheism of the absolute subject, God continually became more and more unreal and the world more and more secular. As bearers of God's image on earth, humans consequently have to understand themselves as the subjects of knowledge and intention, and to see the world as object. If we do not consider God to be the one, absolute subject, in a monotheistic fashion, but look at him in a trinitaristic way as the unity of Father, Son and Holy Ghost, then we can no longer view his relation to the created world as a onesided dominant relationship, but should see it as a manysided community relationship. The knowledge of nature then becomes more participatory than objective.

Liedke[13] proposes to release the biblical *dominium terrae* from the fatal exploitation model, to do it justice by using a co-operation model. Co-operation implies that operation on nature, including technological work, will remain necessary, even in the future. However, nature should be taken seriously as a real partner in this work. Co-operation involves amongst other things, great intensification of the ecological balancing mechanisms; if the partner is better known, the reactions will also be estimated more accurately.

The conflict between humanity and nature has become asymmetrical, especially because of the development of science and technology; it has been brought to a head because nature is barely seen as a conflicting partner any more, but purely as dead material which can be used by humanity without reserve. The recognition of nature as a party in the conflict is the first step in the ecological interpretation of the *dominium terrae*. The next step is to strengthen the underlying partner, nature, by looking for protective mechanisms.

Co-operation also means that socioeconomic values such as increase in production, economic growth and increase in consumption must be replaced by values such as respect, sobriety and 'self-constraint with a view to nature conservation'. However, in appealing for sobriety, it must not be forgotten that one must have enjoyed considerable affluence in order to agree with sobriety.

In Holy Communion (in which the elements of nature and culture, bread and wine, are signs of eschatological salvation) the church possesses an – often forgotten – model of co-operative contact with reality. The hope for an eschatological reality of the reconciliation between man and nature can give hope for co-operative behaviour in the present.[14]

NOTES

1. White, Lynn, Jr 1967.'The historical roots of our ecological crisis', *Science* **155**: 1203-7.
2. Liedke, Gerhard 1979. *Im Bauch des Fisches. Oekologische Theologie.* Stuttgart/ Berlin, Kreuz Verlag; van Dijk, P 1985. *Op de grens van twee werelden. Een onderzoek naar het ethische denken van de natuurwetenschapper C.J.Dippel.* Den Haag, Boekencentrum pp.186 ff.

3. I have argued and documented the cultural historical relevance of the thesis elaborately in van Dijk, 1985 *Op de grens van twee werelden*, pp. 191 ff.

4. Liedke, op. cit., pp. 63 ff. and 91 ff.

5. Liedke, Gerhard, 'Von der Ausbeutung zur Kooperation' in Weizsäcker, Ernst von (ed.) *Humanökologie und Umweltschutz*..

6. Howe, G 1971. *Gott und die Technik. Die Verantwortung der Christenheit fur die technisch-wissenschaftliche Welt*. Hamburg, Furche Verlag.

7. See Heinz Eduard Todt's introduction in Howe 1971, *Gott und die Technik*, p. 23.

8. See also Weima, Jan 1981. *Reiken naar oneindigheid. Inleiding tot de psychologie van de relgieuse ervaring*. Baarn, Ambo.

9. Duintjer, O.D. 1972. 'Produceren en andere wijzen van mens-zijn. Een kritisch onderzoek naar uitgangspunten bij Marx die
liggen in het verlegende van de overheersende traditie' in his book *Wat willen wij met de toekomst doen?* Bilthoven.

10. *Avicenna und die Aristotelische Linke*, Frankfurt 1963; *Das Materialismusproblem, seine Geschichte und Substanz*; and Dijk, P. van 1978 'Ernst Bloch, leven en werk' and 'Atheïstische herwaardering van religie en bijbel', *Kerk en Theologie* **29** No 3, 229ff. and **29** No 4, 299ff.

11. Weima, Jan 1972. *Wat willen wij met de toekomst doen?* Bilthoven.

12. Moltmann, J. 1985. *Gott in der Schopfung. Eine ökologische Schopfungslehre*. Munchen, Kaiser.

13. 'Solidarity in conflict', in Roger L. Shinn (ed.) 1979. *Faith and Science in an unjust World. Report of the World Council of Churches' conference on Faith, Science and the Future*. Vol. 1, pp. 73 ff..

14. See Howe 1971, p. 234.

Chapter 4

Radicalism or Historical Consciousness: On Breaks and Continuity in the Discussion of Basic Attitudes

Wim Zweers

In what follows I will defend two positions:

— a radical reorientation in our relationship with nature is necessary;

— this is actually possible through engaging with certain elements of Western tradition.

Since my analysis will be mainly in terms of basic attitudes towards nature, I shall begin by considering these, as I have done in more detail elsewhere.[1] This will be followed by four propositions including some comments.

1. Basic Attitudes Towards Nature

In attitudes towards nature a particular conception about the fundamental structure of reality is expressed: a view or image of the world or of reality as a whole, more specifically an *image of nature*. At the same time there emerges a picture of what it is to be human: who we are, what is important to us, in short a *self image*. The image of nature and the image of self are closely related, they complement one another, one could even say that they form one another's mirror image. I discern six basic attitudes or models:

1. The *despot*, who subjects nature, if necessary by force, and deals with her at will, unhampered by considerations of morality or moderation; in present times this is the technocrat, who has unlimited confidence in technological possibilities, and for whom there are no limits to growth.

2. The *enlightened ruler*, who still reigns over nature, but who at the same time also recognizes that he is dependent on nature; in the interest of

realizing human ends he strives towards developing nature's possibilities as much as he can, but he understands that exploitation and oppression are out of the question here.

3. The *steward*, who no longer controls nature on his own authority, but manages her on behalf of the 'owner' to whom he is responsible: in the Christian variety that is God, in the secular variety, it is humanity. The tenor is conservative, the emphasis is on conservation of natural resources (i.e. the capital, the interest of which only may be utilized) and the scope is still mainly human-centred.

4. The *partner* works together with nature on the basis of equality, that is in order to realize the 'aims' of both parties as well as possible. There is a striving for integration or harmonization, of fulfilment of social functions on the one hand and of some sort of natural development on the other, both from a dynamic rather than from a static perspective. It is essential to partnership that nature's 'values' and 'interests' have now attained equal importance to those of humanity

5. The *participant*, who views nature as a totality of which he is part, not only in a biological sense, but especially in the sense that there is an experience of solidarity with nature from which he derives a meaning which is at least contributory to his self image. He participates in nature, but as an independent being with both identity and culture. He is able to participate in such a way exactly because of his special capacities as a human being (his norms and values).

6. *Unity with nature*, sometimes referred to as *unio mystica*. The individually experiencing 'me' falls away and merges into a nature which in this conception acquires an (immanent) divine character.

2. DEFINITION OF STANDPOINTS

Proposition 1 is about *anthropocentrism*:

> *The despot has been dominant in the development of western culture since the sixteenth or seventeenth century. This is one of the most important roots of the present environmental crisis, especially in its combination of exclusive orientation towards humanity on the one hand, and reduction of nature to pure factuality and instrumentality on the other hand.*

What is the basis of this view? Which presuppositions concerning images of nature and of humanity (both components of a basic attitude) are necessarily implied in it?

(i) First of all it is an attitude in which nature is seen only as a resource for humanity (instrumental value) and at the same time as a purely factual, material entity. These two are interrelated: not only does the second characteristic form the condition for the first, at the same time it is the result, the consequence of it. Descartes expressed this in his conception of nature or reality as *measurable matter* and *treatable material*.

(ii) Besides this, it is a position in which humans see themselves as the only beings that are more than a mere resource for others, that is, they are first and foremost valuable in their own right. There are many ways to formulate this idea, for example 'the integrity of the human individual', or 'the fundamental and inalienable rights of the human being'. This is often based on very specific human characteristics, such as self consciousness, rationality, morality, all of which are typical human attributes. Take, for example, Kant's well-known principle that one should never view another person only as a means to an end, a view which is generally accepted and unopposed in our culture. This can be summarized as *humanity's monopoly on values*.

The consequence of both these points is clear: a *fundamentally unique position for humanity*. In this view, humans are placed outside, that is opposed to nature, they are essentially different from nature and do not belong to her. That is the core of mainstream western philosophy since Descartes, who again gave it exemplary expression, with his distinction between 'thinking being' and 'extended matter'. This opposition of humanity and nature – one could also say this idea of a fundamental separation between culture and nature – provides on the one hand the basis for the images of nature and of humanity given above, and on the other hand the justification for our actions with respect to nature to be solely determined by human preferences. This whole complex can briefly be referred to as *anthropocentrism*, i.e. the view that everything revolves around humans because they are the only beings that have value in themselves, and that everything else that exists has value for their benefit only. This anthropocentrism forms the basis, the condition for the actions of the despot/ technocrat.

Proposition 2 is about *reformism*:

> *The enlightened ruler and the steward (often at the basis of national and worldwide environmental policy strategies) are not bringing this combination of anthropocentric images of humanity and nature to an end, and can therefore not be considered to be a sufficient answer to the environmental crisis.*

The anthropocentrism of the despot also forms the basis of reformism as this is embodied in models 2 and 3. However, it is attenuated, the sharp edges have been taken off when it comes to the effects. One can observe two aspects:

(i) First of all, there is the insight that even though we may try to control nature, we cannot do to her what we want to do: Descartes was wrong when he said that nature is like wax in our hands. Nature establishes her own conditions, she enforces her limits on us. This is the idea of *nature as a boundary condition*, a condition for realizing human aims and ends. It is in our own interest to take nature into consideration if we want to achieve our aims.

(ii) There is also the question of *accountability*, maybe to God, in whose name we manage earth, or at any rate to humanity, on behalf of which we manage earth – either spatially, i.e. on a world scale (developing countries), or in time (future generations). This is self interest enlarged to include the whole of humanity, but self interest nonetheless. The key word in this case is *sustainability*: sustainable fulfilment of human needs, and since nature forms the condition for this, it also implies a sustainable ecological balance.

These two aspects, that of a boundary condition and of accountability, together form the basis of reformism. One can find it in the Brundtland Report, in the Dutch National Environmental Policy Plan, *Zorgen voor Morgen* ('Concerns for Tomorrow', a scientific document underpinning Dutch environmental policy), in short it forms the basis of most recent environmental policy. Nevertheless, it leaves the basic despotic-technocratic attitude as I have described it earlier untouched.

Proposition 3 concerns *radicalism*:

> *A radical change in basic attitude is necessary, which is described in the partner and participant approach. It is 'radical' because human monopoly on values and the fundamental opposition between humanity and nature have been broken, and nature is seen as a realm offering among other things possible meaning and sense to human life.*

If it is true that despotic-technocratic behaviour forms an important root of the environmental crisis, and if it is also true that fundamental changes are necessary, then these fundamental changes must transform the very foundations and preconditions of this behaviour, not only the surface, which is all that is affected by adapting or adjusting measures from a reformist perspective. This leads to the next basic attitudes: the partner and the participant. The two essential elements of this radicalism are:

(i) *Breaking the human monopoly on values*, by at least recognizing that there exists something like a *value in nature itself*, that is, that nature is not exhausted by her value for humanity but that she can also have her own 'aims', aims which will continue to be present even if humans are not involved in it in any way. This element is emphasized in the *partner model*: here nature makes her own contribution independent of ours, and there is a revaluation, an *ap*preciation of nature even beyond her significance for humanity, though without the implication that humanity and culture should have to undergo a *de*preciation.

Equality of aims (some people would perhaps speak of 'harmony') is essential for partnership, which by definition concerns *two* entities. Thus there has to be something of nature's 'self', her own interest, her intrinsic value, since otherwise it is impossible to speak of the equality which is the basis of partnership. And, if it is a truly 'own' value of nature which is at issue – of individuals, species or ecosystems in their entirety – then this should not only be applied to 'higher' animals, for example, for in that case it is clear that human criteria are being used as the starting point, not nature's own. Instead, each animal, each organism should be looked at according to its own nature.

(ii) *Breaking the opposition between humanity and nature*, by dispelling the notion that humans are placed fundamentally outside nature. This is emphasized especially by the participatory attitude. Participation here is no longer confined to a material and biological character, as is the case in model 2, in which nature acts only as a boundary condition, whereas humanity's essence is found on the immaterial level of culture, that of meaning and sense, norms and values, where there clearly can be no question of participation according to this viewpoint. In the basic attitude of model 5, however, participation is expanded from the biological level to the level of meaning and sense. There is an *experience* of solidarity, not merely knowledge of a material connection. This experience is something from which a meaning can be derived that is contributory to what could be meant by 'human–ness'.

Hence the human self image changes: most important is that we no longer stand outside nature, but belong to her. However, it is not only our self image that has changed, but also our image or concept of nature. There is a rejection of the modern philosophical, Cartesian concept of nature, nature as that which '...includes everything except man, and that which obviously bears the mark of man's handiwork' (Passmore). It is replaced by what I would like to call an *'ecological concept of nature'*: that which organizes and maintains itself and which includes everything, including man. 'Ecological' as a term of reference now includes not only the biological world, but also cultural, social and human relationships.

To summarize, the following essential elements of the radical vision can be distinguished: the partner brings the element of nature's autonomous value into view, the participant maintains this element and expands the perspective into an experience of solidarity with nature, which is thus recognized as having her own value. Hence autonomous value of nature and solidarity with nature form two sides of the same coin: solidarity is unthinkable without autonomous value. Both elements are lacking in the two basic attitudes which together constitute reformism (proposition 2), as is also the case in the despotic-technocratic model which has already been presented as an important root of the environmental crisis (proposition 1).

There is one more thing deserving attention in a discussion of the radical alternative: *rejection of anthropocentrism does not have to lead to (radical) ecocentrism*, insofar as one understands the latter to mean the subordination of humanity to nature. Firstly, as has already been said with reference to the partner model, mutual attuning ('harmonization') of nature's interests and human interests does not need to mean subordination of the latter. It is not a 'zero-sum game' any more than would be the case in partner relationships between humans. It can mean, however, that we have to restrain ourselves, that we have to set limits to ourselves, but even then our interests and aims will play a full part in the weighing process.

There is another, perhaps more fundamental consideration, in this case arising from the participation model. The experience of solidarity, participation on the level of meaning and sense, is a specific human ability: it is one of our characteristic capacities which allows us to 'belong to nature' in this way. Other natural beings know of participation on a biological level only: this level is also applicable to us, but we are capable of more. This leads me to a sort of paradox: thanks to that which differentiates us from other natural beings, it is possible for us to belong to nature in a more encompassing way than the merely biological, at least if we choose to do so. That means at the very least a subordination or neglect of what is human. On the contrary, this is full participation as a human being, with the identity of someone who is in possession of human norms and values.

Participation as a human being also means that one strives towards one's own aims, with the help of science, technology and rationality. This perspective of participation is in no we hostile towards these human capacities or towards the enlightened self interest which they support. However, there is a very important limiting factor: these specifically human aims must not be a last resort, or obtain an absolute character, but should always be embedded in the encompassing notion of participation, which places them in a limiting framework.

Such pursuit of one's own ends, not in an absolute way but from a participatory position, could be called pursuing from within, in contrast to controlling from without. Other natural beings also pursue their aims from within, by definition, so to speak, because they belong to nature. But in the case of humans, we can say that if we place ourselves outside nature with respect to meaning and sense, following the fundamental misconception of a great deal of modern western philosophy, the pursuit of our ends will attain an absolute character: it will become a pursuit through domination from outside, which will lead to the destruction of nature. Therefore, the alternative does not have to be at all incompatible with our enlightened self interest, the latter is only restricted. One can see, then, that the recognition of nature's intrinsic value, together with the realization that we belong to nature, is a way of restricting the pursuit of our own aims. It is an idea which lays a sort of minimal condition for what may and can be done to nature, just as is the case in relationships between humans. One could also say, 'Noblesse oblige'.

Proposition 4, finally, is about *tradition*:

> *Radicalism as interpreted above does not have to mean a rejection of western culture. While duly acknowledging all the differences, it can quite well be viewed as a return to certain elements of 'premodern' thinking, where the world is conceived of as an organized and meaningful entity in itself, within which humans occupy a specific place and which forms the basis for their understanding of themselves.*

I use the word 'premodern' to refer to that mode of thought which understands the world or nature to be a 'cosmos', i.e. an organized and meaningful entity in itself, which is subjected to 'spiritual' principles. Exactly because nature and spirit had not yet taken up such sharply opposed positions, it was possible for man, also a spiritual being, to take part in that world, and therefore to have insight into it on more than just a material, biological level. This concept of nature has been totally lost in modern thought: the spiritual is concentrated in humanity and only the material has been left for nature, and that is the core of the present day concept of nature, which makes it impossible for us to relate to nature in any other way than from the outside.

However, there is also another very different tradition present in western cultural history, a tradition that has indeed had a rather low profile for the last few centuries, with all that that implies of extremes or distortions, but which in the distant past has actually known classical and generally accepted articulations. Now, I agree, of course, that there is at least *some* truth in the traditional view of Greek thinking as the precursor of modern rational-empirical consciousness, but maybe it is also useful to look at its other side, and not to reduce this to what modern Enlightenment thinking could put it to its own advantage. At any rate it is possible to consider another view, at least in a complementary, corrective way. I refer to Löwith[2], who calls Greek thinking 'cosmotheological': man understands himself within the framework of the world, albeit not in the modern sense of the term, but an immanently, divinely ordered world, a cosmos, i.e. an order existing by and on behalf of itself, neither created by a transcendent God outside it nor imposed in a dominating manner by humanity in conflict with it. Human destiny is therefore to achieve a harmonious concordance with this order, especially by way of actions whose fulfilment is found within themselves: contemplative, reflective, even 'aesthetic', and not interfering, transforming, converting to man's sole will. Finally, that this is a possibility at all may be seen as a privilege of humanity, which may indeed be placed within this order, but which nevertheless finds itself in a privileged position within this whole.

This is easily interpreted as a description of the participation model proposed above, and this is what I have in mind when I say that ecological radicalism has historical roots. What in my opinion truly has no tradition, is rather the modern, mathematical-mechanistic-technocratic world view: this is almost literally 'without example', not only from a historical but perhaps also from a geographical–cultural point of view. According to Löwith, this modern world view has been fostered and made possible by Christianity since Augustine, particularly in its characteristic moving towards the self-experience by humanity of an exclusively transcendent God, and the renouncing of the world, which in this way becomes something unimportant, something accidental: 'ein Uebriges', as Löwith says. Humanity thus no longer understands itself from the perspective of the world as described above, but rather from that of God, and the world disappears beyond any horizon of sense or meaning. Without this latter development, the idea of placing humanity outside the world, which is so typical of modern thinking, could not have originated. When, along with the process of secularization, God himself finally disappears beyond the horizon too, human self experience is left as the only basis for both self understanding and a world view. From now on humanity is able to understand itself and the world from hit own standpoint only.

It seems to me that ecological radicalism is now once more trying to include the world in the 'triangle of meaning'. However, this does not have to conflict with a renewed understanding of God in any way:[3] beginnings have already been made in both creation theology and process theology.

Neither need this occur at the expense of humanity. Quite the contrary, it is not a matter of *choosing between* the three realms of meaning 'Gott, Mensch und Welt' (Löwith): in the end we need them *all* for a truly human existence.

NOTES

1. Zweers, W. 1989. 'Houdingen ten opzichte van de natuur' (Attitudes towards nature), *Heidemijtijdschrift*, **100** no.3: 74-80. A fuller treatment can be found in chapter 1, 'Attitudes towards nature', of a book I am preparing. (A 52pp. manuscript of this chapter has been completed in Dutch.)

2. Löwith, K. 1967. *Gott, Mensch und Welt in der Metaphysik von Descartes bis zu Nietschze*, pp. 9-24 .Göttingen, Van den Hoeck und Rubrecht; also Needleman, J. 1975. *A Sense of the Cosmos: The Encounter of Modern Science and Ancient Truth*, p. 22. New York, Dutton.

3. A somewhat fuller treatment can be found in Zweers, W. 1987. 'Christendom en ecologisch perspecteif' (Christianity and the ecological perspective), *De Ronde Tafel*, **17** (Aug/Sep): 34-41.

Chapter 5

THE LIMITS OF SCIENCE

Henk Tennekes

1. THE CONVERSION OF A METEOROLOGIST TO ECOLOGY

Sometimes one wonders if the bureaucrats at the Dutch Ministry of Environment will ever learn. On a train trip to Rotterdam a few years ago I noticed a massive billboard by the side of the railway saying 'Does the greenhouse effect still leave you cold?' The marketing technology of Coca Cola and Peter Stuyvesant is being used to sell computer forecasts on the evolution of the world climate. Apparently we need Beelzebub to exorcise the devil, and the methods of Madison Avenue to defend our environment.

I had just read somewhere that the train costs 1 Megajoule per passenger kilometre. By doing some calculations (1 Joule is 0.24 calories) it was possible to work out that my return journey, Zeist-Rotterdam, cost approximately 33,000 kilocalories of energy, an amount which a human being can live on comfortably for two weeks. It seems that we are willing to sacrifice much to remain mobile. The Netherlands is one large urban sprawl which pretends to be country. Our railways are a metro above ground. Today we have a meeting in Rotterdam, tomorrow we have to go to a congress in Nijmegen, while we have appointments in Amsterdam and Groningen next week.

There I was travelling through the 'Green Heart of Holland' in the train, pleased that our urban planners have left some nature for us to enjoy. Nature? The Dutch have no idea what the term means. The Green Heart of Holland is a rainy grass desert, the sewage dump of the bioindustry. Compared with the concrete jungles that we are used to, this seems to offer welcome breathing space (as long as no liquid manure is being spread), but it is also a landscape suffering under human exploitation. Years ago I took an American friend of mine for a trip along the river Rhine as it winds its way through the grasslands of Holland, in order to give him an impression of the Dutch countryside and the beautiful skies, made famous by the works of artists such as Ruijsdael. I remained silent, hoping that the clouds, the silence and the spaciousness would have the same effect on him as it does on me. Once we had reached one of the most beautiful stretches known to me, my friend asked: 'What is the name of this canal and when are we going to reach the river?' Dutchmen have learnt to appreciate the beauty of rivers confined by dams, canalized by civil engineers. We would not dream of leaving a river to its own devices.

It is very dangerous to treat words such as 'nature' and 'environment' as nouns. Before we know it, we speak of 'the' as we speak of cars, computers or coffee makers. Before we know it, nature and the environment have become things that can be discussed, that can be studied, for which policy can be made where necessary, that can be moulded to one's wishes. Before we realize it, we consider the straitjacket of a river to be a beautiful example of nature, and before we know it we are appreciative of the bureaucrats who saved the green heart of Holland.

Sometimes everyday language can be very precise. The word 'nature' can mean the nature surrounding me, as well as my own nature, my character. If I look at a cloudy sky, I see an image of myself, made by myself in some mysterious way. Inner nature and outer nature: both are incomprehensible to a large extent, capricious, ambiguous and unpredictable. The accessibility of nature to rational analysis, to research, to rules and regulations is fundamentally limited. Once we have restrained nature, it is no longer itself.

As a stranger in the Jerusalem of environmental philosophy, I must search for words which make my thoughts intelligible. I once came across the following definition of metaphysics: it is the threesome of philosophy, psychology and theology. If that is an acceptable definition, then I can call myself a metaphysicist. If my thoughts about nature have no counterpart in my contemplations on my own character, and if my worries about the future of our planet are not reflected in my desperation about a society so dominated by the economic-growth myth that it has become blind to immaterial values, then I would not know where to begin at all.

2. THE PREDICTABILITY OF THE WEATHER

My motivation for becoming involved in these issues is the limited predictability of the weather. During the last twenty years it has become clear that it is impossible to predict the weather more than about a week in advance, notwithstanding the projected technological progress in computers, weather satellites and prediction models. I have expounded on the scientific aspects of this matter elsewhere[1]; here I will limit myself to a short historical sketch.

Directly after the Second World War, John van Neumann developed the first computer, in Princeton. Along with his colleagues (amongst whom was the meteorologist Jule Charney) he speculated on the potential implications of his new invention. The following projects were sponsored: calculations needed for the construction of the hydrogen bomb,and weather prediction. In principle, the atmosphere can be seen as a deterministic system; it should be possible to make perfect weather forecasts if sufficiently powerful computers and sufficiently detailed observations are available.

These expectations were far too optimistic. In 1963, when large international meteorological observation programs were being promoted with promises of weather forecasts for as much as a month ahead, Edward Lorenz, a mathematician at the Massachusetts Institute of Technology who had ended up in meteorology, discovered that computer models of atmospheric circulation are unstable, and that all weather forecasts become unreliable after a few days.

I cannot deny that there has been much progress in the last thirty years. In 1960 we could predict two days ahead, if we allowed for a reasonable percentage of mistakes, while at present we can predict five days in advance, and in ten years time that may have increased to six days. However, the expectations on the maximum attainable prediction period (the so-called 'prediction horizon') have been progressively reduced. In the 1960s there was hope that a prediction horizon of 30 days could be achieved. In 1974, when the national weather services in Europe established a joint computer centre, the official aim was ten days, but now there is a consensus that seven days ahead is the best that one can achieve, even if nearly unlimited technological resources are available. We now know that the goal formulated in 1974 is beyond our reach.

These findings can be illustrated using the increased sensitivity of computer models of the atmosphere. In the first generation of models, it took eight days before observation errors had increased to twice their original magnitude. In the second generation of models (approximately 1970) it took only three days, and nowadays it only takes one day and a half. This is because computer models are continually being improved: they are becoming increasingly complex and detailed, and can imitate the innumerable instabilities of the real atmosphere better and better. The true nature of the weather is more capricious and unstable than the best models that we can make. If we look at it this way, it is actually amazing that weather forecasts have in fact improved. What has happened is that the diagnosis of the initial state of the atmosphere, which is needed to start the calculations, has improved a little faster than the increasing sensitivity of models. But this balance will reverse within ten years: then we will have reached the limits of our technology.

3. WHOLE AND HOLY

A conclusion such as this obviously has far-reaching consequences for the preconceptions, assumptions and conventions we employ as we do research. After all, science is not purely accidental, an incident without meaning, is it? If it is true that we are reaching the limits of our skills, then what is the use of further research? And what is left of our belief in the progress of science and technology?

Perhaps I am running a little ahead of myself when I state that the limited predictability of the weather may be seen as an example of the way in which nature protects itself against the technocrats who attempt to bring it under control. One can speak of a kind of inaccessibility, of ineffability. The presence of a definite limit must have a deeper meaning.

In his latest book[2], the anthropologist Gregory Bateson speculates about the characteristics of an epistemology of the sacred. We use the adjective 'holy' when we are not allowed to tread on sacred ground, when we are not allowed to touch, when we cannot comprehend, when we cannot begin to understand. That is anathema for researchers: they cannot leave anything alone. Nothing is sacred in science. The proverb 'Only fools rush in where angels fear to tread' is seldom found in the mental baggage of scientists. In the meantime, meteorologists who were carried away by early expectations of scientific and technological progress have already been called to order. I can hear the archangel say, 'This far and not one step further'

It is not at all inconceivable that the limited predictability of weather is necessary to safeguard the integrity of the global ecosystem. I would not dare to imagine that our planet is dependent on the so-called intelligence of the human race. The integrity of the atmosphere has to be protected; it has to be kept whole. If you want to keep something whole, you must be careful with it. You must treat it as if it were holy. The atmosphere makes sure that it remains 'holy' by remaining inaccessible to human intervention. The link between 'whole' and 'holy' is very old: both words originate from the Indogermanic 'halig'. Indeed not only 'whole' and 'holy' have the same origin, the adjective 'healthy' also originates from the same stock. Health is related to wholeness; we can never completely understand how it works; and when the medical establishment cannot help us, we try to find holistic healers.

4. Metaphors

The metaphors for whole and holy which I use here can easily lead to misunderstanding. In scientific circles metaphors are considered to be cheap and noncommittal popularizations, a manner of speaking that makes decent scientific analysis impossible. In other circles, however, there is such a need for spiritual support that metaphors which manage to touch deeply felt sentiments are embraced without criticism. I would like to avoid both extremes. To me all language is a figure of speech. We evoke imagery for lack of something better. We use metaphors because of our inability to differentiate clearly between reality and our perception of it. Even within science we do not stand on firm ground. The mathematical equations used in physics restrict themselves to the tiny fraction of our perception of the world surrounding us that is amenable to calculations. Calculation is the imagery of the calculable: when this imagery becomes inadequate we have to switch to other manners of speech, to other metaphors. My pronouncements on whole and holy are not meant to close the discussion, but to open the dialogue. When my calculation skills have reached their limits I must go in search of new metaphors. This can help us in our fight against our annoying inclination towards throwing away all information that we find irrelevant. We need this characteristic to stop us from drowning in everything that we observe. Otherwise it would be impossible to make practical choices in everyday life. On the other hand, we have become so good at the suppression of new impressions that we should be thankful for metaphors which expand our opportunities for research and contemplation.

A perfect example of this issue is the continuing commotion about Lovelock's Gaia hypothesis. Lovelock considers the earth, in a manner of speaking (which is all we can manage), to be a living organism. This is anathema among the computing wizards of science, but at the same time it has practically become a religion to many others. In all this commotion, with accusations of heresy and idolatry flying back and forth, it is easily forgotten that the Gaia hypothesis is an invitation to remove our blinkers and to look at research on the health of our planet from another perspective. This is not because this perspective can claim any monopoly, but because a new way of thinking will help us in controlling our urge to narrow our perception. A new metaphor is a powerful weapon in our continuous struggle against our tendency to conceal our lack of knowledge and understanding behind dogmas and prejudices. If we humbly accept that all our speech, including our scientific knowledge, is no more than imagery, then at least we will not fall into the trap of believing that we can obtain knowledge that is independent of the metaphors we employ to codify it. If science starts from the notion that the processes by which we acquire knowledge are beyond our comprehension, then we should be somewhat less prone to making serious methodological and epistemological blunders. It is therefore encouraging that the Gaia perspective has already achieved many concrete results in research on the health of the earth's climate system. Lovelock's own work on the role of dimethyl sulphide in the homeostasis of our planet is an excellent example.[3]

5. TECHNOLOGICAL INTERVENTION

We cannot leave well enough alone. Now that our computers can forecast the greenhouse effect, we wish to take measures which guarantee that the world climate will become stabilized. We treat the planetary ecosystem as if it can only be saved through human intervention. The way in which the Dutch ministry for Waterways and Public Works administers the bird sanctuary in the wetlands of Holland's reclaimed Zuyderzee is typical of the way that the Dutch view their stewardship of nature: the water level is controlled to the millimetre, in order to make sure that each species of wader will find perfect conditions when it passes by on its annual migration, to make sure that the young willow trees drown in excess water at the right time (in order to inhibit an explosive expansion of the willow population), and that young reed plants can be grazed by migrating flocks of geese at exactly the right moment. If the stewardship of nature is left to humanity, then everything will work out all right.

Having become wiser by his experience, a meteorologist looks at speculations about the management of the global climate system from a very different perspective. Human intervention may be thought of as a desirable proposition, but a meteorologist is inclined to be rather pessimistic about the prospects of attempts to regulate the world climate. No intervention strategy can do without reliable predictions. But our prediction skills are rather limited. Meteorologists have had no choice but to become modest.

Alas, meteorology has little to offer as far as possible technological interventions are concerned. The predictability of the weather is so small that manipulation will remain an illusion. In the 1960s and 1970s, when positivistic optimism was still widespread in meteorology, several countries carried out experiments in which silver iodide was scattered on cumulus clouds in the hope that this would cause rainfall on preselected locations. These experiments were so unsuccessful that the attempts died a slow death almost everywhere. In the same period some scientists speculated on the possibility of suppressing hurricane development by exploding an atomic bomb in the eye of the storm. That did not turn out to be a good idea either, even when the release of radioactive material was disregarded. Science fiction authors continue to make up stories, for example about laying asphalt on half of Saudi Arabia, so that more rain will fall on the leeward side. Such fabrications will remain 'fiction'; 'science' they are not.

As an extension of these arguments, I suspect that it is impossible to modify the world climate by technological measures. The greenhouse effect and the gap in the ozone layer make it plain that human economic activities do not leave the climate undisturbed, but that does not imply that it would be conceivable to develop technical-scientific instruments that can be used to stabilize the climate. Drastic limits to the emission of carbon dioxide, methane and many other gases are necessary, although such actions are no guarantee for the future. We cannot mould the climate according to our wishes. That is no fatalistic statement, based on a poorly thought out ideology, but a sober prognosis, based on the present knowledge of complex systems which, just like the atmosphere, exhibit chaotic behaviour.

This issue can be made clearer by looking at the fundamental problem which faces climate research. The climate of the planet on which we live includes an atmosphere, the oceans, the solid earth and the biosphere. Each part of the system has its own dynamics; moreover, the interactions between the components have their own idiosyncracies. We rightly speak of an ecosystem: there are many cycles, many feedback systems, many interactions and there are many different phenomena. However, disregarding the enormous complexity, there is still a feeling of relatedness. How can we get to know the climate?

Nowadays scientists attempt to answer questions of this kind by making computer models of the system studied. Many scientists have become model builders, in effect designers and engineers. That is an encouraging development: there comes a time where it pays to ignore further details and to start reconstructing the interactions between the various components. However, the holistic goal of model builders is often naive: they do not sufficiently realize that a computer model will always remain a primitive reflection of reality, in spite of all attempts to simulate nature as closely as possible with larger computers and more detail. In practice a computer model always contains all sorts of tricks and empirical rules, no matter how many refinements are added. The empiricism contained in a computer model cannot be adjusted in advance; it is tuned by repeatedly checking the performance of the model against observations, until the model finally functions in a reliable way. Because of the irreversibility of the evolution of life on earth, including man's interventions, the climate is a one-time experiment. Hence the predictions of climatic models are always overtaken by the facts, regardless of how reliable the models are.

6. ILLNESS AND HEALTH

It comes as no surprise that climate models can only be of limited value. They can be useful for diagnostic and prognostic purposes, but they cannot cure all. Are there other ways of thinking which we can use to increase our insight into the nature of the problem? In the metaphor introduced by Lovelock our planet is perceived to be an organism that is made ill by the aggressive and expansive behaviour of humanity. To me this is an attractive metaphor because it refers to a complex, chaotic and creative ecosystem that contains an infinite number of feedback loops and interaction cycles. However, this way of thinking does not provide an outlook on an effective strategy for therapeutic intervention either. 'If Mother Earth is sick, let us cure her' would have to be the motto in that case. But that is impossible, because mankind is not an external physician. We ourselves are within the organism; we form a part of it. In terms of the same metaphor: the liver can hardly be expected to take care of a stomach ulcer, and we cannot assume that the brain is capable of driving a malignant tumour into remission on its own. It is incredibly pretentious of us to sustain the illusion that we are more intelligent than the planet, especially when we have to take into account that it is we who are making her sick. However, even if we could live up to this pretension, we would not achieve anything. The problem is precisely the same as that of model building: the climate is a one-time experiment, and we cannot continue to experiment with it until we have discovered which measures are effective.

If a physician performs a medical intervention, he bases his actions on endless experimentation. He is aware of certain prominent side effects and feedback interactions that may occur in practice, because they have been brought to light during long-term research. For the rest he has to appeal blindly to the self healing capacities of the organism. If a physician had to worry about the way in which an antibiotic disturbs all the cycles that are not directly related to an infection, and if he were not allowed to assume that the organism can usually cope with the disturbance, then he would not dare to be responsible for any intervention.

Each intervention in the climatic system, be it air pollution or emission limitation, deforestation or reforestation, makes an unavoidable appeal to Mother Earth's self healing capacities. However, this is precisely the ability that is only partially accessible to science. The scientific insight into the coherence of a complex natural system is fundamentally incomplete. The idea that we are capable of understanding the coherence of all the feedback cycles on this planet, and can control them, is an enormous logical error. Ultimately, we cannot know what a healthy environment is, just as we cannot give a perfect, unambiguous definition of the concept of 'health'. Scientific knowledge cannot answer questions of this kind.

7. AUTOPOIESIS

Having reached this point, it seems useful to explain once more why I believe it unavoidable that this issue is explained with the aid of metaphors. It seems as though I am using unscientific language, which perhaps creates some interesting images, but which may actually conceal rather than clarify matters. If science deals with 'reality', then metaphors about reality are unscientific. In my opinion, however, this is a grave mistake. We are not standing on solid ground when we do research. Unfortunately we have to begin with our own ideas. We ourselves have to invent the standards by which we are to test our own knowledge, we ourselves have to choose what we find relevant. Scientific work is autopoiesis, just like writing poetry, making music, designing clothes and all the other creative things we do.

Autopoiesis. Maturana and Varela could not have chosen a better word.[4] It makes one think of poetry. The Greek verb *poiein,* which is the origin of our word poetry, means 'to make' or 'to create'. Scientists often forget that poiesis is, strictly speaking, impossible, but poets are very clear about this. Poetry is one continuous struggle with the ambiguity, the ineffability of the words we use. Each word that has any significance at all is surrounded by a swarm of associations; each attempt at poetic precision is an act of defiance against the structure of language. Poetry is a 'hopeless task', as one poet has said.

All of this applies to research and environmental philosophy as well. This problem is not necessarily an urgent one in all branches of science. If, for example, we use Newton's laws of motion to tackle a problem in classical mechanics, it is not likely that anything will go wrong if we (incorrectly) assume that these laws have universal, 'objective' validity. But when we study the quality of the earth's ecosystem, it is altogether impossible to avoid this problem. The reason for this is that the autopoiesis of the global biosphere is inextricably linked to the autopoiesis of our thoughts about the 'threatened' planet (this is also a metaphor – how can one find out if this is used properly?). I use the adjective inextricable because the origin and maintenance of the coherence in the planetary ecosystem, its self organizing and self healing activities must be studied using the self organizing ability of the mental ecosystem that we comprehend least of all, namely our own thoughts. If we did understand the self organizing ability of our brains, then research into the self organizing ability of our planet would be relatively easy; then we would know what we had to look for. However, we do not. To give a concrete example: we have no idea of how the coherence within our thoughts gives us the illusion that there is an 'I'. Descartes' famous statement was — seen from a psychological perspective — a clever attempt to lock the door and throw away the key. It was an attempt to avoid scientific inquiry. If Descartes had thought about this a little better, he might have written something like: 'If I may presume that mathematical proofs are exemplary for human thought processes [which they are not – H.T.] then I can also presume that there is a subject that is capable of objective statements. However, it is a mystery to me how I should approach the problem of proving this. I know that it hurts when I hit my thumb with a hammer, but that's about as far as I can go. The only conclusion that I can draw with certainty is : doleo ergo sum: I hurt, therefore I am.'

All this does not mean that we should give up. We will have to become creative, just like poets: tackle the impossible and acquire knowledge about things that are actually ultimately incomprehensible. Natural scientists should carry out research under the assumption that we understand so little of the environment, that it is almost certain that we will overlook things if we do not keep our eyes open. And environmental philosophers should pay much more attention to metaphysics. This is because it is the coherence between philosophy, psychology and theology that is at issue here. An environmental philosopher who believes that he does not have to concern himself with epistemological and spiritual problems will miss the boat. I wish to argue in favour of a 'deep ecology', but it should be consistent with the deep ecology of my thoughts and the deep ecology of the sacred. This is because the study of the coherence of ecosystems would be impossible if we cut up the issue in advance, or if we divide up the study of ecosystems into disciplines. This would be a flagrant violation of the 'deep ecology of the sacred'. It ignores the relation between whole and holy, and is therefore domed to fail. To paraphrase Francis Bacon's famous statement: 'ecology, in order to be understood, has to be obeyed'. Or as Gregory Bateson said: 'The ecological God is incorruptible and therefore is not mocked'.[5] The principles of Eco-logic will not be mocked. If we do not respect the principles of ecosystems, we will never get to know how they work.

8. THE INTELLIGIBILITY OF COHERENCE

Questions concerning the origin and maintenance of coherence belong to the province of chaos theory. Without outside intervention, coherent structures can be generated only by chaotic systems. The atmosphere creates thunderstorms and hurricanes, the climate system makes midlatitude belts of westerly winds, the Gulf Stream, tundras and tropical rain forests, the economy creates villages, towns and networks of trading routes, and our brains invent new ideas about ourselves and our future.

Chaos leads to order. This does not happen always and everywhere, and not necessarily at the time and place that would suit us best, or in a way that serves our interests, but we know exactly which system characteristics are responsible for this behaviour: the system must be complex and chaotic; only then does it have self organizing abilities.

A technical explanation is appropriate here. Chaos is a characteristic of nonlinear systems, because it arises only when small causes have large effects (in specialist jargon this is called 'sensitive dependence on initial conditions'). In linear systems causes and effects are proportional: an impulse that is twice as large causes a reaction that is twice as large. Hence a linear system can never be chaotic. To use a psychological metaphor: linear systems cannot display behaviour, because that word implies a certain degree of capriciousness and unpredictability. A mother who tells her child to behave, gives an order which contains a logical contradiction. She puts her child in a 'double bind', as psychologists say. Linear systems always react in precisely the same way. In nonlinear systems, however, there exist no straightforward relations between cause and effect. Nonlinear systems do show behaviour. If they are hit twice as hard, they may very well move in an entirely different, unexpected direction. If we were talking about human behaviour, we would call this creativity. Nonlinearity is a necessary condition for chaotic behaviour.

The creation of coherence in a chaotic system not only requires non-linearity, but also a sufficiently large degree of complexity. As a system becomes more complicated, there is an increasing chance that its evolution can no longer be adequately predicted using mathematical computation methods. This is because there is an increasing chance that somewhere inside the system there will be a component that cannot be linearized. Linearization is permitted only if the amplitude of disturbances remains small. However in a complicated system it is unlikely that a disturbance that is small for the component in which it occurs, can also be called small for all of the other components that interact with it. A small disturbance in one component then may easily exceed the danger level for other components. The latter are then free to exhibit their nonlinearity and to generate chaotic fluctuations. In this way the entire system is triggered into chaotic behaviour. This, as we have seen before, limits the predictive performance of mathematical models. This conclusion applies not only to the weather, but also to the economy and to ecosystems.

As it stands at the moment, chaos theory can only make an empirical observation: coherence is created by complex, nonlinear systems which exhibit sensitive dependence on initial conditions. We know *that* it happens, nothing more. Apparently all complex, chaotic systems have the ability to organize themselves. They are creative: they construct coherent structures, and do so seemingly without effort. We know that the atmosphere makes cyclones that show such evident coherence that even a layman can easily recognize them on satellite pictures. We can also make fairly realistic simulations of the birth and life cycle of cyclones with our computer models. However we understand very little about the how and why. At best we can say that our brains have a great need for pattern recognition. Our mind eagerly concentrates on finding coherence in the chaos of impressions that reach our eyes.

This is the core of the problem. Science is almost completely helpless when it has to deal with questions that are vitally dependent on our own processes of perception. Words such as coherence, health and quality say something about our interaction with reality, not about reality as such. We have to rely on the incomprehensible mechanism of the origin of coherence in our brains (for example, in the form of pattern recognition) in order to get insight into the creation of patterns in the world around us. This is asking for difficulties. It is no wonder that science does not know how to deal with it. Science excels at unravelling details. By comparison the mystery of the recognition of coherence has been unravelled to a far lesser extent. However, time is running out. Our planet's ecosystem, which is just as unique and irreversible as our private musings, is forcing us to synthesis, preferably before we have made such a mess of the situation that Mother Earth is forced to let us slide into extinction.

9. INSIDE AND OUT

If I look at it in this way, I cannot help but conclude that we should not distinguish between object and subject if we wish to make progress in the study of the planetary ecosystem. The dualism that we have been brought up with is a sin against a fundamental characteristic of ecosystems, namely their wholeness and indivisibility. The division between subject and object is a violation of the laws of eco-logic. And we cannot afford to fool around with those. Hence I will choose another point of departure: I respect and accept that the intelligibility of coherence in ecosystems is limited in principle, and that this inability is somehow related to the fact that we are part of the system that we wish to understand. This applies to both our planet's climatic system and to our scientific knowledge. We cannot stand outside it and we cannot study it from a distance. Our knowledge about the world is recursive, exactly like our knowledge of ourselves. Precisely because our thought processes are recursive, we cannot escape from describing the dynamics of ecosystems in terms of the dynamics of our thought processes. We ourselves are also self organizing systems: everything we do, including research and scholarship, is coloured by our need to affirm the coherence in ourselves.

If we want to make any progress in our study of the limits to the intelligibility of coherence in nature, we will have to search in this direction. The self-organizing ability of a complex chaotic system exists by the grace of the many feedback loops and sensitivities of its internal dynamics; it cannot be imposed from the outside. Coherence exists within a system, not outside it. From the moment that we try to place ourselves outside the climate system, for example by pretending we are capable of acting as its stewards, we can no longer contribute to the self healing powers of the planet. This is the source of my affinity with deep ecology. The limited predictability of the weather reminds us that we are in no position to manage anything. We cannot even manage ourselves. The study of the health of the climate system and the integrity of our thought processes can only be fruitful if we show respect for the unfathomable secrets of our own nature.

10. ECO-LOGIC

In view of these considerations, it will not come as a surprise that I am concerned about our primitive knowledge of the formal logic of ecosystems. Conventional logic sets out a chain of rational arguments, and in this way eliminates erroneous hypotheses about the possible relationships between causes and effects. The logic of ecosystems (eco-logic, for the sake of brevity) is related to the cyclic character of all ecological relationships. If I may borrow the idiom of Gestalt psychology: the spherical form of our planet does not condone linear logic and does not tolerate towering hierarchies. Using the idiom of theory control: eco-logic consists of a large number of feedback loops, in which causes and effects are closely interrelated, because the effects become the causes of the causes. Economic growth cannot fulfil this requirement, no matter how sustainable, because it does not possess adequate feedback mechanisms. Economic growth disguises the disastrous consequences of the explosive growth of the world population. Unbridled population growth is perhaps the greatest danger that threatens our planet. Sustainable adaptation and permanent adjustment are better labels for the boundary conditions imposed by the global ecosystem.

When we carry out research (that is, when we perform activities within the ecosystem of our knowledge), it certainly is no excessive luxury to heed the requirements imposed by the logic of ecosystems far more carefully than we have done up to now. This is because eco-logic is unrelenting: if you violate its laws, your research will be doomed to fail from the start. Then it will provide a nice 'solution' for an irrelevant problem, or it will drown in the tangle of relationships between causes and effects. I have given various examples of this on the previous pages. One aspect I have not yet discussed is that eco-logic forces us to consider the influence that the solution to a problem may have on the initial analysis. If this feedback is ignored it is possible to make the strangest blunders. Hence almost all the proposed 'solutions' to the motorway traffic jams in urban areas lead to increased traffic congestion. In the same way, the maxim about polluters having to pay for their emissions forces businessmen into accelerating their activities to such an extent that they are capable of paying high environmental levies. In that way, this dogma may yet become responsible for boosting obsessive economic growth.

All research should begin with a thorough study of the various alternatives for the starting point of the analysis. Conventional logic cannot help us with this. It takes us from A to B without giving one moment's thought to the question as to why we should start at A. A more rational approach to that selection process would be a big step in the right direction. Then meteorologists would be less quick to claim that large atmospheric models are necessary to understand the climate system, and representatives of all sorts of disciplines would lobby less persistently for research funding from the environment budget. Where do you actually begin research into the planetary ecosystem? We do not even know how we should approach this question in a scientific way, that is systematically and rationally. But there is no cause for despair. Quite the opposite: my (subjective) assessment of the vigour of ecosystems is that they can easily cope with setbacks because they are typically extravagantly wasteful. This is true of the atmosphere which has a thermal efficiency of one percent at the most, it is valid for tropical forests, in which humming birds burn up their own weight in nectar each day, it applies to the millions of spermatozoa that compete with one another as they find their way through an ovarium, and it holds for a poet whose attempts to formulate the ineffable remain incomplete, notwithstanding a thousand verses.

If science is wasteful and poorly organized in the way it tackles problems, then it finds itself in good company. Perhaps science itself is an ecosystem. The fact that it is much more effective at inventing new questions than at finding answers is a comforting idea.

11. ENOUGH WORRIES

By now it will have become evident that metaphors are unavoidable because we have nothing better, and that the use of imagery is an explicit reference to the wholeness and holiness of ecosystems. To a meteorologist the concept of eco-logic, seen as a metaphor, is not very different to the way in which atmospheric circulation works. We are well aware of the fact that we are using a hollow metaphor when we claim that a blocking high pressure ridge keeps the storms away from us. The true intelligence of computer models of the atmosphere is that they are not dependent on simplistic logic of that kind. I would sleep much more soundly if the unavoidability of complicated feedback loops in the logic by which we attempt to understand the climate system was taken more seriously in climate research.

Why are scientists so eager? I find it rather embarrassing and rather inconsistent that we dare to harp on about rapid expansion in climate research, even though it has become painfully obvious that the uncontrollable expansion of human activities is the cause of the poor health of our planet. Chasing after additional funding is a symptom of our aggressiveness, however minor. Unwittingly we aggravate the problem, despite our good intentions.

My worries increase when I think about the side effects. Intensifying research supports the illusion that science and technology can solve all problems, as long as they receive sufficient money. Research sustains the progress myth which pervades modern society, but it is that very myth that tempts us to close our eyes to the consequences of our actions.

I do not want to create any misunderstanding. Like others I plead for a considerable increase in climate monitoring, in earth observation satellites and research programs. However I try to keep myself in check. I do not want to make promises that I will not be able to keep. I refuse to become a slave of my expansive instincts. I try to be a scientist: I wish to think before I act.

12. EPILOGUE

A recent edition of *Scientific American* carries the pretentious title 'Managing Planet Earth'. The United States Environmental Protection Agency has launched a programme to stabilize the climate system. The arrogance and conceitedness of such plans are suffocating. Who are we to think that we can control the planet? We cannot even keep ourselves under control. There is no boss within an ecosystem, virtually by definition. Why are we so easily tempted by ecological totalitarianism? Is Homo sapiens doomed to learn from his mistakes, simply because he is not clever enough to approach his learning processes in a different way? Why is it so difficult for Homo sapiens to be a little modest? It is high time that we tried something that seems almost impossible to us: that is, to use our brains. That is the only ecosystem we have available for understanding the global ecosystem. A small step, but a giant step for mankind.

This chapter is based on a lecture entitled 'The conversion of a meteorologist to humanism'. Wim Zweers, the coeditor of this book, questioned this title. 'Why humanism and not ecology? Or do you suggest that there is no difference?' No: if I mean what I say when I state that no-one can be boss in an ecosystem, then an anthropological starting point is inconsistent with eco-logic. This is because it presumes that we people are more knowledgeable than other components of the planetary ecosystem. It is not at all clear that this is so. Yes: if I follow Teilhard de Chardin and give credit to the experiment in the awakening of consciousness that Homo sapiens represents, then we are obliged to do the impossible. We have to relate our attempts at 'consciousness raising' to the ecological conversion of our intellectual habits. The adventure that we personify partially lies in our own hands, no matter how difficult this assignment is. There is no escape from this responsibility.

One only starts to think about these things when one has banged one's head against the wall time and time again. The conversion of a meteorologist to ecology is no simple matter. He will begin to think about the limits to the intelligibility of nature only when it has become impossible to avoid doing so. Once he has become entwined in epistemological problems, he will not be able to avoid the conclusion that the logic of ecosystems applies to the nature surrounding him, as well as to his own nature. His thought processes also form an ecosystem. In his attempts at ecological contemplation he will have to learn to live with the limited rational approachability of everything of which he is part. 'Only fools rush in where angels fear to tread': it is high time that we made a thorough study of the holiness of nature.

Notes

1. Tennekes, H. et al. 1990. *De vlinder van Lorenz* ('Lorenz' Butterfly') and Tennekes, H. 1990. *Dan leef ik liever in onzekerheid* ('Then I prefer uncertainty'), both Bloemendaal, Aramith.
2. Bateson, G., and Bateson, M.C. 1987. *Angels Fear.* New York, MacMillan.
3. Lovelock, J. 1988. *The Ages of Gaia.* New York, Norton. 4. Maturana, H.J. and Varela, F.J. 1988. *The Tree of Knowledge.* Boston, Shambala.
5. op. cit., p.143.

Chapter 6

MODELS AND MODERNISM: BETWEEN ANXIETY AND HUBRIS

Chung Lin Kwa

I shall begin by telling three stories, three present day moral fables. The first concerns something that some people may still remember. In the beginning of 1990 northwestern Europe was plagued by storms, far more than are usual in spring. In Amsterdam many trees fell spectacularly over the canals. What was most noticeable was that the storms lasted such a long time: two months. In March of the same year the Dutch TV satirists van Kooten and de Bie had themselves filmed in a wind tunnel where storm force 12 was simulated. They showed us what we could expect henceforth as a normal situation. At the time, there were serious predictions that it might continue to be stormy for the next twenty years – allegedly because of jet streams which usually remain in the region of the north pole, but which had now approached our region. However, the explanation is not important. Van Kooten and de Bie were attempting to depict anxiety, the anxiety that we may have to live like that from now on, fear of an unstable nature that could play such a trick on us.

The second story is about some mysterious, very old ruins in Africa: the so-called Zimbabwe Ruins. This large complex of towers and walls built of stone is found in southern Zimbabwe. Striking decorations and other finds indicate a fairly advanced culture, which must have existed for at least several centuries. The complex is unique in the whole of subsaharan Africa. When Cecil Rhodes and the first English settlers discovered the ruins, they surmised Phoenician settlers, indicating that in their opinion the settlement was old and highly civilized. It was obvious to them that this was an 'implanted' civilization, which presumably had been slowly watered down by interaction with the native black population. The different archaeological explanations of these ruins have an interesting history in themselves, which falls outside the scope of this book. Present day archaeologists believe that a native culture from the tenth to the twelfth century was involved. The key question is obviously why the civilization ceased to exist. The explanation held to be the most probable now, is that the people of the Zimbabwe Ruins used up their natural resources and were forced to emigrate. This type of hypothesis about other vanished civilizations is fairly popular among archaeologists at the moment. The idea that a civilization caused its own end by destroying its environment is thought to be applicable to other similar archaeological mysteries.[1]

The third story is about the recent history of so-called weather modification programmes. The possibility that it was feasible to alter the climate in favour of humanity stimulated high expectations in the 1950s and 1960s, especially in the United States. At the beginning of the 1950s, meteorologists believed that it would be possible to tame hurricanes within ten years, and that the African climate would be altered within twenty years to produce a fertile continent with a rich population. In 1966, Thomas Malone, a leading meteorologist, declared in a speech to the American Association for the Advancement of Science that the following four results had been achieved:

(i)		Knowledge of the physical processes in the atmosphere was so advanced that mathematical models could be made to simulate the behaviour of the atmosphere, as well as of human influence on it.

(ii)	The computer had become so advanced that it had reached the same level of complexity. The solution to the difficult problems concerning linear instability was within arm's reach.

(iii)	Meteorological measurement networks had become so advanced that models could be provided with all the necessary information.

(iv)	Field experiments had become so advanced that a real causal interpretation could be given to predicted changes, instead of only being able to speak of correlations.

It was concluded that the rational basis for research on wished for changes in the climate was present. Humanity was ready to take a great step forward.[2] Malone's optimism now seems ridiculous. A few years after his predictions, doubts began to set in, and Tennekes's account makes it clear that our present position is very remote from this.

The three stories are moral fables: let us take a look at their moral content. For all three this concerns the relationship between humanity and nature. The last story illustrates what now clearly seems like hubris; however, in fact it is typical of the modernistic programme of 'makeability' of society, a makeability that is also applicable to nature. The moral message of the story is that if we do our best and believe in science and rationality, we can take the world in our hands and guide it like an engineer, as a greenhouse builder controls the climate in his greenhouse. At the same time that Malone made his optimistic statement, the Dutch believed that it was possible to plan the economy rationally. The Central Planning Bureau's macroeconomic models are in a way analogous to the meteorological ones mentioned above. They used to be (and still are) utilized by the Social Economic Council and by political parties as a check for all sorts of plans which may be of influence on the Dutch economy.

The United States provides a classic example of the belief in these moral fables, at least at the time that Malone made his statements. In 1967 and the following years the USA thought that they could win the war in Vietnam, the war against cancer and the war against poverty, by using science, technology and rational planning.

The second moral fable, about the Zimbabwe Ruins, is a typical present day fable. It says that technological success is punished: by ruin. In 1967 David Gates, an influential American biologist, said to members of Congress during a hearing: 'We will go down in history as an elegant technological society struck down by biological ignorance.' He recommended that the members of Congress should finance a large ecological programme, to build up the expertise to turn the tide. One of the members of Congress asked if they could build an early warning system in order to prevent a disaster. Gates answered in the affirmative.[3] The key to this fable is that if we repent, everything will turn out all right. We may have to pay a fine – the fairytale tells us that we live beyond our means – but there are new sciences present that can tell us what we should do to survive. If not, we are only setting up our own memorial, such as the one in the jungle of Zimbabwe.

It is ironical that the 'learning system' that Gates proposed implied similar models to those that Malone referred to. The type of control humanity was trying to develop by making them was also similar: large and comprehensive. An important difference was that the control aimed at by Gates had a different stake: survival, while Malone was thinking of exploitation. But exploitation came close on the heels of survival as one of the aims of ecologists, at the end of the 1960s. So after closer consideration the two moral fables have more similarities than differences.

However, there has been an irrefutable shift from an offensive to a defensive strategy. In the 1950s and 1960s it was thought to be possible to optimalize the global climate to suit humanity, but now the discussion is dominated by the question as to whether it is possible to curb or stave off displeasing changes. The greenhouse effect of the same name is an ambiguous metaphor: both bringing under control and bolting belong to the possibilities.

The moral fable with which I began, that of van Kooten and de Bie, seems to have given up the idea that we can still do something about the storm, i.e. the unchained powers of nature. We must prepare ourselves for them, learn to live with the anxiety and make the best of things. The fable is not dismissive of science. The plausibility of meteorological predictions is accepted, as is the given 'explanation'. However, the relationship between prediction and explanation on the one hand, and control on the other hand, is no longer applicable. Van Kooten and de Bie's fable shows that the modern control ideal has lost its naturalness – I understand the ideal of control to mean the idea that we (via a 'complete' knowledge of natural laws, combined in a model) can achieve universal control by local interventions.

The question is now whether abandoning the ideal of control will lead to passive acceptance. I myself do not think so, and would like to explain this by juxtaposing two strategies to achieve safety, as they have been analysed by C.S. Holling.[4] He called the first one a failsafe strategy, based on the design of optimal systems which are so stable that they cannot possibly break. The second strategy he proposed calling 'safefail'. This strategy would try to limit the effects of failure, to be achieved in part because everyone working with the system would be prepared for failure, and would know what to do in the event. The first strategy works best if there is a lot of knowledge about the system involved, the second if the knowledge is limited. In many cases a specific combination of both strategies is applied. What becomes clear when the two strategies are placed side by side, is that in situations where there is only limited knowledge of a system (e.g., the world climate system and the greenhouse effect), a policy aimed at increasing knowledge is not the only rational strategy, disregarding as it does the limits which are always fixed to knowledge (see Tennekes in the previous chapter). In such a situation a politics of increasing knowledge can be seen as only one form of allaying anxiety. A policy aimed at looking at other than normal possibilities of acting is just as necessary. These considerations do lead to an abandonment of the ideal of comprehensive knowledge and total control of natural systems. Possibilities of acting are most probably more tightly defined in space and time than would be wished for by the nourishers of the modernistic control ideal.

NOTES

1. H Kuklick, oral information in a lecture delivered at University of Amsterdam, 1990.

2. Malone, Thomas 1967. 'Weather Modifications: Implications of the New Horizons in Research', *Science,* **156**: 897-901.

3. Kwa, C.L., 1987. 'Representations of Nature Mediating between Ecology and Science Policy: The Case of International Biological Programme', *Social Studies of Science,* **17**: 413-42.

4. Holling, C.S. 1976. 'Resilience and Stability of Ecosystems', in Jantsch, E. & Waddington, C.H. (eds) *Evolution and Consciousness. Human Systems in Transition,* pp. 73-92. Reading, Mass., Addison-Wesley.

Chapter 7

SCIENCE: A MODEST HOPE

Pieter Schroevers

Henk Tennekes has taken on those who still believe the world can be made exactly as we want it to be. There are worrying aspects to this belief; it is quite unconcerned about mistakes, for science and technology are waiting at any time to solve the problems, aren't they? It seems to me that we should abandon such ideas and subscribe to appeals like Tennekes'. However, the subject can also be viewed from another perspective also. In what follows I shall argue that ignoring every possibility of altering the future in a conscious way has its disadvantages as well. Such thinking leads to matters being left to go their own way, even if we know there are serious risks in such a course of events, and know what to do to counter them – a situation in which the world clearly finds itself today.

Tennekes discusses the unpredictable in the natural sciences. As a meteorologist, he watches his fellow researchers, switching off at five o'clock in the afternoon to go home, becoming a part of their computer through their forecasting work, which is based upon knowledge collected in the past. He wants to liberate them from such a fate by using the 'logic of unpredictability'. He called this 'humanization' in the speech at the congress on which this book is based. However, his pronouncement could be extrapolated from its context at the congress to other fields of science, and it may be questioned whether this is always right. If unpredictability is our starting point, then as a logical consequence the use of the past as a guideline for action must be condemned. Would that be humanization of something that would be inhuman without it?

During the same congress I intended to pay a quick visit to the Boymans Museum during lunchtime. The congress was being held right next to the museum and for some reason I was interested to see one particular seventeenth century painting. I went straight to the relevant part of the museum and found myself suddenly surrounded by the explosion of creativity which occurred in this country some 300 years ago. It was a dive into the past, although I realize very well that I look at it with the eyes of someone who also has knowledge of all the history that came after. For that reason my dive into the past cannot be seen solely as backward looking. It includes my position as a human being of the twentieth century. I look at the past from the outside, my view is 'scientificated', so to speak. The same thought can be applied to a performance of old music, to a walk along an Amsterdam canal, and especially to our experience of the landscape, which in the Netherlands is an expression of social history. Everything around us – nothing excepted – has a kind of historical context, and the recognition of it is essential to our thoughts about the reality surrounding us, even – no, especially – as people situated in our own time. I would call this a humanization as well, yet I can see some difference between making weather forecasts and a large number of other things. Today, two hundred years on, I can be touched by the way Mozart played around with notes on a day in 1770, whereas I am not in the slightest interested about the weather that day. What I am trying to say is that the 'repetition of the past' can have a different meaning for different fields of human activity, and that experiences in one field cannot always be transferred to another.

At the moment 'sustainable development' is a topic for discussion. An international committee of great authority introduced the term, and policy documents that ignore this starting point are rarely taken seriously any more. Not that it is such a new idea; the whole environmental movement has always said the same thing, only using different words. It is, however, becoming more and more generally accepted and used in the pursuit of politics. 'We don't want to go back to the time of sod huts or the steam engine', it wants to tell us. The future will be different from the past, and we want there to be development. But this development must guarantee sustainability. It must respect the things of the past, among them *Homo sapiens*, and act accordingly. Such thinking makes using elements of the past as a guideline for action related to the future unavoidable. Neglecting this will mean letting things take their own course, and our present insights force us to recognize that that could end badly. Paying attention to the past seems to be of real importance, it has to do with the survival of humanity. Of course it is true no one can predict the future, but that does not matter here. The point is that looking back can give some decisiveness, a decisiveness which is certainly required.

All these things are connected with value. Here I do not mean an economic or otherwise quantifiable value, but an inner realization of the meaning of things around us. Imagine you let a plate fall and it breaks into pieces. Once this plate was made by a person, it has been transported, sold, transported again, used, cherished, washed up numerous times and tidied away. It has got history, and suddenly it all perishes: the plate is broken. What do we do? We go to the shop to buy a new one. But history is not to buy. In some cases we are very aware of it: a painting from the Boymans Museum cannot be replaced. But what about an ordinary plate? Our day and age has an alienating effect, in converting irreplaceability more or less into an apparent replaceability. It dims the recognition of values, and hence decreases the historical context in which things can be placed. This is applicable not only to things themselves, but also to the way they came about. This latter is actually more important in a world trying to achieve sustainable development, in which it is essential to use old knowledge in a new way. If the knowledge has disappeared the product has become irreplaceable. This is the case with nature. We know what we are forfeiting, and we know the direction that new economic developments should stick to if we want to maintain or retrieve it. The values of the past serve as a guideline for the future. 'Repetition of the past' has a different meaning for different fields of human activity, as I said before. In ecology it is essential. It is a condition for sustainable development. To me, 'ecologization of a scientist' means taking this seriously.

The use of causal models in global problems can be looked upon as an optimistic way of looking into the future. The past has yielded a number of quantifiable facts: by integrating them into a model and by applying extrapolation techniques, this knowledge can be shifted to the future. The logical consequence is that we know the solutions of our problems beforehand; they are no problems at all. And if we do not know quite everything, not to worry, further research will help. This leads to the arrogance of technocracy, the optimism of 'enlightenment thinking', which set the train of thought far into the twentieth century and which still does it in a lot of cases. If, however, Tennekes' warning 'distrust every prognosis' is taken too literally, it is possible to get into trouble as well. It is no longer possible then to give directives for development; one can only anticipate the broad outline of world occurrences based on what is going on already. But most of today's worries are the result of these broad outlines. For example, the unequal growth in the world, which our analyses are able to expose, allows overdevelopment and underdevelopment to exist side by side. In Brazil it leads to erosion, in the Netherlands to the accumulation of nitrogen in the soil. Our anticipatory actions allow us to create both development aid and purification plants. But these do not touch the real problem, they even enlarge it by legitimating the existing structure of inequality. It is an example of the well-known 'Prisoner's dilemma'. The recognition of our inability to anticipate future developments can lead to nothing but pessimistic thoughts, aptly described by L.C. Heldring in his 'Paradiso lecture' some years ago. Moreover if we *do* act with foresight, we can only do so through using our experience. Then, too, we are 'repeating the past', and hence coming to the same technocratic solutions as our opponents. The difference is smaller than we should wish. In both cases a social paradigm is the underlying steering factor; the paradigm that has given form to our western expansion for several centuries, 'Everyone is allowed to do everything, as long as it is not proved to do harm'. The one uses it as an optimist, because he believes that it will improve the world, the other as a pessimist because he has no other choice: but they both do it.

Our history knows another 'social paradigm', common over large areas of the world not so long ago: 'nothing is allowed unless it is possible to indicate that it does no harm'. We all remember the well-known speech of the Chief of the Suquamps Indians as an example. But the same used to be applicable in medieval western Europe, and we are beginning to realize that a similar kind of attitude would be very welcome, at least towards some of our interferences, if we really want sustainability in our development. Reflection on the past is an essential part of this attitude, and it has to be directed to future activities. In other words science has a role to play here. But it will be another type of science, if compared with quantified models. I myself call it the science of common sense. Everyone develops his or her own impression of the world. Of course there are good and less good opinions. A good opinion is consistent in itself and can be measured according to its level of realism. By discussing it systematically and by redefining its main points, we polish up such an image bit by bit until there is something we can agree on. To be sure, such a way of thinking does not explain the world, but it can at least clarify what we do not want. It has been in discredit for quite some time, and it certainly knows its limits. But these days, it can be very useful in our search for a way towards sustainable living to be critical about the future, on the basis of experiences in the past, with the imposing of limits as an important aim.

There are people (not Tennekes) who tell us not to worry about the increase of carbon dioxide in the atmosphere, because nobody is able to predict the outcome of the greenhouse effect. They deride the prophets of doom, who depict what will happen if we do not rapidly alter our behaviour, and who derive their judgements from quantified future models. But this seems equally objectionable to me. The Dutch Environmental Movement said 'We do not know what is going to happen, but we believe that we do not have the right to consciously destroy a regulatory system, created over millions of years. And, whatever the consequences, we are the ones who are responsible.' To me such a statement is more scientific than either extreme. It shows respect for the values of nature, and also recognition of history.

To conclude, science means thinking in terms of models, simplified pictures of the complexity of the world. And these models enable us to think about the future by using knowledge of the past. There is nothing wrong with that. But there exist many types of science, and hence of models. The quantifying causal model is only one of them. And every model has its limits, none can be used all the time and everywhere. Scientific thinking ought to be in the first case clean thinking. It means that scientists should continually discuss their own starting points. Many scientists use objectionable trains of thought, Tennekes rightly opposes them. But let us ensure we are not overcritical in dealing with this problem. We cannot mould the future, but we should at least discuss it.

Chapter 8

THE MOUSE IN THE CAT'S CLAWS: A FRAMEWORK FOR A HERMENEUTICS OF NATURE

Petran Kockelkoren

1. INTRODUCTION

Most people nowadays agree that we should relate to nature in a way other than we usually do, but somehow it seems impossible for this verbally shared insight to filter through into our daily activities. There is a gap between our intellectual conception of nature and our bodily perception of her which can hardly be bridged. I agree with the diagnosis of the Dutch philosopher Otto Duintjer that in our culture a onesided emphasis on discursive understanding has been gained at the expense of a participatory approach to nature.[1] The disconnection of understanding and participation was initially only a methodological maxim underlying the practice of science. However, after the scientific revolution society went through a process of scientification. Along that way a distanced attitude towards nature penetrated almost every domain of everyday experience. When philosophers ask questions regarding nature nowadays, most of the time this commonly experienced distance serves as the self-evident starting point. Thus it even seems natural to pose the question: how can we be certain that an animal experiences pain when we burn its paw? Answer: we do not know! The motive for my account is the desire to get rid of that fatal distance and to restore a more participatory approach to nature.

How can we come closer to nature? Duintjer's plea for a participatory approach to nature contains an important presupposition, namely that there is something to participate in. In the way the natural sciences approach nature this possibility is ruled out right from the start because the empirical method presupposes objectification. As a condition for its own existence empiricism constructs a mute objective world. In the scientific view nature cannot but appear as dead stuff and as a stock of raw materials waiting to be technically processed. The possibility of approaching nature as a fellow subject rests on a different presupposition. In other words: the question as to whether a subjective approach will do more justice to nature than an objective approach cannot be answered empirically; it is, at least for the time being, a matter of presuppositions. Even if nature were expressing itself in many different ways, we would, within the context of the methodology of the natural sciences, still not be able to understand it, since this context does not allow for nature to manifest itself expressively. How can we find a framework which *does* allow for this? Only when we have developed such a contrary framework can we see whether aspects of nature which have hitherto gone unnoticed may yet be understood. This leads directly to the following question: can we get to know nature otherwise than by the empirical ways of the natural sciences? In other words: what are the conditions for the possibility of understanding nature as a fellow subject? Only within a frame like this, in which methodological distance gives way to participation, may the question as to whether an animal suffers pain when its paw is burnt eventually be answered, because it is only then that other criteria for the validity of shared experience apply than those of commonly accepted empiricism, which is at a loss with regard to this question.

For me, searching for an alternative to empiricism leads to hermeneutics. Hermeneutics has had many different historical manifestations. The development of hermeneutics as a method involuntarily mirrors the development of our culture as I outlined it above: in hermeneutics too a decrease in participation can be seen to go hand in hand with an increasing emphasis on discursive understanding.

In ancient Greece Hermes, from whom the word hermeneutics is derived, was the messenger of the gods. He voiced the intentions of the gods for mankind and so revealed their destiny to them. Hermeneutics was the priests' art of divination, of divining meaning. From phenomena in nature, such as the flight of birds and the rustling of the wind in the tree tops, meaningful patterns were derived into which human behaviour had to be fitted. Nature was understood as an inherently meaningful whole in which people participated.

In the western tradition the art of understanding the sacred soon became separated from understanding nature. The main reason for this was that in the Christian world view, God had set out His intentions in a text, the Bible. Hermeneutics became exegesis of text, the pre-eminent theological method. Within this context, nature was at best used as a supplier of allegories or as a concealed text.

In the nineteenth century, Wilhelm Dilthey, the patriarch of modern hermeneutics, removed hermeneutics from its theological context and broadened it into the general method of the cultural sciences. Hermeneutics remained the explaining of texts, but it was no longer necessarily restricted to the exegesis of the Bible. Starting from written texts or, if these are not available, from other symbolic expressions such as pieces of art, tools or rituals, we can gain some understanding of a distant culture or an age gone by. Dilthey himself was quite attached to the non-discursive components of understanding, in particular to the dimensions of feeling and willing, but later hermeneuticians, from Gadamer to Habermas, discarded precisely these non-linguistic aspects of understanding as romantic frills and concentrated exclusively on discursive understanding and the conditions for its possibility. At present the term 'hermeneutics' refers to the method of explaining text. Nature is no longer included in hermeneutics, unless it is understood as text. In any case, for human beings the ability to acquire knowledge in a discursive way is dominant.

I would like to attempt to revive hermeneutics in its ancient form of understanding nature on her own terms. By doing so, I inevitably land in a double track. On the one hand it is necessary to develop a notion of the expressivity of nature, which makes nature understandable as an inherently meaningful whole. On the other hand it is also necessary to develop an epistemological vision of human abilities to acquire intimate knowledge of nature. For if meanings lie hidden in nature even before humanity enters on the scene, our prevalent meaning-bestowing faculties will fall short and an integrative hermeneutics will have to be developed which includes not only the discursive level but also affection and body consciousness as gateways to nature's meaning.

When making this plea for the notion of an expressive nature and for an integrative hermeneutics in line with this notion, I remain on the level of presuppositions, that is on the level of drawing the outlines of an alternative relationship between humans and other species. This leaves unanswered – for the time being – the question as to *what* meaning might ultimately be hidden in nature. Before tackling this problem though, I want to dissociate myself from some other attempts to reach for a hermeneutics of nature, which also have a certain historical legitimacy.

Following the metaphor of 'the book of nature', for instance, we could regard nature as a text. Ilse Bulhof does so.[2] According to her, a text does not obtain its final meaning until it is seen through the eyes of the reader. There is no end to this process of bestowing meaning on the text, since there will always be new readers. In the same way the meaning of nature can never be interpreted exhaustively, since nature would be gaining her very shape through human interpretation. The contact with those who relate to them, incessantly reshapes things into being what they actually are. This gives humans a lot of responsibility. Yet Bulhof's approach is exclusively anthropocentric. She leaves hardly any room for nature's self expression.

According to another interpretation of the metaphor of nature as a text, it is not necessary to pose any expressivity of nature in her own right in order to be able to understand her. Again, when explaining a text, one does not rely on the intentions of the author, since the meaning depends to a great extent on its contextuality and hence exceeds the intentions of its maker. One could therefore try to grasp nature's meaning without regard to its presumed self expression. This interpretation does however pose a serious problem: other natures not being available, what could possibly be the context in which nature can appear within this analogy?

I do not want to go along with either of these approaches to a hermeneutics of nature. On the contrary, I shall stand up for nature's own expressivity and for an integrative hermeneutics on the part of humanity. Frankly speaking I am not even interested so much in the contents of the meaning expressed in and by nature, as in the kind of reciprocity and susceptibility required for understanding any meanings coming from the other side in our encounters with nature. I am intent on analysing the susceptibility which can restore our disturbed relationship with nature. In this way it is possible to secure the respect we owe to forms of life other than just humanity, once they are admitted into the circle of expression and understanding of meaning. To me the necessary alternative practice is the most important, but before that the way must be cleared on the level of presuppositions. To begin with, an alternative image of the relationship between man and nature must be developed which allows for a practical understanding of nature. The most suitable starting point for this is Helmuth Plessner's hermeneutic philosophy of nature, which is based on the works of Dilthey. As soon as we have gained more insight into this, we will take a closer look at its consequences for the practical understanding of nature.

2. A HERMENEUTIC PHILOSOPHY OF NATURE

a. Wilhelm Dilthey

To Dilthey, feelings and manifestations of will are integral components of hermeneutics. Even if we wish to understand a written message, we will have to take into account its emotional aspects and the will expressed in it. It is the task of the cultural sciences to develop such a hermeneutic susceptibility, in which the different abilities to acquire knowledge are balanced. According to Dilthey the purpose of the cultural sciences is 'individuation', that is, becoming a complete person. This purpose is contrary to the purpose of the natural sciences, which strive after control in the wake of explanation. 'Understanding' and 'individuation', respectively 'explaining' and 'control', are the keywords when characterizing the cultural and the natural sciences. The former is concerned with life, the latter with nature. 'We understand life, we explain nature',[3] is the catch phrase which characterizes all Dilthey's work.

Dilthey was a true Kantian, in that to him 'nature' was merely the object of the natural sciences. This means that nature is characterized by abstract concepts such as 'substance, causality, space, time, mass, motion'. Opposite this reduced entity called nature stands life, with all its expressivity. To Dilthey, however, life means only human life, and this explicitly leaves out those natural objects we usually call living, such as organisms.[4] The following quotation leaves no room for speculations on this point: 'Something which cannot be understood can have no meaning or value. A tree can never have meaning'.[5]

In other words, though Dilthey propagates an integrative hermeneutics aimed at individuation, he does not extend it to the understanding of nature. In contrast to human life, nature is depicted only as an inorganic, physical substratum which humans have to take into account in the conditional sphere of continuing their existence. By categorizing nature *a priori* as meaningless in its own right, Dilthey cuts humanity off from its natural roots. As a consequence he himself is left with the discord of anthropocentric cultural sciences on the one hand and devitalized natural sciences on the other. Led thus far and no further by Dilthey, Plessner took it upon himself to develop a hermeneutical method for the understanding of nature.

b. Helmuth Plessner's presuppositions

Plessner initially came into contact with the problem from a very different angle. Plessner's first major work, *Die Einheit der Sinne* (The Unity of the Senses, 1923), contains systematic research into the role of sensory perception in the construction of human experience. Though Kant had already made it clear that the human faculties for acquiring knowledge contribute constructively to the perception of nature, he was biased in favour of the intellectual faculties. Plessner, in his turn, emphasized that the senses are not just passive receivers of external impressions either. Like the intellectual faculties, the senses constitutively contribute to the perception of the world. Plessner made up for Kant's shortcomings by uncovering an a priori of sensory perception that precedes the a priori of intellectual understanding.

With this line of thought Plessner overthrew more than he could handle in the scope of his research into the senses. If the a priori of reason is founded upon an a priori of the senses, it must be rooted in nature. The transcendental subject tumbles down, so to speak, from its noncorporeal sphere, and in doing so loses its primacy in epistemology. As a consequence we must no longer go in search just of the possibility of our understanding life, but of the possibility of life that is able to understand. We are, in other words, no longer studying the possibility of knowing, but the conditions which make a knowing existence possible. Thus the cognitive a priori must be replaced by a material a priori, which is rooted in deeper layers than the merely intellectual level. Experience and perception constitute an indispensable substratum of cognition, and moreover, experience and perception are shared by humans and other forms of life, albeit each in its own specific way. Hence Plessner did not have any choice but to develop a complete philosophical biology and anthropology, and that is what he set out to do in his main work *Die Stufen des Organischen und der Mensch* (Man's Place on the Stepladder of Organic Life, 1928).

In this book Plessner develops his hermeneutic philosophy of nature, which is of importance to us. In his study of the senses Plessner had already suggested that an anthropology of the senses should lead to a hermeneutics, because if the senses relate not passively but constructively to their surroundings, life expresses itself in a sensory way and these sensory forms of expression are intelligible. With this Plessner falls back on the unity of 'life, expression and understanding' proposed by Dilthey, while at the same time extending it to include prehuman organisms as well. 'Leben versteht Leben' (Life understands life), Plessner propounds in the footsteps of Dilthey,[6] and using this motto he unfolds his hermeneutics of an expressive nature.

Up until now I have spoken of nature in a rather undefined way, as if it were a massive entity expressing itself. Following Plessner's example I would like to define nature as the complex whole of interspecies understanding, in which plants, animals and human beings relate to one another. Lifeless nature then forms the lower limit, the minimum of self expression and intelligibility.

Self expression and intelligibility go hand in hand in living nature. From his teachers in phenomenology, Husserl and Scheler, Plessner adopted the notion of the intentionality of consciousness. From the phenomenological point of view, consciousness is not a mere passive receptacle of impressions coming in from the outside, but rather actively outward bound, towards discerning meaning in the already given. In phenomenology this act of constituting meaning is summarized under the head of the 'intentionality' of consciousness. To Plessner, however, consciousness is not something exclusively human. Human reflexivity is just one way, although of course a highly developed one, for an organism to relate intentionally to its surroundings. On less complex levels of vital organization intentional directedness must be present too, though it is, of course, different from humans 'having explicit intentions'. Plessner presents his own conception of intentionality as 'the realizing of borders'.[7] The organism's border is not something external (set from the outside), but is fixed in the act of self positioning. In this act of self positioning a specific relationship is constituted between the organism and its environment. The border fixed by the organism itself forms the horizon of the understanding of the organism in question. This last point must be further elaborated.

c. An example

To move away from abstractions and to get a better grasp of the subject, we will now consider an example of the reciprocity of the intentional realizing of borders and of the concomitant interspecies understanding. The example concerns the pattern of interaction between a mongoose and a cobra. The mongoose is an African predator the size of a large squirrel, the cobra is a snake. Plessner himself is not very lavish with examples, so it is not one of his own; it comes from a book by Norbert Wiener, the cyberneticist, not exactly a participatory scientist, but definitely a keen observer.

When a mongoose and a snake come across each other, the same pattern of interaction may be observed every time:

> The mongoose begins with a feint, which provokes the snake to strike back. The mongoose dodges and makes another such feint, so that we have a rhythmical pattern of activity on the part of the two animals. However this dance is not static but develops progressively. As it goes on, the feints of the mongoose come earlier and earlier in phase with respect to the darts of the cobra, until finally the mongoose attacks when the cobra is extended and not in a position to move rapidly. This time the mongoose's attack is not a feint, but a deadly accurate bite through the cobra's brain. In other words, the snake's pattern of action is confined to single darts, each one for itself, while the pattern of the mongoose's action involves an appreciable, if not very long, segment of the whole past of the fight. To this extent the mongoose acts like a learning machine, and the real deadliness of its attack is dependent upon a much more highly organized nervous system.[8]

Leaving it to Wiener to account for the machine metaphor, a lot can be made comprehensible in terms of Plessner's philosophy. The borders realized by the two forms of life must be understood as the scope of their respective ranges of behaviour. The mongoose's range of behaviour is not only more extensive than that of the snake, it is also of a different quality: whereas the snake carries out a series of separate actions, the actions of the mongoose are arranged as parts within an encompassing horizon of behaviour. Feints are only possible if we presume the mongoose to have an elementary form of self representation for the duration of its action. Plessner would speak in this context of the difference between centrally and decentrally organized animals; that is, of the difference between animals that can relate to their own borders, like the mongoose does, and animals that lack such central self representation, such as the cobra. However, this is only a side issue: the importance of this example lies mainly in its illustrating the reciprocity of the intentional realizing of borders – understood as scopes of action – and understanding.

The animal expresses itself in the same act in which it confines its behaviour to its self imposed borders. At the same time, however, the range of action realized by the animal constitutes its horizon of understanding. Organic intentionality works both ways: expressive and receptive. Because the mongoose has a broader horizon than the cobra, the mongoose conceives the snake's behaviour as relatively invariant. The other way around, the mongoose's range of behaviour exceeds the snake's horizon of understanding, with fatal consequences. The horizons which the different forms of life constitute determine how the world can present itself to them. Plessner, however, is averse to what he calls 'zoological idealism'.[9] Forms of life intentionally determine how the world can present itself to them, but not *what* presents itself. With his theory of interspecies understanding, Plessner steers a middle course between philosophical idealism and realism.

d. *The material a priori*

Though these considerations resulting from an example have given us some idea of where the theory of interspecies understanding leads, we have not yet achieved Plessner's real aim, which is to find out the material a priori of the different forms of life. What are the structural differences between plants, animals and human beings?

The intentional realizing of borders is the starting point of Plessner's philosophy of nature. A simple realization of borders can be observed in plants. A plant opens and closes its flowers in accordance with the position of the sun, and by doing so it maintains a constant temperature, independent of fluctuations in its surroundings.

In animal forms of life the primary realization of borders, as observed in plants, is 'mediated'. In another jargon one could speak of 'feedback'. Through this mediation or feedback a specifically animal-like relationship with that which lies beyond the border appears, namely one that includes relating to the border as such. Thus physically equipped the animal can intentionally circumscribe its own scope of action, as the case of the mongoose illustrates.

The animal cannot, however, step outside its own horizon, since this would require a second act of mediation, in which a distance to its own centre is created. But this is precisely the mode of human existence. By a second mediation of the realization of borders we can relate to this act of realizing borders itself. While the patterns of behaviour of even the most highly developed animals are fixed within certain margins, humans can freely design their behaviour from an 'eccentric' position, i.e. from 'outside the centre'. This is what changes behaviour into action. Action is behaviour designed from an outside position towards oneself. This enables humans to vary the horizon of their behaviour at will, so that many different kinds of action become possible.

On further inspection, Plessner presents the different levels on which life expresses itself within a dialectical scheme. The plant, which has an 'open' relationship with the diffuse things beyond its border, is positioned on ground level. Then, through mediation, the animal is able to relate to its borders but at the same time this forces it back within its borders, resulting in a 'closed' way of life. If mediation takes place once more, the human level of existence is reached: on the one hand the eccentric position acquired by humans makes it impossible to confine them to any border whatsoever, on the other hand they feel the need to define borders to give themselves the fixed outline that nature has denied them. Hence they are forced to be 'open' and 'closed' at the same time. With the help of this dialectical categorial scheme Plessner believes that he has grasped the material a priori of the different manifestations of life.

Before we turn to the implications of this outline for understanding between species – especially between people and other forms of life – one important remark must be made: the categories of the material a priori, which Plessner uses to classify the manifestations of life of plants, animals and human beings, do not define these forms of life essentialistically. Although

Plessner's scheme of the material a priori constitutes an ontology, this ontology is an empty one, in the sense that it only defines the scopes within which the organisms of the different levels of complexity can express themselves; it does not compellingly prescribe the way any organism *must* express itself. The same certainly applies to humanity. Plessner calls the human way of life 'eccentric', or literally 'out of the centre'. Our eccentricity divides us: on the one hand we are physically a part of nature, on the other hand we relate to her from a virtual outside. Man is his own outsider. As a result he has not been given a fixed identity; he must make himself into what he is, a process which can never end, since he will continue to transcend himself again and again. Hence it can never be defined what man is; the only thing that *is* fixed is that he must be himself in one way or another. What does this mean for our understanding of nature?

e. Human understanding of nature

Man is an inextricable part of nature, but due to his eccentricity he lacks direct access to it, because even with respect to his corporeality he remains his own outsider. Hence we have an ambivalent relationship with our bodies: each of us *is* a body and at the same time *has* a body. Because of this ambivalence, even our sensory access to nature is always mediated. This mediation takes place via the other person. The position of outsider which a human being can occupy with respect to him or herself is not only some abstract construction of the mind, but is already occupied by the other person. By looking at ourselves through the eyes of other people, we are able to objectify ourselves, in the same way as we learn to objectify the rest of the world.

The mediation necessary because of our eccentricity crystallizes in a symbolic order. Because of our eccentricity we always occupy a metaposition with respect to our own behaviour and therefore we can design our own behaviour, thus transforming it into deliberate action. These plans for action are handed over to others in the form of symbols. The word 'dog' stands for an action scheme that is triggered as soon as a real dog is encountered. Every symbol being a recipe for action that can be transferred to other people, the symbolic order presents a large repertoire of these. As a result of the structure of the symbolic order nature appears in a culture-specific way.

Language, but also technology, art, etc., are exponents of human eccentricity and thus they are the mediators of our understanding of nature. Because of the limited scope of this article we will not discuss art and technology, but we will have to take a closer look at the inter-relatedness of language and our understanding of nature. Nature, both lifeless things and nonhuman forms of life, is named and classified in the context of human action. In the same way that the range of behaviour constitutes the framework in which animals approach their environment (think of the interaction of mongoose and cobra), our framework for encountering another species is our design for action precipitated in a symbol. Within the outline of such a design animal behaviour as well as the expressions of other forms of life and even of lifeless things appear as relatively invariant in relationship to its own actions. This is comparable to the encounter of the mongoose and the snake in which the snake got killed because the mongoose could grasp the scope of the snake's behaviour, whereas the opposite was not the case. In the same way, whenever humans come across a less complex form of life, this encounter can be classified by means of a concise design for action. Words stand for well defined courses of action with respect to that which takes place in the environment. These designs for action, which should really be open horizons for encounter, are laid down in rigid concepts and are thus reified (i.e. they are treated as solid facts). Because of the relative invariance they have in common, interactions with other forms of life can be rigidly classified under the uniform denominator of objects, thus giving rise to the so-called objective world that is dependent on the symbolic order.

However, this is precisely what Plessner's subjectifying view of nature is opposed to. The diversity of nature's self-manifestations is not done justice by the singular differentiation between subject and object. Nature is much more versatile in her self-expressions than the simple concept of a confrontation of the human subject on one side, with the objects on the other side, allows for. Nature should rather be understood as a multitude of dissimilar subjects which together weave a multilayered web of meanings. The reifying or solidifying effects of language – not language itself of course – must be eliminated in order to make it possible for human action with respect to nature to achieve the character of an open horizon for understanding other life forms, in which fellow subjects of a different disposition than the human get a chance to express themselves too.

With his philosophy of nature Plessner lays the foundations for a subjectifying framework for understanding nature which might be an alternative to the objectifying approach of the natural sciences. Nonetheless, at present this alternative framework is nothing but a draft on the level of our presuppositions. At best this has made a breach in the wall of our exclusive intellectual approach to nature, but in order to attain an alternative practice we will have to enter the wide open spaces that lie behind this wall.

3. A Practical Understanding of Nature

a. Integrative hermeneutics

How can we break open the reifications to which language tempts us, so that the prediscursive abilities too can be integrated into the understanding of nature? It must be a matter of integration because the development of a prelinguistic understanding may not be considered an alternative to a scorned linguistic communication; it should rather be considered an equally valuable ingredient of all understanding. To achieve such integration we must first gain more insight into the way language and corporeality are related. The comparison between human and animal may shed some light on this.

When a fox in the wood picks up a life-advancing or life-threatening signal, its body is brought into a state of readiness right away: its hormones are mobilized, its heart rate accelerates, its muscles become tense, ready to mate, fight or flee. Naturally the fox can be mistaken; it may have picked up a false alarm. But still, within its own horizon of behaviour, its reaction is adequate, since the signals it reacts to do immediately concern its bodily survival. For humans this is mostly different. Precisely the same general mobilization of the body may be brought about by purely imaginary threats or temptations. The reason for this is that we often react to symbolic representations. Though our lives are by no means in danger when our favourite self image is verbally attacked, we will still begin to feel aggressive and to perspire. The human body is like a marionette hanging on the strings of language. The body is the accomplice of the discursive regime.

This intertwinement of corporeal and discursive order cannot be avoided or nullified, however, because our eccentricity and its concomitant symbolic order are not just a layer on top of an animal substratum which has undergone no transformations. The philosophy of eccentricity breaks with the classical images of man and nature which regarded an animal as a plant plus something extra and man as an animal equipped with reason or whatever else was considered characteristic. Reflexivity is but one exponent of eccentricity, and it is not the origin of our disunity. We are discorded to the core; even in our corporeal and emotional roots. Only we humans are dual with respect to our corporeality, by virtue of our ability to both express ourselves relationally and direct ourselves instrumentally. Only we can indulge in our feelings, can be passionate and sentimental. It is absolutely impossible to return to an immediate holistic corporeality and affectiveness by disconnecting or peeling off the linguistic level. Language is not a yoke, placed on an animal body, that can be shaken off. It is, however, possible to alleviate the effects language inevitably has on the body. By means of its vocabulary, language can also provide horizons for encounters with other life forms in which the body can receive its rightful share and in which it can unfold itself optimally. The point is not to abolish discursive understanding, but to find the right balance between language, corporeality and affectiveness.

According to Plessner language on the one hand liberates us, because it allows us to transcend the situation our body is in, while on the other hand it constricts us, because the 'outside' we perceive is dictated by language. Language unlocks the world in a way specific to the culture we live in, but at the same time it locks out complete sectors of all that might be perceived.[10] It offers recipes for action laid down in words, but the contents of these recipes are dominated by pragmatic motives. Language cannot cope with the subtle ramifications between the different levels of expression of life itself. It simplifies, selects, reorganizes. Eskimos distinguish between different types of snow, each type corresponding with a different strategy for action; conversely inhabitants of Amsterdam call all kinds of birds 'siskins' and hence a duck a 'floating siskin'. The reduction of all meanings expressed by nature to what can be handled culturally has far-reaching effects on the body, the receiver – in spite of itself – of the surplus of meaning not covered by language. If a culture restricts itself to discursive understanding, ignoring pre-discursive expressions of meaning, the body gets the worst of it. Every culture needs to discipline the body to a certain extent, in accordance with its pragmatic priorities, but disciplining need not degenerate into enslavement. The symbolic order of one culture can be more susceptible to prediscursive expressions of meaning than that of others. Linguistic understanding can create more or less room for the extra-linguistic components of understanding. In our culture, however, this certainly takes place only very scantily, causing the body to have a rough time. For this reason, the road to understanding nature first of all requires a rehabilitation of body-consciousness and of affectiveness, both understood in their eccentric ambivalence, i.e. not as an unbroken (or holistic) alternative to the presumed disrupting influence of the intellect.

Duintjer draws up the balance sheet for our culture, with its obsession with verbal communication. He differentiates between five dimensions of experience which have fallen into disuse as a result of our exclusive identification with rational-empirical consciousness. I will present them in my own order. In the first place the possibility of perceiving internally our own bodies with their living organs, energy flows and blockades: we often fail to notice the internal signals of our bodies until we cross the threshold to illness. Next comes the sensory openness to our surroundings: while walking in the woods we are often more occupied with the bodily reactions to the images unfolding in our heads (like a continuous illuminated news trailer), than with our surroundings; while tripping over tree roots we rehearse precarious conversations. If these two neglected dimensions of experience are restored, the road is opened up again to the third level of experience, namely a mature emotional life: moods, emotions etc. are subject to the heart's own logic; but in our culture sentimental popsongs set the tone. Finally Duintjer mentions two more dimensions which have both fallen victim to the arbitrary division between the physical and the metaphysical realm and are now treated as supernatural nonsense accordingly: in the fourth place there is the dimension of dreams, visions, creative imagination, mythical consciousness; and in the fifth place the cosmic dimension, which can be entered through prayer or meditation. While the world of myths and dreams is populated differently by different cultures, the cosmic dimension is universal. It opens up the dimension of the inexhaustible: the space embracing all possible worlds including the above mentioned levels of experience.

In Duintjer's enumeration of neglected dimensions of experience one very important dimension is missing: that of rationality. Discursiveness and rationality are not the same thing. A onesided emphasis on discursive understanding is at the expense of the integrative approach to man and nature for which I would like to reserve the honorary title 'rationality'. The truncated form of rationality we use nowadays does not deserve this title at all. This is why I take Dilthey's appeal for 'individuation' – for becoming a complete person through integrative hermeneutics – seriously, as the shortest way to a rational relationship with nature. The burning question remains, however: how can we do this?

b. *The common ground of understanding*

Human corporeality and affectiveness are not the same as those of animals, not even if we could switch off our intellect. This makes the relationship between human and animal fundamentally asymmetrical. However, it is not only humans who are in that position. The mongoose also has a fundamentally asymmetrical position with respect to the cobra. Nature is full of asymmetrical relationships; in interspecies understanding these are often the rule rather than the exception. 'Life understands life', not on the grounds of equality but rather in spite of all the differences in self expression and modes of understanding. Nevertheless, mutual understanding can only take place against the background of a common order which both parties to the exchange share. This common order of expressions and understanding is not found in language, as anthropocentric thinkers like to believe, but in the order of the body. What links all forms of life is the vulnerability of their incarnation. Obviously humans experience their corporeality differently from other animals, but they share the vulnerability of the body. Life is constantly threatened; in order to be able to share this experience with other forms of life we, human beings, must not take a step backwards and retreat into the conceptual sphere, but we must dare to move forwards, deeper into corporeal nature with all its grief. Merleau-Ponty spoke of 'la chair du monde', 'the flesh of the world'.

The shared flesh is the precondition for all hermeneutics and for a morality which springs from our shared fragility. This is why the question whether an animal suffers pain when we burn its paw, is absolutely wrong. This question can only be posed in a discursive atmosphere, from which all corporeality has been banned. To enter into this atmosphere we must first take leave of all that links us through the flesh. The question posed presents itself as the opening move of a moral discourse but on close inspection it is a symptom of a distanced attitude, in which the principle of morality with regard to nature has been discarded beforehand.

But do we really want to disconnect ourselves from our bodies? This is an option which is open only to a human; only we can transcend our being a body because of our eccentricity. For centuries, discursiveness and consciousness, even spirituality, have been wrongly considered synonyms. One became increasingly human the more one managed to break away from natural roots. The ideal of the philosopher was *apatheia*. What could possibly counterbalance this? The only likely candidate would be a philosophy of love, in which love is not conceived as a sentiment but as a total surrender to one's finite existence, as a daring choice for incarnation.

The phenomenologist Max Scheler said valuable things about the development of the emotional life under the guidance of love.[11] In both ancient Greek philosophy and Buddhism, love is depicted as the guide which leads the soul upwards, away from the chains of corporeal existence; love aimed at transcending the pain of our incarceration in the flesh. Christianity, on the other hand, is characterized, according to Scheler, by a reversal of the direction in which love leads us. Not only does love lead upwards to God, God himself loves life and surrenders himself to corporeal existence with all its restrictions. Loving is 'amare in Deo': participating in the act of the divine incarnation, because only through this – and not through a premature leavetaking from the body – do we transcend our self-imposed borders in the direction of our fellow subjects, forms of life other than the human included.

That this conception of love is also found outside the religious sphere is shown by Ton Lemaire in his little book on tenderness.[12] For instance when he talks about caressing: caressing is cautious bodily contact, which on the one hand expresses respect and awe for the other person's transcendence, but which on the other hand at the same time invites the other person to coincide with his body, as it is only in this that transcendence may be realized. Only man is capable of this paradoxical unity of transcendence and incarnation. Love – that is, the way human eccentricity pre-eminently shows itself on the level of feelings – makes the world of the flesh lucid in its expressivity. There is no need to look elsewhere for the essence of life, prying into a 'higher' sphere apart from the body, as Plato and many others after him did. Granted for the sake of argument that such an essentialistic approach makes sense, the essence must be conceived as being embodied right from the start. This is why Scheler, in the footsteps of Augustine, calls love 'the a priori of knowledge'. If we approach the world with a non-participating objectifying attitude – as the scientific method requires – the objects will hide themselves from us and show us only an inaccessible surface: but as soon as we treat them lovingly, they open up and show themselves from within. Yet the appeal for a sensitive intellect does not remove us from the scientific world view, nor does it present an alternative for it. On the contrary: one should rather say that the scientific enterprise has difficulty understanding itself and recognizing its own deeper motives the moment its methodology renounces participation. Subjective involvement with the 'object' of research often *does* play a decisive role, but this aspect is usually not brought to the fore in the justification of the resulting scientific theories, since justification in the domain of science – unjustifiably – only allows for criteria bearing on the discursive order. Hence we are more concerned here with bringing to the light an aspect already present (at least in the context of discovery) but mostly discarded, and drawing up quality requirements for it, than with adding new ingredients to the practice of science.

We can only understand the self-expression of nature if we accept our being corporeal and finite, and this also applies to science. 'Non intratur in veritatem, nisi per charitatem', i.e. 'One cannot enter truth, except through love', Scheler quotes Augustine. Usually we tend to get caught in the ambivalences of our sentiments. Love leads us in developing our emotional life. A mature emotional life enables us to comprehend the plenitude of meaning in nature which must remain concealed as long as we do not dare assent to our own naturalness.

c. Becoming human through understanding nature

What is the meaning that lies hidden in nature? In my appeal for a hermeneutics of nature I do not want to evoke the illusion of an Arcadia where the lion lies next to the lamb. On the contrary, nature is as paradoxical as its fruit: man. She is generous and cruel at the same time. Nature is excessive in her gifts: each year every oak produces countless acorns, but how many of these actually develop into a tree? Nature gives in abundance but she is very wasteful of individuals. In a newspaper article entitled 'There is more dying than living in nature', Midas Dekkers (a well-known Dutch biologist) wrote, 'Four fifths of all the animals born in spring die in winter. Five million sparrows die, five thousand foxes go to pieces, as do a hundred thousand seagulls, a billion insects disappear, in the Netherlands alone; there is more dying than living in nature. On top of this the men in the slaughterhouses kill off another million imprisoned animals.'[13]

To these dramatic figures we can add the incalculable suffering of human beings. The level of sensitivity required for a hermeneutics of nature can only be bought at a high price: taking leave of the idyll and accepting co-responsibility for suffering, even though the latter has never been inflicted by you on purpose.

This is why the title of my essay, 'The mouse in the cat's claws', was taken from Bataille. The quotation literally reads, 'Instead of worshipping we might see the mouse in the cat's claws.'[14] With these words Bataille, in my opinion, indicates that the starting point of philosophy should be the experience of suffering in nature, the experience of the vulnerability and the injurability of corporeal existence, and not, as is usually the case, some cerebral self understanding which sees the 'I' as the pivot on which the world hinges. In his book on the prehistoric cave paintings of Lascaux,[15] Bataille penetratingly describes our being as grievously torn apart, on the one hand unable to participate completely in the animal kingdom while on the other unable to withdraw from it for good. Man will always remain aware of the gulf dividing his life, a gulf which he can at the most delineate in shamanistic rituals, but which he can never annul.

No wonder that we recoil. And yet the road through nature is also the way to our transcending ourselves. To be able to understand we must say goodbye to all that is so reassuringly familiar and face the world from the point of view of our insurmountable alienation. 'Grief is the mind's eye',[16] Plessner says. Being different hurts, but it is also the precondition for true partnership. 'Der Mensch versteht sich aufs Heterogene' (Man understands himself only through encounters with the heterogeneous), is Plessner's summary of human existence. Yet here, of course, also lies the seed of joy and pleasure. There is after all more to life than suffering. In embracing one another's naked existence, in the healing which results from affirming that which is so painfully different, suffering is transcended.

Self understanding and becoming whole can only be achieved if one willingly listens to that which is different. Viewed in this light, the philosophical controversy between anthropocentrism and ecocentrism is merely a pseudo-problem. Human understanding of nature is anthropocentric, but as a result of our eccentricity we will not become aware of our own centre unless we open up to what is different from ourselves. Thus ecocentrism and anthropocentrism presuppose each other.

Ultimately we derive our self understanding as incarnated consciousness from our openness towards other organisms. Spirituality which, afraid of suffering, forsakes nature, is nothing but self betrayal. This is the same conclusion Otto Duintjer eventually draws. At first he looked upon the cosmic dimension – the awareness of which he places at the top of the list of neglected experiences – as the inner void from which worlds spring forth inexhaustably but which can only be reached through detachment from the world. Later on, however, he tended more towards equating this cosmic dimension with inexhaustible life, with 'Mother Nature'. Both points of view stem from the same root: our human eccentricity, which makes it difficult to endorse life wholesale. True spirituality, however, does not unfold itself in spite of organic suffering, but by living through it. Therefore we have to be willing to link ourselves up with our vulnerable bodies, so as to be completely present, no matter how difficult that may be. Only the others we encounter in bodily presence can invite us to a reconciliation with life. There are still fellow-terrestrials who, because their expressiveness differs from ours, can teach *us* what it means to be human. Let us listen to them before through our negligence of life their voices fall silent forever.

NOTES

1. Duintjer, Otto 1983. 'Produceren en andere wijzen van menszijn', *Tijdschrift voor Filosofie*, **45**, no. 3: 421-58, Leuven; and 'Over natuur, vervreemding en heelwording'. In Achterberg, W. & Zweers, W. (eds), 1984, *Milieucrisis & Filosofie*, pp. 189-207. Utrecht, Van Arkel.
2. Bulhof, Ilse N. 1992.*The Language of Science: a study of the relationship between literature and science in the perspective of a hermeneutical approach: with a casestudy of Darwin's The origin of species.* Leiden, Brill.
3. Dilthey, Wilhelm,1968. *Die geistige Welt. Einleitung in die Philosophie des*

Lebens. Gesammelte Schriften V. Band. p. 144. Stuttgart/Gottingen, Teubner Verlag.

4. Dilthey, Wilhelm,1981 (1910). *Der Aufbau der geschichtlichen Welt in den Geisteswissenschaften.* p. 283. Frankfurt: Suhrkamp.

5. Ibid., p. 321.

6. Plessner, Helmuth, 1975 (1928) *Die Stufen des Organischen und der Mensch.* p.22. Berlin, de Gruyter.

7. Ibid. For Plessner's key-concept of 'intentional realization of borders' see: *Stufen* III.5 (99-105) and IV.2 (126-32).

8. Wiener, Norbert, 1948/1961. *Cybernetics: or Control and Communication in the Animal and the Machine.* p.174, Cambridge Mass., MIT Press.

9. Plessner, 1975 (1928), p. 259.

10. Plessner, Helmuth, 'Der Mensch als Lebewesen', *Merkur,* June 1967; also included in H. Plessner (ed.) *Die Frage nach der Conditio Humana* 1976, Frankfurt, Suhrkamp, pp. 111-23, especially pp. 112-13. Quote: 'Jede Sprache ist ein Gitter, durch dessen Stäbe wir als Gefangene in ein illusionäres Draussen schauen'.

11. Scheler, Max, 1974 (1915), *Liebe und Erkenntnis.* Bern, Francke Verlag.

12. Lemaire, Ton, *De tederheid.* Bilthoven, Ambo.

13. Dekkers, Midas. 'In de natuur wordt meer gestorven dan geleefd', *NRC-Zaterdagsbijvoegsel,* 9-3-1985.

14. Bataille, Georges,1954. *L'experience interieure.* Paris, Editions Gallimard.

15. Bataille, Georges, 1986 (1955). *Die Hohlenbilder von Lascaux, oder die Geburt der Kunst.* Stuttgart, Klett-Cotta.

16. Plessner, Helmuth,1979 (1948). 'Mit anderen Augen', in *Zwischen Philosophie und Gesellschaft.* .pp. 233-48, quote on p. 239. Frankfurt, Suhrkamp.

Chapter 9

TOWARDS A HERMENEUTICS OF NATURE: ON THE NECESSITY OF ENDURING DISTANCE

Maarten Coolen

1. KNOWLEDGE OF NATURE'S INHERENT CHARACTER

How can I know something that is different from myself? It may seem rather strange to start a discussion about the possibility of a hermeneutical approach to nature with a question like this. However, we do expect from a hermeneutics of nature that it will provide us with something we regard the hypothetical-deductive natural sciences as incapable of doing: a knowledge of the plenitude, the sense and the meaning of the inward coherence of nature, in which it reveals itself exactly as it is by and in itself. This we do not demand from the modern natural sciences. We content ourselves with the fact that they can only provide knowledge of the way in which nature appears when we objectify nature by departing from the principles of analysability and obedience to laws, which are exactly the principles by which knowledge within these sciences is constituted.

The reason why modern natural sciences have to ignore any potential sense and meaning natural occurrences may have by themselves is that we have to abstract from any concrete content directly given to us in everyday life by analysing it into a number of factors each of which can be determined logically independent from the others. These are subsequently placed in a new relationship, it is true, but this new order is constructed by the scientific researcher himself. The separate data obtained in this way are connected with each other by means of law-like relationships, thus bringing about a structure of which the form can be represented in mathematical terms. In this process events are conceived of as manifestations of these nomological connections. These relations are added to the data after the latter have already been established. In the hermeneutical tradition such relations are therefore called *external* relationships, in contrast with *internal* relationships; the latter exist between the constituent parts of a meaningful whole, in which case the parts can only be thought of *in terms of* the whole.

Law-governed connections are tested in experiments; in such testing one necessarily has to intervene in the course of events in nature. It is often inferred from this that the natural sciences do not have any respect for nature at all, and that technology stems from humanity's need to subject nature to its own arbitrary actions. I do not agree with that. In the natural sciences and in technology too, it has in the end to be assumed that nature has a typical quality of its own: for we should not forget that in both we are seeking the workings of nature itself, although under conditions imposed by us.[1]

However, it is not in wrong to say that the manner in which the natural sciences study nature has to be at the expense of an understanding of the purport of the internal relations potentially present in nature. On the one hand, in modern natural sciences nature is placed as an object opposite to the knowing subject, turning it into something alien to and distant from humanity. On the other hand, nature is regarded as matter that appears only in accordance with law-governed connections formulated by the subject, which makes it appear that nature can be completely subordinated within the domain of human action.

The more nature is present as something 'for me', the greater my knowledge of it becomes; the more its own typical qualities are at issue, so much more it withdraws itself from my cognition. That is, put in a rather exaggerated fashion, the paradox for which the natural sciences cannot offer a solution. How, then, am I able to learn to know nature, exactly insofar as it *is* different from humanity? And how can I, at the same time, bridge the distance between myself and nature created by nomological objectification? It is to these questions that we may hope to find answers in a hermeneutics of nature.

The humanities in the hermeneutical tradition (in German: *Geisteswissenschaften*) are directed towards understanding (German verb: *verstehen*)[2] the values, aims and meanings people attach to external events, by looking at what they have given rise to in the way of cultural objects of any kind. Certainly it would be a fine thing if we could extend the hermeneutical approach to bring to light the sense and meaning that are present in the forms of nature. In my short contribution I wish to discuss some problems we stumble upon when trying to reach such an extension of hermeneutics.

2. NATURE AS A COHERENT ENTITY OF MEANING

We must not fall into the erroneous assumption that the conception of nature as a coherent entity of meaning has not arisen until recent times. Already in the 1920s there were biologists who supported a holistic approach to animate nature, in which phenomena are understood in the light of the purposes they serve for the whole organism or the whole class of living beings. Their objective was to overcome both mechanism and vitalism.[3] In the mechanistic view organisms are approached as mechanisms of which the behaviour can be completely explained in terms of law-like connections. The vitalists, remarkably enough, also kept to the principle of government by laws, except that they additionally postulated the existence of a non-material life force, which in typical phenomena of life acts as a cause of an event along with purely physical-chemical forces, but which at the same time defies further natural scientific research.

In latter years some biologists have defended a view that is in line with holism: they hold that in the life sciences a second type of explanation is needed in addition to the law-like relationship, namely the teleological or functional explanation. Not only are living beings separated from their surroundings by an external boundary – like a stone in a river – but they realize this boundary *themselves*. This is brought about through feedback within the organism; with higher animals the central nervous system plays an important role in accomplishing this. The physical-chemical processes in which the organism participates, do, of course, allow a full nomological explanation, but then one ignores the function they have in the realization of the boundary by the organism in question. A good example of this is that of plankton organisms, which daily cover large vertical distances in the sea: in the morning downwards, in the afternoon upwards. The physical-chemical processes that take place here can be entirely explained in terms of nomological connections. Nevertheless, one may ask: why do these organisms do this? Are they not able to withstand light, or is that the way they find what can serve them as nutrition? What is the biological purpose or meaning of these processes?

One may find this way of searching for meaningful internal relationships leads to rather meagre results, but it does have the advantage that it is still directed at meaning that is inherent in nature itself. In the hermeneutical approach to nature that Ilse Bulhof has proposed recently, things are quite different. She wants to extend the hermeneutics that has been developed to interpret cultural objects to include things not made by humans, such as nature. As examples she mentions the interpretation of a landscape by a poet or by a cultural anthropologist. What then matters is the articulation of the meaning the landscape has in a specific personal experience or in a historical-cultural context.[4] In the sunrise the poet sees the very beginning of a new love, whereas the cultural anthropologist sees in the formation of the landscape the traces people have left behind. My objection to this is that the meaning discovered in this way is a human one that has subsequently been added to nature.

The extension of the hermeneutics from culture to nature which I am seeking is quite different. A hermeneutical approach to nature must bring to light the *intrinsic* sense or meaning of nature, not merely what humans put into it because of their cultural background. This is why I am against conceiving nature as a text that asks to be interpreted. Anyone who has more in mind than a metaphor in holding this position will soon fall into an anthropomorphic misinterpretation of nature as a text. Mostly, the ultimate aim of the philosophers who advise us to 'read in the book of nature' is not to obtain greater knowledge of nature's own typical qualities, but more knowledge of God or about human beings.[5] Although text and nature both form coherent entities of meaning the contents of which I can try to recover, the foundations that support the internal relations in the coherences of meaning are of a completely different kind in either case.

In a text a person tells how he sees a certain state of affairs; the whole is therefore founded in the world of experiences that person has had. When I read the text, I am not trying to evoke the same experiences in my mind as the author may have had, but instead I am attempting to gain some insight into what he is talking about and into the world of experiences that underlie his view of it. In order to be able to do this it must be assumed that human actions are characterized by intentionality. When studying nature it is important to descry in the inner relational coherence what is involved in an organism being alive; at the basis of this coherence of meaning lies the specific way in which this organism as a living being realizes its boundary between itself and its environment. The processes that take place in living organisms are to a large extent unmistakably purposive. But it would be wrong to interpret this as a form of intentionality in which the goal the organism is oriented to is also represented as a goal. An organism cannot explicitly set itself the target to realize a specific state through its behaviour. I shall return to this in the following section.

Perhaps some may find the effort to reach a hermeneutics of nature as discussed in this section unsatisfactory, while an approach that takes the expressiveness of nature as a starting point, such as that attempted by Petran Kockelkoren in his contribution to this book, may be more to their liking. That is what we shall turn to now.

3. Expressivity of Living Beings

The hermeneutical humanities *(Geisteswissenschaften)* should, according to Wilhelm Dilthey, the father of this type of science, concentrate on human situations insofar as people *live* in them and have expressed themselves in them; by understanding what has been expressed in various cultural constructs, human life can shed some light on itself.[6] We can understand ourselves and others only through the fact that we and they take part in expressing the modes in which people live. What takes place in the course of human history manifests itself in all kinds of material objects. Scholars in the humanities have a special interest in trying to tell from these sensorily perceptible data what occurrences between people have taken place. For example, when a war is being carried on, there are tanks on the battlefield and politicians and military men appear on television making statements during press conferences. For a historian giving a historical account of a war, it is legitimate to use phrases in which he tells us about the feelings of indignation the attacked country holds towards the aggressor, in consequence of which the tenacious resistance by the defending army may very well be understood. Since feelings of indignation are not directly sensorily perceptible it is (i) necessary that they find expression in something external – in our example the occurrences during the war. Further, we cannot talk about feelings of indignation without (ii) having experienced ourselves what it is to be inflamed in indignation. And we must also (iii) assume that our experiences are in relevant respects comparable with those undergone by the people whose actions we wish to understand. If these three conditions are fulfilled, we may legitimately claim that talking about feelings of indignation can contribute to the understanding of the war in question.

Summing up, life and experiencing life (German: *Leben* and *beleben*), expression *(Ausdruck)*, and understanding *(verstehen)* form the triad that makes up the philosophical foundation of Dilthey's hermeneutical humanities *(Geisteswissenschaften)*. We understand what has happened in other people's lives and in our own lives, by seeing the inner meaning of life through the external constructs in which life has expressed itself.

But we have to take into account that when Dilthey talked of life expressing itself, he had only human life in mind. Would it now be possible to extend this coherence of life, expression and understanding in such a way that it becomes sensible to say that we can also understand expressions by living beings other than humans? In this short discussion I shall confine myself to animals and take as an example the understanding of the experiencing of pain by animals. The first two conditions are, it seems, easily fulfilled. We can tell from the animal's outward expression that it is in pain. Also, we have ourselves experienced what it is to be in pain. The third condition, however, in which the assumption is made that there exists a reciprocity between the one who understands and the one understood, our attempt to extrapolate hermeneutics to natural phenomena runs up against difficulties. Such a reciprocity between humans and animals does not exist. From Helmuth Plessner, a philosophical anthropologist who in his writings never tires of bringing the body's constitutive role in all our actions and all our cognition to our notice, we learn that we should not equate our human experience of pain with the experience of pain animals have. Although we share with the animals that we are embodied beings, our embodiedness happens to be of a completely different nature than the embodiedness of animals.

How is it different? Any organism that can move itself about has a relationship with its body. But only a human being can procure the means of turning the body into an instrument and thereby putting it into service in order to achieve a certain goal: only a human can take a position towards such a relationship to the body. We can look at ourselves as it were from outside, as if we were an entity different from ourselves. With respect to human life the body has two traits in common with language:[7] on the one hand, the instrumental character of the body (and of language) helps a human being to be free, because he or she can use it in this or that manner in the course of self realization; but, on the other hand, the body (and language) is a prison, because one remains thrown back on the specific qualities of the body (language) while being in contact with reality.

There is another phenomenon related to this. The human being, unlike animals, can refer to itself as 'I'. The perspective from which humans look on themselves as an 'I' is often wrongly understood. It is something very different from a primitive kind of egocentricity, in which surroundings are seen as entirely centred around the self, and the self is the pivot on which the world turns. A being that is totally absorbed in relating everything to itself, as animals are, does not have the possibility of distancing itself from this central point it occupies in its environment. Therefore, this centre is impenetrable: it does not have an 'inside'. When a human being understands the self as an 'I', a breach is made in this solid closedness: an opening 'inwards' is made, by which that person's position in the world and with respect to the self loses its centredness and becomes eccentric (in the strict sense of the word: ec-centric); one can then say that there is an inner self to which one can relate. Exactly by being able to say 'I', humans cannot be egocentric in an innocent manner any more.[8]

A human being can take a position at a distance from the body, which an animal will always be spared. An animal is at one with its body; insofar as it 'has' its body, this is entirely bound to the situation in which it has to fulfil specific locomotive demands, as is the case in pouncing upon a prey. Only a human can also exert control over his body in other ways, by using that body in all sorts of situations so as to realize something through actions, because a human being is sheathed in the body, quite different from an animal, which coincides with its body. We have a double relationship to our physical existence: we *are* our bodies and we *have* our bodies. But we must be on our guard against conceiving this 'having' only in terms of usefulness: to Plessner the body is also an instrument which can be played on.[9]

The human self awareness manifest in being able to say 'I', and the human being's distance from his or her own body are connected with the human ability to take as a starting point the assumption that the other person can have experiences and give expression to himself in the same way as oneself. Not only can I look at the other person as I see myself through my own eyes, I can also see myself through the other person's eyes. Through this capacity, the self-centredness to which an animal is confined is broken. Only people can have this sort of reciprocal relationship.

The realizing of its boundary by an organism which we have dealt with before may be construed as a self-positing.[10] However, we should take care not to interpret this in an all too human manner. It must be emphasized that when an animal posits the boundary between itself and the outer world, it does not posit this boundary *as* a boundary. This circumscription is given to the animal along with its belonging to its species; it has no power to choose or alter it. It cannot tread outside of its own field of view. Humans can do exactly that, because they can take a position at a distance from the centre of their own actions. While an animal has a fixed horizon that allows it to have a repertory of behaviour that it cannot change, a human being because of this eccentric position is continually able to change the horizon within which he or she understands and acts. An animal's environment is closed, whereas the human world is open.

What can we learn from this difference in corporeality between human and animal when it comes to understanding what an animal is expressing? That we human beings are able to understand that an animal can experience pain is so not only because we too can be in pain. For that to be possible our eccentric position and our open horizon are also required, which provide us with a distance to the pain, as a result of which we can suffer from it if it is our own pain, or be compassionate if the pain is of another person or of an animal. Our experience of pain is always double: we find ourselves in pain, and we suffer from our vulnerability. Analogous remarks may, of course, also be made in connection with the experiencing of joy. Here a fundamental asymmetry exists: we understand what the animal experiences, but our experience of something similar is always thoroughly human. With hindsight it turns out that with animals expression and experience have a different structure from that of human beings: centred as opposed to eccentric. I cannot share Kockelkoren's view in the matter of the asymmetrical relation between the mongoose and the snake being comparable with the relationship between human and animal.[11] In my opinion the mongoose does not understand the expressions of the snake. It has a repertory of potential behaviour through which the expressions of the snake's behaviour are completely drawn within the perspective of its own self-realization. Understanding expressions of another species lies within the capability only of a being that, like a human, can set a distance to its realizing by itself of its own boundaries. Comprehension simply cannot be possible without a capacity to relate to the horizon of self from which things are understood, as much as to the horizon of the other being. That is why an understanding between species only exists in the case of humanity in relation to other living beings.

When we humans try to understand what animals experience, we must avoid interpreting their expressions anthropomorphically, that is as manifestations of an eccentric mode of being.

4. WHY STRIVE FOR A HERMENEUTICS OF NATURE?

Why is it desirable to strive for a hermeneutics of nature? Because in this approach to nature we allow ourselves to be acquainted with nature as if it were a fellow subject? I appreciate what is intended in such an answer; nevertheless, the consequence is that the typical asymmetry in the understanding of nature arising from humanity's eccentric position tends to disappear. On my account I would prefer to say that we wish to learn to know nature in itself, or the specific way in which other living beings have selves of their own (which is different from the human way of 'being for oneself' or being a subject), of which sense, value and meaning can be brought to light in a hermeneutical approach.

How then can we learn to know the intrinsic character and value of other living beings? This is possible through our own experience and interpretation, provided that we accept the fact that they have a mode of being different from ours. Only if we take this unavoidable epistemological anthropocentrism seriously can we succeed in avoiding the anthropomorphic short circuit lurking in every hermeneutics of nature

'Grief is in the mind's eye.' I would like to read this pronouncement by Plessner[12] as meaning that in the end only a being that can suffer is able to understand another being. A prerequisite of grief is detachment from nature, from one's own and from that of the other, as well as an eccentric position in the world. It is up to us to take upon ourselves this special position, which animals have been spared. Whoever wants to understand sense and meaning in nature will have to endure the distance from nature which is necessary to that end.

A deeper understanding of ourselves as natural beings – our special eccentric position included – may bring us closer to the very nature of nature. When we pay more attention to things as they are in themselves we can also take account of them in a better way. The hermeneutical approach to nature may therefore be seen as an attempt to find a foundation that enables us to act respectfully and responsibly with regard to nature, starting from the value it has by and in itself.

NOTES

1. Coolen, Marten 1989. 'Enkele filosofisch-antropologische notities over hot maken'. In W. Achterberg (ed.), *Natuur: uitbuiting of respect?* pp. 46-64. Kampen, Kok Agora.

2. In this essay I translate the German *verstehen* by 'understand' (cf.. von Wright, G.H. 1971. *Explanation and Understanding,* London: Routledge & Kegan Paul.) in spite of the fact that in a Kantian context 'understanding' is the translation of the German *Verstand*, which has a very different meaning.

3. Some names: J.C. Smuts, J.S. Haldane, A. Meyer-Abich.

4. Bulhof, Ilse N. 1988. 'Hermeneutiek en natuurwetenschappen'. In T. de Boer et al. (eds), *Hermeneutiek: filosofische grondslagen van mens-en cultuurwetenschappen* pp.240-61, see p.241. Meppel, Boom. 1988. The further elaboration of the examples is on my account.

5. See e.g. Verhoog, H. 1989. 'Lezen in het boek der natuur'. In W. Achterberg (ed.), *Natuur: uitbuiting of respect?* pp.145-59, especially pp 145-6.

6.Dilthey, Wilhelm 1970.*Der Aufbau der geschichtlichen Welt in den Geisteswissenschaften,* p 98 ff. Frankfurt am Main, Suhrkamp.

7. For the aspect of language referred to, see Petran Kockelkoren's contribution to this book, section 3a.

8. Plessner, Helmut 'Der Mensch als Lebewesen', in *Gesammelte Schriften VIII; Conditio humana,* pp. 314-27; see p. 319. I have also made use of his book 1928.*Die Stufen des Organischen und der Mensch,* especially p.100 ff. and p.288 ff. Berlin & Leipzig, De Gruyter.

9. Plessner, H. op. cit., p. 321.

10. See Kockelkoren's contribution, section 2b.

11. The example is found in section 2c, the commentary remarks in section 2e of his contribution.

12.Plessner,H. 1979. 'Mit anderen Augen', in *Zwischen Philosophie und Gesellschaft.* pp. 233-48, quotation on p. 239; Frankfurt am Main, Suhrkamp. Also quoted by Kockelkoren.

Chapter 10

POTTER'S BULL AND CASTRATED PIGS: CONSIDERING THE IMPOSSIBILITY OF A HERMENEUTIC NATURAL SCIENCE.

Susanne Lijmbach

1. INTRODUCTION

One of the problems of contemporary philosophy of nature is that pair of concepts, nature and culture. In many philosophy of nature texts 'nature' stands for reality independent of humanity. 'Culture' stands for meaningful reality. The word 'meaningful' is used because culture is created by man and its meaning derives from this fact. Our behaviour and knowledge of both nature and culture can be compared with one another in the same way. Behaviour involving nature is always instrumental behaviour, in which nature is only a means (instrument) of realizing human ends (meanings). In contrast with this, behaviour involving cultural reality is tuned into the meaning of that reality. According to these philosophers of nature, nature is seen as an instrument not only in cattle farming and animal experimentation, but also, for example, in art. Even to Potter the bull is seen purely as a means of satisfying his and other people's aesthetic needs. We treat Potter's painting, a cultural phenomenon, with care. In stark contrast to this, the bull's life may have ended in a gruesome way. In science, the contrast between nature and culture is also depicted as a contrast between natural and cultural sciences. For example knowledge of the bull is knowledge of the biological processes taking place in the bull, such as genetic and physiological processes; knowledge of Potter's painting is knowledge of the way in which Potter has depicted the bull, knowledge that amongst other things can refer to the meaning of bulls and/or their aesthetic meaning to Potter and to people of his age and of ours. In the above I have attempted to indicate the way in which nature and culture are characterized in the philosophy of nature.

It is this gulf between nature and culture, and thus between behaviour and knowledge of nature and culture, which people involved with the philosophy of nature are attempting to bridge. This they do by means of hermeneutics and a hermeneutic science of nature, comparable with the understanding of culture and cultural science. Supporters of a hermeneutic of nature and a hermeneutic science presume that natural phenomena are meaningful expressions, which should be understood and acknowledged as such, analogous to cultural phenomena. A specific example of this is that the frequency at which pigs squeal changes once their spermatic cord has been castrated.[1] Hermeneutic animal scientists take this change in frequency to be an expression of pain, pain being a phenomenon which is meaningful to the pigs themselves. These scientists believe that it is possible to develop hermeneutic scientific knowledge about such expressions of feeling in pigs.

The rest of my paper will be a defence of the following proposition: a hermeneutic experience of nature is a necessary precondition for any type of knowledge of nature. However, firstly, the meaning that I shall refer to is the meaning of nature to us as people, and secondly, in hermeneutic science it is not nature, but the human experience of nature that is the subject of research. I shall explain my proposal using human contact with and knowledge of animals as an example.

2. HERMENEUTIC EXPERIENCE AS THE BASIS OF KNOWLEDGE

I presume that the criticism of biased observations as the basis of scientific theories is well known. According to this criticism, observation is an activity which people take part in on the basis of already accepted theories, paradigms, or cultural or social backgrounds. Numerous scientific-historical studies have been carried out on the way in which theories, paradigms or culture have kept the development of scientific disciplines within specific boundaries.

Animals too are always viewed within a specific horizon. For this reason, ethologists speak of different paradigmatic images of animals.[2] In her research into Darwin's use of metaphors, Bulhof has also shown how Darwin and later evolutionary biologists became 'bewitched' by terms which are derived from animal breeding programmes and plant cultivation, such as the term 'selection'. They view the development of plant and animal species from the perspective of mother nature as a breeder and cultivator selecting the strongest animals and plants with which to continue to breed and cultivate.[3]

However, what applies to observations also applies to other sensory and bodily experiences of our surroundings. Potter was not surprised by the aesthetic pleasure he experienced when watching bulls, but he used a specific framework of aesthetic interpretation, a framework in which beautiful and ugly forms, colour and proportions all have a specific place. Other sensory and corporeal experiences, such as aesthetic and emotional ones, can be compared with observations which are not detached. It is the presumptions incorporated in these interpretative frameworks which we use to observe and experience nature and in which nature has meaning that I would like to emphasize when saying that the hermeneutic experience of nature is a necessary precondition for every type of knowledge of nature, even biological knowledge.

According to Gadamer, this necessary hermeneutic experience is linked to human linguistic abilities: our surroundings can only be expressed as a meaningful world through language.[4] Even though I agree with this, it does not mean that I view our relationship with, for example animals, as purely discursive. If we hear the squealing of pigs being castrated or if we take pleasure at seeing a bull, then the words 'pain' and 'beauty' are not merely words which represent the sound that the pigs produce or the forms and colours of bulls. Instead 'pain' and 'beauty' are both linked with a specific category of sensory-bodily experiences. However these sensory-bodily experiences only have meaning within the conceptual framework in which we are able to speak of our feelings. Even internal, human nature is only meaningful within a framework of interpretation.

In the introduction I said that the relationship between nature and culture is often understood as follows: on the one hand nature has no meaning in itself and is seen only as a means of realizing human goals; in contrast to this cultural phenomena are meaningful and our relationship with them is partially determined by their own meaning. This contrast between nature and culture needs further differentiation.

The use of nature as a means of realizing our aims also takes place on the basis of experiences of nature which are meaningful to us. In general we see nature's meaning here as technical activity with respect to nature. The nature of technological activity, for example, what is and is not allowed, is embedded in culture. Nature as a means of realizing our aims is part of our culture. The same can be said for art. The fact that it is now possible to make chimaeras, crosses between two animal species, says just as much about our culture as Potter's 'The Bull' did in his day and age.

By embedding technical activity in cultural activities, it is possible to consider nature as something other than an instrument. Potter's experience of beauty when looking the bulls was essential to him, and this experience has a very different meaning to that of a fervent biotechnologist who sees a 'beautiful' bull. By reducing both experiences to the same denominator of nature as an instrument, the difference disappears, so that both painting and genetic manipulation become technical activities. Thus the possibility that nature also has non-instrumental meaning to people is denied. Furthermore, if the experience of the squealing pigs is an expression of their pain, this can be seen as an argument against the use of animals as instruments. Apparently pigs seem to have a meaning other than as instruments to people.

3. THE MEANING OF NATURE IS A MEANING TO PEOPLE

In the meantime I have already touched on the second part of my proposition, namely that the meaning of nature, which we experience in our relationship with it, is a meaning which is derived from the meaning of nature to us as people. Up to now I have proposed that a hermeneutic experience is only meaningful thanks to interpretation or conceptualization of the surroundings. The second part of my proposition is that our relationship with nature is always asymmetrical, because only humans interpret natural phenomena, which are only of meaning to them; minerals, plants and animals do not interpret their own phenomena and behaviour. To them the phenomena and behaviour have no meaning.

In nature one cannot talk about the meaning of phenomena to nature itself, because a meaning is always an interpreted meaning, that is, possible alternative meanings also exist.[5] The behaviour of animals can naturally have different meanings to us, as the different paradigms in ethology indicate only too well. However these remain meanings for us *as humans*. A causal explanation of the behaviour of animals is also an explanation full of meaning, e.g., a meaning for ethologists.

In order to speak of meaningful expressions of, for example, pigs, a medium is required in which the same expressions can also have different meanings to pigs. In humans, the medium is spoken and written language. Our linguistic abilities allow us to conceptualize our surroundings and our inner nature in different ways, and to be able to discuss these with others and agree about them. I do not mean to say that the meaning of all our expressions is firstly discussed and agreed on before it can be understood by others, but that it is possible to agree on understanding each other's expressions by discussion. Since a comparable medium is lacking in minerals, plants and animals, this excludes the possibility, for example, that pigs themselves experience pain as a meaning of their behaviour. When we speak of the pig's pain on the basis of our experiences of their squeals, then the pain is our human interpretation of the squealing, an interpretation which we humans can agree on, but which the pigs themselves cannot establish and which the pigs and ourselves cannot agree on.

On the basis of the above it is possible to comment on the different ways in which the philosophy of nature discusses the meaning of the behaviour of animals to the animals themselves:

a. According to some people, animals do not have a language which is comparable to that of humans, although some animal species do have a conceptual ability and express this in their behaviour. Many studies should have proved that animals are able to form concepts of, for example, colours or things surrounding them.[6]

In such research the behaviour of the animals always coincides with its interpreted meaning. I question whether this is a meaning to the animals themselves, or whether the meaning is only understood by us. If we do not understand a specific behavioural pattern, then how are we supposed to discover its meaning if the animals can only 'answer' with another behavioural pattern which may be just as strange? It is not possible to observe concepts, that is mental occurrences which are expressed in behaviour. In particular, they are elements of a public scope for interpretation whereby agreement can be reached on the meaning of a specific type of behaviour. In the case of such studies, I would conclude that if one believes that animals' behaviour has some meaning to themselves, then one must firstly reflect on the meaning of 'meaning' in relation to concepts and behaviour and in comparison with concepts such as result, response and reaction.

b. Besides this there are philosophers of nature who use a totally different meaning of the word 'meaning'. According to them meanings exist not only through a communal language or symbolic order, but through a symbolic bodily order. Thus the squealing of pigs does not mean pain because the pigs *interpret* their bodily experience in the same way as humans do, but because pigs *express* their bodily experiences in the same way as humans, in this case an expression which we people interpret as pain.

The problem encountered via this line of reasoning is depicted in the concept of 'communal bodily order'. It seems plausible to me that biological (including behavioural) continuity exists between people and animals. However in the case of pigs experiencing pain, this is not seen as a biological phenomenon, but rather as pain as we know it, a horrible, negative, bodily experience. This reasoning presumes that there is communal order between animals and people as far as – meaningful – corporeal experiences are concerned, even though animals may not be able to interpret these as such. This line of reasoning seems to differentiate between meaningful bodily experiences and our hermeneutically understood experiences, as if people experience pain and then interpret this experience as pain. In this way it possible to speak of a painful bodily experience in animals, without them being able to experience it as such themselves. This differentiation brings us back to the scientific philosophical debate several decades ago, i.e., to the period in which it was presumed that observations and experiences were unbiased, and that these could then be explained and interpreted by people. As I have already said, bodily experiences are inevitably hermeneutical experiences, that is, experiences which fit into a specific framework of interpretation. We do not experience pain and then question its meaning: a painful experience is an experience which has already been interpreted.

4. THE HERMENEUTICAL SCIENCE OF EXPERIENCES OF NATURE

The above may lead to the conclusion that to me the squeals of pigs being castrated is nothing more than a sound with a particular frequency. However this is not the case.

What I am actually saying is that we can interpret the squeals in different ways. To begin with we can interpret them using the conceptual scheme in which we speak of the world of things and happenings which we experience through the senses. Terms such as noise and frequency are included in this scheme. Amongst other things, knowledge based on this is physical knowledge applicable to sound waves and their frequency. A hermeneutic science of this is also possible, that is a hermeneutic science of natural science. However neither I or the advocates of a hermeneutic of nature mean this. We can also interpret squealing pigs within the conceptual scheme in which we speak about our emotional experiences. Terms such as compassion, enjoyment, sorrow, excitement, anger etc. can all be included. What I appeal for is hermeneutic knowledge of this, hermeneutic knowledge in the sense of methodical understanding of these experiences.

The ethologists mentioned at the beginning of this chapter interpreted the pigs' squeals according to the concepts of natural science, on the basis of which they were able to establish that the frequency of the noise changed when the spermatic cord was cut. They then translated this conclusion to the framework in which we speak of our emotional, mainly bodily experiences. Precisely this step cannot be justified, and is not justifiable. The same is true of the bulls, since the biological knowledge about bulls cannot be translated into knowledge about the beauty of bulls. Possible knowledge about animals' pain can only be developed on the basis of animals' emotional experiences and a communal relationship between people and animals as far as these communal expressions are concerned. As has already been said, it is very problematic to presume such a communal relationship. With respect to this, ethologists speak of an analogy between people and animals which as yet has not been proved. The ethologists' conclusion concerning the pigs was most probably based on this analogy and not on the determination of the noise's frequency. We do not require determination of the frequency of noise in order to state that castration of people who have not been anaesthetised is painful. Along with the analogous line of reasoning, the squealing of pigs leads directly to the statement that pigs suffer pain.

Does this mean that we cannot say whether pigs suffer pain, and that this is purely a human experience, because of the uncertainty of the existence of a communal emotional order between people and animals? No, we can reliably say that they do, and we do so and act accordingly in everyday life. However science is different to everyday life, since it is a critical analysis of everyday knowledge and behaviour. Hence in the hermeneutic science of our experiences of animals we are for example concerned with critically testing our everyday experience that pigs suffer pain. This test is not a matter of introspection, because that can only lead to a confirmation of the experience. Instead it is a question of comparison and consistency of these and other experiences of people and animals. For example we should clarify why we do everything to minimize laboratory animals' pain and discomfort, even though we still carry out animal experiments before a new medicine for humans is released on the market. The first activity presupposes that animals as well as humans suffer pain, while the second activity means that we are not allowed to cause pain to people in the process of research. Does this not mean that 'pain in animals' is different from 'pain in people'?

The clarification of such terms, which we use to articulate our experience of animals, is the subject of a much needed hermeneutic research project. Such research is necessary immediately because we see, for example, that the emotional reactions of people to the discussion about the permissibility of biotechnology in animals, is put down as 'only' emotional, subjective or irrational. I believe that these reactions are expressions of criticism about the naturalness of the cultural background of the biotechnological sciences and the technologies which will develop from these. This is mostly a cultural background in which animals are seen only as instruments to obtain meat, milk and eggs, and in which emotional criticism is at the most interpreted in terms of social acceptance, without the contents of this criticism being explored further.

My advice to philosophers of nature who are worried about our society's treatment of animals is as follows:

(i) Extend the discussion about animals to the level of our cultural ideas about animals, ideas which are built into the concepts of biotechnology and of which we are critical.

(ii) Articulate, criticize or build on these ideas using hermeneutical scientific methods.

(iii) Develop a treatment of animals on this basis, which does justice to our well-founded emotional experiences concerning animals as well as to the technical treatment of animals.

NOTES

1. van Putten, G. 1986. 'Ethologisch onderzoek naar pijn en lijden' (Ethological research on pain and suffering), *Biotechniek* **4**: 61-63.
2. Rollin, B. 1989 *The Unheeded Cry*. Oxford, Oxford University Press.
3. Bulhof, Ilse N. 1988. *Darwin's Origin of Species: Betoverde wetenschap* (enchanted science). Ambo, Baarn.
4. Gadamer, H.G. 1972.*Wahrheit und Methode* pp. 419-21. Tübingen, Paul Siebeck.
5. Winch, P. 1958. *The Idea of a Social Science* Chapter2. London: Routledge & Kegan Paul.
6. Noske, B. 1988. *Huilen met de wolven* (Crying with the wolves), pp. 167-94. Amsterdam, Van Gennep.

Chapter 11

Can Liberal Democracy Survive the Environmental Crisis? Sustainability, Liberal Neutrality and Overlapping Consensus[1]

Wouter Achterberg

This chapter deals with the problem of legitimacy which, in liberal democracies, results from the pursuit of sustainability or sustainable development as an effort to find a structural solution to the environmental crisis. After giving a rough outline of the political context in which this problem develops, I will discuss the concept of sustainable development as well as some attempts to elaborate it into guidelines for the structural solution or control of environmental problems, and I will give some examples of structural changes in the organization of society which could be the result of the implementation of these guidelines. Thus, the necessity of the legitimacy of a consistent environmental policy, directed at sustainability, becomes clear in a concrete manner. Subsequently, the liberal ideals of political legitimacy and neutrality, and especially Rawls' idea of an overlapping consensus as a theoretical elaboration of these ideals, will be dealt with. Finally, I will explore whether and to what extent Rawls' idea is useful, or can be made useful by alteration and supplementation, for justifying a structural environmental policy which derives from sustainability as a norm. Special attention will be paid to the situation in the Netherlands.

1.Introduction

It seems that a serious environmental policy has not yet got off the ground in liberal-democratic countries, or at least not fast or radically enough. By a serious environmental and nature policy I mean a policy that aims at structural changes within society in order to achieve an enduring solution to environmental problems, or at least to create a situation in which they can be controlled. Such a policy is directed not only at maintaining nature as a basis of our social activities for generations to come (sustainability of our use of the environment) but also at protecting, maintaining and developing nature for its own sake (sustainability of nature; Achterberg 1990).

Probably, radical changes in our system of producing and consuming will be necessary, that is to say, changes in the nature of our social market economy, industry, traffic and agriculture; in short, in our entire way of life. Opposition to these changes is likely to be considerable for some time. This is hardly surprising: acquired rights, established interests and deep-rooted life styles threaten to be infringed.

Therefore, a necessary condition for a structural solution to the environmental crisis is that it is permanently supported by as many people involved (citizens) as is possible. Participation in the decisions which affect one's own life is a central political value of democracy anyhow. But for strategic reasons too, a structural solution to environmental problems can only be a democratic one: the required sacrifices and the changes of life style connected with it can never be lasting if they are imposed in an authoritarian way. These sacrifices and changes demand voluntariness, understanding and the (conditional) preparedness of all people involved.

Nevertheless, liberal democracies appear destined to have a hard time as far as a structural solution to environmental problems is concerned. How hard can be illustrated as follows. The government is either inclined to take too little action or no action at all because it is permanently paralysed by continuously changing majorities against every proposed serious regulation or policy (which is certainly partly due to the short term vision of both politicians and voters), or it is forced to impose more or less radical measures, which might be defended as serving the general interest, but have no or insufficient public support. Both horns of this dilemma are unattractive, to say the least. Either way nothing is really solved, and this is morally unacceptable. The second horn in particular merits some attention.

The imposition or at least the selective encouragement by public policy, of one or more of a set of closely connected conceptions of the good life, which give pride of place to sustainability but on which there is no consensus in a pluralistic society like ours, is in general morally doubtful. It clashes, for instance, with the basic intuition of liberal (political) morality, according to which the government should be neutral or impartial towards alternative conceptions of the good life. Since neutrality is an important element of the liberal-democratic conception of the function of government, a plausible justification of its seeming loss of neutrality is necessary. The starting points of such a justification must be public as well as generally accepted. Where and how do we find these starting points?

Further, authoritarian impositions are *prima facie* reprehensible because they require coercion and force, and they are risky too, as they are most probably ineffective: every government has only limited means to control and enforce compliance with the great many environmental measures that would be necessary, whereas to refrain from enforcement would affect the legitimacy of the environmental policy and, in the long run, even of public policy in general.

How can one explain the predicament of liberal democracy noted above? It seems to be rooted in structural shortcomings of the democratic political system, particularly in so far as it has taken shape as a pluralism of competing interest groups, which has been called 'polyarchy' by Robert Dahl. Polyarchy can be conceived as the embodiment of interest group liberalism.

> Interest group liberalism is really a formula for a politics of incrementalism and compromise between *organized* interests. In such a system the less organized and the unorganized lose ground, particularly in hard economic times. The elderly, the poor, the unemployed, and the ill are grossly underrepresented. So too, of course, are future generations and other species. Furthermore, interest group liberalism does not allow for moral arguments. Decisions are quantified, disagreements resolved by splitting the difference. Policies favor the most organized groups, whose members tend to be wealthy and tend to seek concrete, economically self-interested, and immediate gains.(Paehlke 1989: 200)

In such a system only moderate solutions are sought. 'Moderate solutions are piecemeal, partial and technical. They rarely address the need for fundamental changes in our production, consumption and "disposal" habits' (Paehlke 1989: 211). The difficulties of democracy, conceived as the embodiment of interest group liberalism, with the solution of environmental problems can be made clear on the basis of this description of its core.

There seems, however, to be a way out. Its general nature is suggested by Barbour:

> Democracy does... face serious challenges in times of social conflict. The answer, I suggest, lies in the development of *common social purposes*, not in the reduction of participation or increased reliance on government authority

and technical expertise. Only when there are common loyalties to more inclusive goals are people willing to compromise private ends in the public interest, as occurs during time of war or threats to the nation. (Barbour 1980: 124)

Assuming that we are in the comfortable position of having time to wait for this development to happen, the remedy is, then, the forming of a new consensus on a broadened conception of the general interest or the common good. An example of such a conception, which is also non-anthropocentric, is presented by the Dutch environmental economist Hans Opschoor:

The environment has to be recognized as an essential, fundamental part of the *infrastructure* of social activities and processes... the government should realize that it has the task for guaranteeing the continuity of this infrastructure, and not just for the present generation, and not just for human beings..., even if this is to be at the expense of the present generation's economic interests. (Opschoor 1989: 184-5)

Dryzek takes a somewhat stronger position here. He suggests that a prerequisite for the effective solving of environmental problems is 'a consensus about the primacy of ecological values' in society (Dryzek 1987: 130). He deems this difficult because liberal democracy

cannot be driven by a single goal. Therefore the fate of ecological values in a polyarchy is to be severely compromised by other values... The paradox is that, unless the members of polyarchy accept a common ecological purpose, then all other human purposes are endangered. (Dryzek 1987: 130)

We see, then, the possibility of a 'third way', however paradoxical, past the dilemma noted above. Perhaps 'primacy' is too strong. But at the very least the fundamental importance of ecological values for the public realm should be generally acknowledged. And they should be off the political agenda, in the sense that they should not be subjected to the calculus of the benefits and burdens of social co-operation. This implies, as we will shortly see, that the consensus about them has to be overlapping in Rawls' sense. Also the paradox is less marked than Dryzek suggests: the background consensus about the institutional core of liberal democracy can, in the light of the urgency of the environmental crisis, be reactivated and, perhaps, extended to the normative principle of sustainability without jeopardizing the liberal ideal of neutrality. Precisely, Rawls' view about an overlapping consensus is very useful for this purpose.

Before coming back to Rawls I will first examine what the outlines of the structural changes resulting from a serious environmental policy, i.e., a policy aiming at sustainability, could be like. Finally, the relationship between overlapping consensus and sustainable development will be discussed.

2. SUSTAINABILITY

In the literature concerning the environmental crisis and the ecological movement, two visions of the nature and solution of environmental problems are traditionally distinguished. First, there is a 'superficial' or reformist vision ('environmentalism'). According to this vision, environmental problems are mainly management problems, soluble within the context of the dominant political and economic system, and without any rigorous change in our values and culture.

Second, there is a profounder vision, aiming at more structural change ('ecologism', for example 'deep ecology'), according to which a radical change in our attitude towards nature, and therefore also in our political and social system, is necessary (see for example Dobson 1990: 13 and 33).

Both visions, to be distinguished from the classical conservationist vision, should be considered the extremes of a continuum, representing all the possible visions, from superficial to radical, on the nature of and solution to the environmental crisis and, in connection with it, on the relationship between humanity and nature. The value perspective of environmentalism is anthropocentric, that of ecologism is fully ecocentric. Ecocentric in this sense does not mean subordination of human values to those of nature, but complete recognition of nonhuman nature's intrinsic value. I will not concern myself with the classification of all sorts of positions on this scale, but only with the vision that starts from sustainability or sustainable development as the right path towards the solution of environmental problems. This view can be elaborated in such a way that it tends towards environmentalism, and can be extended as well, as suggested above, to include proposals that recognize nature's intrinsic value.

The concept of sustainable development has become widely known in particular through the report *Our Common Future* (1987) from the United Nations' World Commission on Environment and Development (WCED; also known as Brundtland Commission, after its president). Sustainable development had been recommended as a strategy before, for example in the World Conservation Strategy (International Union for Conservation of Nature and Natural Resources [IUCN] et al. 1980), although in this report the emphasis was on living resource conservation. In the Dutch National Environmental Policy Plan and Nature Policy Plan it has also been adopted as a central guiding notion (see below).

What does 'sustainable' mean? An activity, structure or process is sustainable, if 'for all practical purposes it can continue forever' (IUCN et al. 1991: 10). The WCED discusses sustainable development and describes it as follows:

> Sustainable development is a process of change in which the exploitation of resources, the direction of investments, the orientation of technological development and institutional change are all in harmony and enhance both current and future potential to meet human needs and aspirations. (WCED 1987: 9 and 46)

The WCED does not pretend that this process will be easy or straightforward: 'Painful choices have to be made. Thus, in the final analysis, sustainable development must rest on political will' (WCED 1987: 9 and see also xiv).

Elsewhere, the WECD describes sustainable development more concisely:

> sustainable development is development that meets the needs of the present generation without compromising the ability of future generations to meet their own needs. (WCED 1987: 43)

The guideline or criterion for sustainable development that the Commission applies is the next generation's prospect of disposing of a stock of resource that is at least as large as the one inherited by the present generation. The capital to be left behind not only comprises goods and the like, produced by man, but also natural resources or the total of these: the 'natural capital' (WCED 1987: 52 ff and 57 ff; and Annexe 1 under 2). Apparently, the WCED regards capital produced by man and natural capital as interchangeable, and to be valued in the same terms, namely in terms of their usefulness to the quality of human life. This is a disputable perspective, quite apart from the extremely anthropocentric attitude which is expressed by such a view. This anthropocentrism, incidentally, is frankly expressed by president Gro Harlem Brundtland in the preface: 'Our message', she says, 'is, above all, directed towards people, whose wellbeing is the ultimate goal of all environment and development policies' (WCED 1987: xiv). But the report also strikes different, non-anthropocentric notes. For example: 'the case for the conservation of nature should not rest only with development goals. It is part of our moral obligation to other living beings and future generations' (WCED 1987: 57; see also 13, 65, 147, 155, and perhaps 348). The emphasis, however, is on the resource perspective, apparently 'for those who demand an accounting' (WCED 1987: 155).

In this report, a comprehensive programme, inspired by much hope and great optimism, has been proposed. As a matter of fact, it is as much concerned with the first as with the third world, with the economy as with the environment, and with the present, particularly with securing and improving the life chances of people in the poor countries, as with future generations. It is not surprising, then, that an unambiguous explanation of the term sustainable development is hard to come by.

The term has been criticized as ambiguous and open to a wide range of interpretations, many of which are contradictory. The confusion has been caused because 'sustainable development', 'sustainable growth' and 'sustainable use' have been used interchangeably, as if their meanings are the same. They are not. 'Sustainable growth' is a contradiction in terms; nothing physical can grow indefinitely. 'Sustainable use' is applicable only to renewable resources: it means using them at rates within their capacity for renewal (IUCN et al. 1991: 10).

The authors of this report, *Caring for the Earth*, then suggest 'sustainable development' to mean: 'improving the quality of human life within the carrying capacity of supporting ecosystems' (IUCN et al. 1991: 10). So much for terminological clarity.

It may be interesting to consider the situation in the Netherlands, where the perspective of sustainable development has been adopted for environmental policy. The discussion about starting points of environmental and nature policies and their elaboration resulted in a number of important policy documents, including the National Environmental Policy Plan (NEPP, as well as the updated version NEPP Plus) and the Nature Policy Plan (NPP), both accepted in the Parliament (2nd Chamber) by a very large majority in, respectively, September and November 1990. In this context, both policy plans deserve our attention.

The NEPP has adopted the starting point of sustainable development from the report *Our Common Future*. Sustainable development has to satisfy the needs of the present generation, without endangering the opportunities of future generations for satisfying their needs.

The main objective of environmental management is to maintain the environment's carrying capacity on behalf of sustainable development.

The carrying capacity of the environment is damaged if environmental quality can lead to irreversible effects within a generation, such as mortality or morbidity among people, severe nuisance and damage to well-being, the extinction of plant or animal species, the deterioration of ecosystems, damage to water supplies, soil fertility or cultural heritage and impediments to physical and economic development. The environment's carrying capacity is, of course, not exceeded if one single effect occurs, such as, for instance, the extinction of a species. But it is exceeded if these effects occur on a large scale as is currently the case... Sustainable development involves finding a balance between environment and development. (NEPP 1989: 92)

The NEPP makes it a longterm policy objective to solve or gain control of environmental problems within the timescale of one generation. The general criteria that are applied are: closing substance cycles, less intensive using of energy resources, and furthering the quality of products instead of their quantity. Unfortunately, these criteria are only elaborated in a technical-scientific way.

So far, the NEPP seems to breathe an enlightened-anthropocentric spirit. This is largely true. The NEPP contains a non-anthropocentric objective too, however, although it is hardly reflected in the measures proposed: 'For environmental policy it is important that sustainable development implies a level of environmental quality which does justice to the values of public health and wellbeing and to the intrinsic values of plants, animals and eco-systems.' (NEPP 1989: 42)

The non-anthropocentric side of the policy is stated more emphatically in the NPP. In this document, the principal objective of the government's nature management policy is formulated thus:

...sustainable maintenance, restoration and development of the values of nature and landscape (NPP 1990: 36)

This objective is to be pursued in view of the meaning of nature and landscape for humans as well as out of respect for the values attributed to nature on its own... Policy efforts should not only be directed at the protection of values such as public health and well-being, but also at the intrinsic values of plants, animals and ecosystems (NPP 1990: 36).

The basic idea of the NPP is directed at the realization of a physically stable 'ecological main structure' within a period of 30 years. This consists of core areas (highly valued nature reserves, including ancient rural landscapes), nature development areas and connecting zones. This main goal is complemented with a 'buffer policy', which has to guarantee the quality of the environment within the main structure, as well as with a policy directed at the protection of species in the areas outside the main structure.

In this connection, it may be interesting to note that article 21 of the Dutch constitution says: 'the government's concern is aimed at the quality of life of the nation and the protection and improvement of the environment.' Although this article deals with a basic social right of Dutch citizens, which involves a duty of the state to guarantee the welfare of these citizens in this respect, it does not imply – if we take it literally – that this is a duty exclusively towards humans, *in casu* the citizens of the Netherlands. Be that as it may, the authors of the NEPP and the NPP appear to interpret this duty in a broad, non-anthropocentric sense!

If we may conceive the broad parliamentary support of the NEPP and the NPP as more than merely pragmatic and *ad hoc*, and if, as a consequence, the NEPP and the NPP have not just a symbolic meaning, then we may speak of the beginning of a consensus of the type that could play the desired legitimating role.

Taking sustainability and sustainable development seriously implies accepting limitations and sacrifices on the part of the citizens. In the prosperous part of the world this will mean: a cutdown in consumption (and in this sense an 'economy of enough'), a change of lifestyle and radical structural changes. To illustrate how far the changes can go, I will give some examples which at the same time draw more attention to the political-philosophical implications of a serious environmental policy.

First the problem of **(auto) mobility**. Many people agree that the use of automobiles must be reduced, in favour of other means of personal transport which require less energy and raw materials, cause less pollution and other nuisances and take up less space. Financial incentives, fuel price and tax increases for example, (i. e. measures that only make driving a car more expensive), will not be enough according to traffic experts, particularly if we also have to take population growth into account. A volume-oriented policy is necessary therefore, even if this means nothing except a sharp decrease in parking facilities. The question is, however, whether this will be enough in the long run. It is likely that there can only be a real prospect of an enduring result if the need for transportation is affected (CREN 1990: 30.). This need does not stand on its own, however, but is incorporated in a pattern of producing and consuming, of working and spending leisure time; moreover, it has become closely connected with relation patterns in the private sphere. Reduction of the need for transportation therefore necessarily requires alteration of life patterns and different patterns of physical planning. Thus, the CREN report remarks that

> if the distances between the locations where people live, work and spend their leisure time are minimized, ...then the use of cars can be diminished and substituted by non-motorized transport. *More compact* cities can constitute an answer to the demand for reducing the need to move. This requires a more stringent policy regarding physical planning. (CREN 1990: 30)

The implications go even further, as can be seen from the following remarks from Mr. Alders, the Dutch Minister of Housing, Physical Planning and Environment, quoted in the Dutch newspaper *NRC - Handelsblad*:

For years, nearly all political parties, including my own, have been pursuing a policy of social individualization. What has the result been? That in many families nowadays both partners have a job. But not always in the same place, which increases the need for transportation facilities. Therefore we have adjusted the physical planning. But now, we, from Physical Planning, have begun to ask ourselves, very tentatively, whether we have been wise to do this; whether we should not have dealt with the consequences of individualization in a different way. But this doubt from our side does not alter the cultural processes. (8-9-1990)

This example mentioned by Mr. Alders makes it clear that cultural changes are necessary for solving environmental problems.

Furthermore, cars have a psychological, or rather a symbolic function. This can become clear when we consider the nature and the normative backgrounds of (auto)mobility. Our western societies are built upon and permeated by Mobility. Walzer distinguishes four 'mobilities' (1990, 11f.): (i) geographic mobility (ii) social mobility (going up and down the social ladder, in one's own life or in relation to one's parents or children, but also mobility as a result of emancipation and individualization processes); (iii) marital mobility (broken marriages, broken families, etc.) and (iv) political mobility (floating voters etc.). The cultural processes mentioned by Alders mainly refer to (i) and (ii), and also, but to a lesser degree, to (iii).

The four mobilities mentioned by Walzer are deeply rooted in the liberal ethos, they are, for instance, a 'triumphant' (Walzer 1990: 17) manifestation of individual rights and civil liberties.

In the liberal view, ...the Four Mobilities represent the enactment of liberty, and the pursuit of (private or personal) happiness. And it has to be said that, conceived in this way, liberalism is a genuinely popular creed. Any effort to curtail mobility in the four areas... would require a massive and harsh application of state power. (Walzer 1990: 12)

The conclusion must be that the serious application of even the most modest criteria of sustainable development can lead to explosive situations.

Our society is not only based upon and permeated by mobility, but also based upon and permeated by **growth** and development, in the field of economics as well as that of science and technology, which mutually reinforce each other again. From the view of sustainable development, economic growth has to be limited at least selectively. What is the cause of this urge for growth? According to Opschoor, our society is characterized by an inherent urge for growth at every level (Opschoor 1989: 92 f. and 138 ff.). Most people in our society behave as if the rule 'rather more than less, particularly for myself' is their leading norm. This often results in myopic egoism and consumerism. Individual companies maintain their market position by trying to beat their competitors. As a consequence, they have to keep up or increase their market share and feel compelled to innovate and to pursue profit. The government also applauds economic growth, if only to be able to control the tensions flowing from social inequality.

In all this, a central role is played by the decentralized market which through the price mechanism co-ordinates the separate decisions of consumers and producers (individual companies), whereas the government watches and, if necessary, restores the efficiency of the market process or carries out compensatory actions from considerations of justice. The functioning of the market mechanism severely contributes to the presence and continuation of environmental problems. The imperfections include negative external effects (transfer of costs), time preference, subordination of weak interests or interests that cannot be expressed in terms of money, and finally, the failing supply of collective goods, including a healthy and safe environment. The government is the institution *par excellence* to repair these imperfections by furthering or making a start with the supply of collective goods, by way of regulations, levies and subsidies, by volume-reducing measures; in general, by incorporating more 'planning elements' (Opschoor: 152) into its public policies. Opschoor summarizes as follows:

> the market economy is no longer allowed to dictate the direction in which society develops. Economic processes should be subordinated again to socially relevant criteria. This makes demands as to the political controllability of these processes, on a national and an international level. (Opschoor 1989: 128)

This subordination not only implies changes in the rights and duties of individuals and enterprises, particularly in property rights, but also a far reaching channelling or correction of the market mechanism – more far reaching than we have been used to and than is considered desirable these days by, particularly, the many adherents of 'deregulation', a 'withdrawing' government operating 'according to market mechanisms' (all the more so since the democratic revolutions in Eastern Europe). It is true that we should not take an increase in the canalization and correction of the market mechanism too lightly, even though in our mixed economy the first steps in that direction were made a long time ago. Why should we not take them lightly?

First, because the market offers great advantages, such as the stimulation of efficiency and inventiveness. Second, because the market in a liberal democracy, in any case, counts as one of the central institutions of society, and is as much a triumphant expression of individual rights and civil liberties as the above-mentioned mobilities and as representative democracy itself. In the political philosophy of liberalism, redistributions are accepted to compensate for undesired inequalities caused or reinforced by the market, which implies in principle the acceptance of a mixed, that is, a social market, economy (see, for example, Dworkin 1978: 129-134). However, it is not clear or self-evident that the much more rigorous cuts and corrections, necessary because of a serious environmental policy, can be defended on the basis of the same philosophy. A strong opposition against the limitation of market processes is to be expected and therefore there is an urgent necessity for a shared public basis on which to ground the **legitimacy** of restrictions and corrections. This would be true *a forteriori* when the more controversial aspects of the pursuit of sustainable development come to be realized, such as control of population growth, or even reduction of the population, and giving high priority to the maintenance of the diversity and integrity of nature as an end in itself.

The insight that the perspective of sustainable development is connected with the normative-political principles which could justify liberal democracy may be important in view of the legitimation of serious environmental policies. The path towards this insight leads via the liberal idea of neutrality and Rawls' idea of an overlapping consensus. This is what the next section is about.

3. LIBERAL NEUTRALITY AND OVERLAPPING CONSENSUS

First of all, I want to give a general outline of the relationship between political legitimation, liberalism and neutrality. A central element of liberalism as a political philosophy is the idea of legitimacy. This means that the social and political order must be generally acceptable, that is to say, justifiable towards all people on whom this order has – perhaps even coercively – been imposed.

Furthermore, common consent to the fundamental organization of society should at least be conceived as a necessary condition of its political legitimacy (Waldron 1987: 140). General consent does not only serve the aim of political stability. Some attach an independent moral value to the possibility of justifying the social and political system towards as many participants as possible (Nagel 1987: 219).

There is a difference of opinion within the liberal tradition about the nature of this common consent; some say it should be actual (whether or not tacit), while others begin from hypothetical consent. I assume that the idea of hypothetical general consent is the most plausible one, because it is the least problematic.

Hypothetical general consent implies that the political and social order must be acceptable for all people as reasonable beings. More precise: all people involved *would* give their consent to normative principles of the organization of society because and as far as they confine themselves to reasonable (rational) grounds. What sort of principles are, in this connection, likely to meet with common consent?

Principles that can be justified in terms of 'common ground' (Rawls) among reasonable people who otherwise have different interests, values, life styles and ideas of the good life. This 'common ground' comprises the principles that can be shared and recognized as such by people with such divergent points of view – principles concerning fundamental interests and values. We can call these interests and values 'neutral', because, in the eyes of reasonable persons who may all have different conceptions of the good, they can serve as a common basis for the justification of the moral principles which have to determine the basic organization of society.

The principle of neutrality, introduced in this way, mainly refers to justification. Thus, some authors speak of 'justificatory neutrality' (Kymlicka 1989: 884) or 'neutrality of grounds', described by de Marneffe as the idea that:

> the principles of justice that regulate basic social and political institutions must be justifiable in terms of moral and political values that any reasonable person would accept as the basis of moral claims regardless of his or her particular conception of the good. (de Marneffe 1990: 253)

He distinguishes 'neutrality of grounds' from 'concrete neutrality', which he conceives as 'the principle that the state may not limit individual liberties in ways that advance one particular conception of the good' (de Marneffe 1990: 253).

These are the outlines of a theoretical programme for liberal political philosophy. Especially Rawls and Dworkin have greatly contributed to its development. I will chiefly confine myself to Rawls, in particular to his development of the concept of neutrality into the idea of an overlapping consensus.

During the last few years, Rawls has reinterpreted and elaborated his famous theory of justice (1971) in such a way that he now finds himself among the adherents of some form of justificatory neutrality, called 'procedural neutrality' by Rawls. The essence of his views on this point is shown by the following quotation.

If we apply to it [the conception of 'justice as fairness'] the idea of procedural neutrality, we must do so in virtue of its being a political conception that aims to be the focus of an overlapping consensus. That is, the view as a whole hopes to articulate a public basis of justification for the basic structure of a constitutional regime working from fundamental intuitive ideas implicit in the public political culture and abstracting from comprehensive religious, philosophical and moral doctrines. It seeks common ground – or if one prefers, neutral ground – given the fact of pluralism. This common, or neutral, ground is the political conception itself as the focus of an overlapping consensus. (Rawls 1988: 261-2)

Naturally enough, Rawls hopes as well that 'justice as fairness' as a political conception meets the requirement of neutrality of aim: the basic structure, for example, is at any rate not designed to favour particular comprehensive visions. He considers neutrality of effect or result – for example, the government is not allowed to do anything which in fact results in unequal treatment of different parties – to be impossible in practice (Rawls 1988: 26). Now I will comment on the quotation.

Rawls' conception of justice, 'justice as fairness', is his answer to the fundamental problem of political justice: what is the most appropriate conception of political justice which can determine the conditions under which social co-operation is rationally and morally acceptable between citizens who are considered free and equal individuals who live and work together throughout their lives? (Rawls 1985: 234). In the history of democratic thought, a range of divergent answers have been given to this question.

The conditions of social co-operation should be 'fair', and what this exactly means is explained in the famous principles of justice, which, in Rawls' latest version, run as follows.

(i) Each person has an equal right to a fully adequate scheme of equal basic liberties, which is compatible with a similar scheme of liberties for all.

(ii) Social and economic inequalities are to satisfy two conditions:

    a. They must be attached to offices and positions open to all under conditions of fair equality of opportunity;

    b. They must be to the greatest benefit of the least advantaged members of society (Rawls 1982a: 5).

Under normal circumstances, the first principle has priority over the second one, while (ii)a. prevails over (ii)b.

The principles regulate the basic structure of society, that is, the principal political, social and economic institutions and their mutual relationships, which determine the fundamental organization of society (with a view to the realization of the values of liberty and equality). The main institutions referred to here are the constitution, the market, property and family. Rawls' conception of justice chiefly concerns the basic structure of a modern constitutional democracy. 'Justice as fairness' is a *political* conception, partly because it only refers to the basic structure and partly because it articulates and orders fundamental intuitive ideas (about liberty, equality, fair conditions for co-operation), much alive in the democratic tradition and embodied in the political institutions of a constitutional democracy. It is obvious that 'justice as fairness' is also a *liberal* conception of justice (Rawls 1987, 18 and n. 27). Rawls tries to make clear that 'justice as fairness' is the most appropriate conception of political justice, by reformulating the idea of a social contract and the accompanying state of nature in terms of a hypothetical general agreement that is reached in an original position from behind a veil of ignorance. This means that the idea of concluding a social contract is considered by Rawls a 'device of representation' (Rawls 1985: 236), a dramatic staging of an imaginary bargaining situation in which all parties who are to come to an agreement about the principles of the fundamental organization of society, are rational, free and equal indeed, but have to deliberate without all kinds of information on their particular endowment, social position, conception of the good (life) etc. The impartiality thus embodied in the bargaining situation excludes bargaining advantages and guarantees, according to Rawls, a generally accepted agreement on the principles of justice. The justifying power of this construction reaches as far as the incorporated normative notions (rationality, liberty, equality, impartiality, 'sense of justice') carry. I will not go into the much-discussed problems of this derivation here.

The political and non-metaphysical character of Rawls' conception of justice has already been pointed out above. In his later works, he stresses this political character more and more. This is mainly due to the growing insight that modern democratic regimes, in world views, religions, philosophical and moral attitudes, are characterized by pluralism. This is an enduring pluralism that cannot be suppressed by the government except by forceful means. Pluralism, in this context, implies clashing and often incomparable conceptions of the good (life); these are conceptions about the meaning, value and purpose of life, says Rawls (1987: 4.) Therefore, an agreement about the fundamental organization of society is only possible as an 'overlapping consensus'. This is a consensus about a political conception of justice, a consensus 'which is affirmed by the opposing religious, philosophical and moral doctrines likely to thrive over generations in a more or less just constitutional democracy, where the criterion of justice is that political conception itself' (Rawls 1987: 1).

The political conception of justice is intellectually accessible and acceptable proceeding from the above-mentioned comprehensive doctrines (Rawls mentions a religious doctrine encompassing the principle of tolerance, and metaphysical liberalisms such as Kant's and Mill's, in which autonomy is the highest value in personal as well as political life), but can also be rationally acceptable in itself. The loyalty to the conception will, therefore, be able to survive a shift in the balance of power between the adherents of the comprehensive visions of the good. This is also why Rawls speaks about a consensus rather than a 'mere *modus vivendi*' in the sense of a compromise between individuals or interest groups, the stability of which lasts only as long as the balance of power in the underlying constellation of interests endures.

The political conception of justice has the extremely important function of ensuring in a pluralistic democracy (as described above) a minimal but stable social unity over generations (an element of sustainability is as it were incorporated in the notion of an overlapping consensus, which considerably enhances its usefulness for our purpose!) Just because the shared values embodied in this conception probably ensure the existence of different visions of the good life from one generation to the next (this means that they will be able to find support again and again), it is unlikely, Rawls hopes, that they will be easily substituted for by different, more specific values which belong to the individual conceptions of the good. There is one restriction, however: the political conception of justice is only neutral towards admissible visions on the good, the visions that are compatible with the political conception itself.

4. OVERLAPPING CONSENSUS AND SUSTAINABLE DEVELOPMENT

'The aims of political philosophy depend on the society it addresses', Rawls writes (1987: 1). Due to the environmental crisis which threatens human existence and nature in general, our society finds itself at a turning point of its development. It would be appropriate, then, if political philosophy also concerned itself with the viability of a society embodying the fundamental arrangement of a liberal democracy, which finds itself at this turning point. To me, Rawls' idea of an overlapping consensus and the way he shapes it, seems to be useful in developing a theory about this. It is possible that Rawls' conception of justice, as he has elaborated it so far, has to be supplemented or modified on various points which do not directly concern the environmental crisis. Several proposals for such an adjustment have already been made; Rawls himself has put forward an extension of the range of application of his conception to the international order (1989: 251, n.46), an extension which is inevitable anyhow (Pogge 1989) if we take sustainable development seriously. I mainly use his conception here as a plausible and adequate core or basis: it is the focus of an overlapping consensus that is already working, while it can be extended and modified in the light of the environmental crisis and the perspective of sustainable development.

The term 'turning point' has come up. This is no coincidence. It is not only the seriousness of the environmental crisis that suggests this term – there is something else as well. Rawls often talks about the existence of 'reasonably favourable conditions, administrative, economic, technological and the like, which make democracy possible' (1987: 4 and 7; 1982a: 11). One of these conditions is 'the fact of moderate scarcity' (1987: 22; in Rawls 1971 this was already an important objective 'condition of justice': 126 f.). If there were only one thing we could learn from the environmental crisis, it is that it is doubtful whether scarcity *is* that moderate, particularly in the long run, and certainly, if, in spite of population growth, a fair international distribution of wealth or resources is pursued. There is reason enough, then, from the perspective of Rawls' own conception, to consider how the overlapping consensus can be supplemented with new elements in order to enlarge the durability of this consensus itself and thus of liberal democracy as well. The new elements have to be determined from the perspective that, in the end, it will only be possible to overcome scarcity through a different way of life (apart from technical miracles etc.). At least, this different way of life will have to be oriented towards sustainable development, with the emphasis on sustainable. We have already seen that, in the Dutch context, there is a consensus about sustainable development. The conception of sustainable development has to be worked out more specifically, and this will probably give rise to many disagreements. It is not impossible that such elaboration will involve changes in and adjustments to basic institutions. I will give some examples, which have already been mentioned on pp. 145-6.

In the field of fundamental rights and liberties, a conflict might arise between the protection of the (mainly physical) integrity of the individual and freedom of movement (which Rawls also considers a part of the complex 'freedom and integrity of the individual'; for example, 1982a: 50) or a conflict between the right to personal property (Rawls 1982a: 12) and the freedom and integrity of the individual. Hopefully, these conflicts will not immediately lead to restrictions on these liberties. According to Rawls, such restrictions are acceptable for the sake of other liberties which would come off badly otherwise; the purpose of these restrictions has to be the development of an adequate system of basic rights and liberties for individuals, and I add to this: with an eye to those of future generations! The conflicts should at least result in a more detailed regulation of rights and liberties, whereby, unlike restriction, their 'central range of application' remains unaffected (1982a: 9 f).

Increased channelling of the market is another point on the agenda. This can imply e.g. a regulation of the right to own means of production and natural resources (according to Rawls 1982a: 12, the right to own means of production does not belong in the list of the basic rights). It will probably also imply regulation and the introduction of more planning elements. This is a restriction of the market mechanism, since it is not a matter of correcting undesired market effects afterwards.

The justification of these and other restrictions and adjustments, at the level of the basic structure as well as at a less basic level, demands that both of Rawls' principles of justification (in an extended form, therefore also applied internationally) are supplemented with a third principle, which corrects the effects of the other two in such a way that the basic possibility of sustainable development is secured. This means that the application of the two principles of justification depends on the condition that the third principle can be complied with. At least, this is the case in normal circumstances; the intention is not, for example, to sacrifice the present generation for the sake of future generations.

This third principle is not an 'alien' supplement because sustainable development itself is connected with the intuitive idea of justice, for example, between the generations. The third principle, a *transmission* principle, says, (in the words of Richard and Val Routley, whom I do not follow, incidentally, either in their explanation or in their justification of it): 'We should not hand the world that we have used and exploited on to our successors in a substantially worse shape than we 'received' it' (Routley 1982: 123).

As a justification of this principle, two arguments can be put forward. The first reason why we are not allowed to hand the world on to our successors in a worse shape is that this violates the principle of equal opportunities, applied to the relationship between generations. This is an anthropocentric argument.

An intergenerational principle of equal opportunities is defended by authors such as Barry, Page and Richards (see their articles in MacLean and Brown 1983; Barry 1989: 185-203; see also Achterberg 1989). Barry and

Richards only refer to the Kantian element of justice as impartiality, which, incidentally, is also accepted by Rawls (represented in the original position by the 'veil of ignorance'). Of course, we can, in this intergenerational context, no longer speak of justice in a sense that implies reciprocity, which is a central element in Rawls, connected with the derivation from the original position, conceived as a bargaining situation, albeit a hypothetical one. Nevertheless, this is not just an arbitrary or *ad hoc* interference in Rawls' argumentation. Precisely because one or more (in this case objective) circumstances of justice are dropped, there is a reason to eliminate the emphasis on reciprocity from the argumentation. I have little to add on to the arguments of, particularly, Barry and Richards on this point, although the discussion could do with a more serious account of Parfit's paradoxes and problems (Achterberg 1989). I do not know whether Rawls himself could agree with this modification and with the intergenerational application of the principle of equal opportunities.

Moreover, the modification concerns the weight of legislation and policy aiming at solving or controlling the environmental crisis. Rawls does not seem to consider them important enough to incorporate their normative starting points in a political conception of justice (1990, first lecture: 7). Justifiably, the Dutch constitution says something different (see above, p.142). A good reason for this can be found in the quotation from Opschoor on page 138 above.

The second reason why we are not allowed to transfer our world in a considerably worse condition to our successors is that nature as well, in the world that we have received and used, must have the opportunities to survive (integrity) in its diversity characteristic of the biosphere. This is a non-anthropocentric argument. Nature *deserves* these opportunities when its 'self-standingness' and its own or intrinsic value have been recognized (see p. 142 above).

The notion of justice in a sense that implies reciprocity is irrelevant here. The intuitive idea of justice means here that justice is done to nature by giving or leaving it the opportunities to an independent existence and a development of its own, just as we appropriately do justice to other entities, of which we recognize the intrinsic (or inherent) worth (for example humans or animals, who are sentient beings). A comprehensive theory of justice, which offers scope for direct moral concern for natural entities other than sentient animals, is presented by Wenz (1988).

The second reason requires that Rawls' frame of argumentation itself is supplemented, since the element which is introduced can only be justified by abandoning this frame, particularly regarding the restriction to 'the thin theory of the good' (the good or goods about which all who know themselves to belong to the same generation, can be expected to come to an agreement on grounds of rationality). In fact, this is important to the first reason also. After all, in as much as the pursuit of sustainability is a morally relevant pursuit that goes further than mere survival, it must be connected with ideas – our ideas, of course: that is our responsibility for future generations! – of the good: in human life, in human culture, and in nature. An environmental policy aiming at sustainability must help to secure favourable conditions for the protection, maintenance and development of this good (Achterberg 1990).

If we conceive the transmission principle in such a way that it also implicitly refers to the intrinsic value of natural entities, a non-neutral element (i.e. that cannot be neutrally justified) is introduced into the conception of political justice. This may not be harmful if in the context concerned, such as the Dutch, there appears to be the beginning of a consensus about that element. I take it for granted that the notion of an overlapping consensus about a political conception of justice is a useful concept, even if this conception has a partly different content than in Rawls and the justification of the conception itself is also different in Rawls.

Finally, we may apply the results of the previous section to the consensus in the Netherlands about sustainable development, *assuming* that we can conceive this consensus as more than just pragmatic or *ad hoc*. This consensus may be considered as an overlapping consensus in the making, and not just because Rawls' overlapping consensus is part of it – I start from the plausible assumption that the overlapping consensus described by Rawls himself also applies to liberal democracy, as is found in the Netherlands. The consensus about sustainable development is also overlapping because it is a consensus: (i) about a political conception of justice towards future generations (and towards nature, too, if our moral sense is in any way fit to be incorporated in a *political* conception of *justice*), and (ii) which is the object of an agreement, in Dutch society, between adherents of divergent comprehensive conceptions of the good (life) and is, or seems to be, rationally accessible and acceptable proceeding from these conceptions.

Its principles are in reflective equilibrium with our 'considered judgements', that is, with judgements about the starting point or main objective of an environmental, or nature, policy, which are laid down by the government in the NEPP and the NPP, undoubtedly after ample consideration, and subsequently accepted in Parliament.

Further, the conception articulates and arranges intuitive ideas (about opportunities for posterity, future generations and nature) which are rather new, but have already become current in public culture (religious and secular conceptions of stewardship, the idea of integrity or 'wholeness of creation'; basically, the popularized views from the Brundtland report and the earlier *World Conservation Strategy* [1980] also belong to these ideas).

If (i) and (ii) are right, we may also assume of the conception of sustainable development, conceived as a political conception, that it is able to fulfil the function which Rawls ascribes to a political conception of justice: the enhancement of social unity and the stability of pluralistic society over generations.

The political conception of sustainable development is largely based upon central elements in the political philosophy of liberalism. Therefore, it can play a legitimizing role within a liberal democracy, which is necessary in view of the radical changes connected with the solution to or control of the environmental crisis.

5. CONCLUSION

The results of this chapter, which aims to be a contribution to the development of normative 'green' political theory – a significant and urgent task for political philosophers, as, I hope, will have become clear in the meantime – can be summarized as follows.

The idea of an overlapping consensus, as elaborated by Rawls, seems useful for two reasons.

(i) It can be used to explain and analyse the problem of legitimacy which confronts liberal democracy if it decides to follow a radical environmental policy, aimed at sustainable development.

(ii) If we look at what Rawls considers to be the focal point of this overlapping consensus – the political conception of justice – and to his arguments for it, then we discover the possibility of an important theoretical, albeit partial, contribution to the solution of the problem of legitimacy.

The political conception of justice is broadened with the introduction of a third principle, the transmission principle. The justification of that principle is partly formed by a controlled modification of Rawls' argumentation for his two principles. Insofar as this principle is taken in a non-anthropocentric sense, Rawls' argumentation is at least heuristically useful. For it points to the direction in which the justification can be found, namely by developing the 'thin theory of the good' into a conception of a more broadly conceived (non-moral) good, which comprises human society, culture and nature. In fact, an overlapping consensus about elements of such extended conception of the good, seems at least possible.

NOTE

[1] This essay was first published in English in Andrew Dobson & Paul Lucardie (eds.), *The Politics of Nature: Explorations in Green Political Theory.* London, Routledge 1993.

REFERENCES

Achterberg, W. 1989. 'Identiteit en Toekomstige Generaties', *Algemeen Nederlands Tijdschrift voor Wijsbegeerte* **81**: 102-118.
— 1990. 'Ethiek en Duurzame Ontwikkeling'. In CREN (=RMNO), *Duurzame Ontwikkeling.* Rijswijk, Report no. 40: 39-47.
— 1992. 'Environmental Ethics and Liberal Morality'. In Musschenga, A. W. , Soeteman, A. and Voorzanger, B. (eds.) *Morality, Worldview and Law.* Assen, Van Gorcum, pp. 241-53.
Barbour, I. G. 1980. *Technology, Environment and Human Values.* New York, Praeger.
Barry, B. 1989. *Theories of Justice.* London, Harvester-Wheatsheaf.
CREN (Council for Research into the Environment and Nature, now RMNO, Raad voor het Milieu.-.en Natuuronderzoek). 1990 *Duurzame Ontwikkeling* Report no. 49, RMNO, Rijswijk.
Dobson, A. 1990. *Green Political Thought.* London, Unwin Hyman.
Dryzek, J. S. 1987. *Rational Ecology.* Oxford, Blackwell.
Dworkin, R. 1978. 'Liberalism', in S. Hampshire (ed.) *Public and Private Morality.* Princeton, Princeton Univ. Press.
IUCN, UNEP, WWF 1980. *World Conservation Strategy.* Gland, Switzerland.
— 1991 *Caring for the Earth. A Strategy for Sustainability.* Gland, Switzerland
Kymlicka, W. 1989. 'Liberal Individualism and Liberal Neutrality', *Ethics* **99**: 883-905.
MacLean, D. and Brown, P. G. (eds.) 1983. *Energy and The Future.* Totowa, Rowman & Littlefield.
Marneffe, P. de 1990. 'Liberalism, Liberty and Neutrality', *Philosophy and Public Affairs* **19**: 253-74.
Naess, A. 1989. *Ecology, Community and Lifestyle.* Cambridge, Cambridge Univ. Press.
Nagel, T. 1987. 'Moral Conflict and Political Legitimacy', *Philosophy and Public Affairs* **16**: 215-40.
NEPP (National Environmental Policy Plan). Ministry of Housing, Physical Planning and Environment 1989. The Hague, SDU.

NPP (Nature Policy Plan). Ministry of Agriculture, Nature Management and Fisheries 1990. The Hague: SDU.

Opschoor, H. 1989. *Na ons geen zondvloed,*.Kampen, Kok Agora.

Paehlke, R. C. 1989. *Environmentalism and the Future of Progressive Politics*. New Haven, Yale Univ. Press.

Pogge, T. 1989. *Realizing Rawls*. Ithaca, Cornell Univ. Press.

Rawls, J. 1971. *A Theory of Justice*. Cambridge, Mass., Harvard Univ. Press.

— 1978 'The Basic Structure as Subject'. In A.I. Goldman and J. Kim (eds.), *Values and Morals*. Dordrecht: Reidel.

— 1982a. 'The Basic Liberties and Their Priority'. In McMurrin, S.M. (ed.) *Liberty, Equality and Law*. Cambridge, Cambridge Univ. Press.

— 1982b. 'Social Unity and Primary Goods'. In A. Sen & B. Williams (eds.) *Utilitarianism and Beyond*. Cambridge, Cambridge Univ. Press.

— 1985. 'Justice as Fairness: Political not Metaphysical'. *Philosophy and Public Affairs* **14**: 223-51

— 1987 'The Idea of an Overlapping Consensus', *Oxford Journal of Legal Studies* **7**: 1-25.

— 1988 'The Priority of Right and Ideas of the Good', *Philosophy and Public Affairs* **17**: 251-76.

— 1989 'The Domain of the Political and Overlapping Consensus', *New York University Law Review* **64**: 233-55.

— 1990 'The Idea of Free Public Reason', Two Lectures. Irvine: University of California.

Routley, R. and V. 1982. 'Nuclear Power - Some Ethical and Social Dimensions', in T. Regan & D. Van De Veer (eds.) *And Justice for All*. Totowa, Rowman & Littlefield.

Sagoff, Mark 1988. *The Economy of the Earth*. Cambridge, Cambridge University Press.

Waldron, J. 1987. 'Theoretical Foundations of Liberalism', *Philosophical Quarterly* **37**: 127-50.

Walzer, M. 1990. 'The Communitarian Critique of Liberalism', *Political Theory* **18**: 6-23.

Wenz, P. 1988. *Environmental Justice*. Albany, State University of New York Press.

The World Commission on Environment and Development 1987. *Our Common Future*. Oxford, Oxford Univ. Press.

Chapter 12

CAN LIBERAL DEMOCRACY HELP US TO SURVIVE THE ENVIRONMENTAL CRISIS?

Frans Jacobs

In the previous chapter Wouter Achterberg asked whether liberal democracy can survive the environmental crisis. My contribution can be seen as a commentary on his arguments, and I would first like to summarize these under five headings. My commentary will express my own ideas on how the environmental crisis should be approached. I shall attempt to show how liberal democracy and the environmental crisis can be tuned into each other. It is possible to summarize Achterberg's arguments as follows:

(i) A government which carries out policies directed at sustainable development appears to lose its neutrality with respect to specific conceptions of the good life. This is anti-liberal and will therefore most probably lead to a lot of opposition.

(ii) However, appearances can deceive: there is an overlapping consensus on the necessity for sustainable development. It is not contrary to the fundamental principles of liberal democracy to take non-neutral measures, as long as they are not controversial.

(iii) Besides, overlapping consensus already exists on the principle of equal opportunity (in the sense of Rawls); it only has to be extended to include the life chances of future generations and maybe also to include the sustainability and diversity of nature.

(iv) If we add the 'transmission principle' ('We are not allowed to hand over the world which we have used and exploited to our future generations in a (much) worse state than the one in which we received it') to Rawls' two principles of justice, it will attract broad support.

(v)   Only such voluntary agreement, based on common social aims, with the severe measures made necessary by the transmission principle, provides sufficient public support, without the democratic government running into a dilemma: the government would either not dare to do anything because of its fear of the expected opposition, or it would take harsh measures to attempt to break the opposition – most probably without result.

I find the third step of Achterberg's paper rather implausible (the overlapping consensus about the principle of equal opportunity). Why should the presence of an overlapping consensus be a condition for upholding the principle regarding future generations, and maybe even nature, without which consensus the governmental policy would not be neutral?

Let us look at an analogous situation: a fictitious country in which the life chances of a minority are continually threatened by a majority. Their houses are set alight, the women are raped, etc. Would the government in question only have the right to do something against this if there was an overlapping consensus? Would the majority also have to agree with the measures? By violating the fundamental rights and freedoms of the minority, the majority would clearly be acting contrary to Rawls' first principle of justice. Likewise, Achterberg does not believe that a government should remain neutral, either in intention or effect, with respect to life styles in which the rules of morality in the narrow sense are systematically broken. Taking action against the violent majority is not a form of perfectionism, and only if this were the case would an overlapping consensus be required. (In my opinion, the idea of overlapping consensus is for Rawls mainly important as a way of legitimizing governmental perfectionism.)

This makes it possible for me to cast a new light on other steps of Achterberg's argument. Taking the first step, if sustainable development is a fundamental requirement of life for future generations and even for present generations, then there is no chance of the government losing its neutrality by stimulating sustainable development. According to Rawls, tolerance is not dictated with respect to intolerance, and to a certain extent we, who are opposed to sustainable development, are comparable with the violent majority, of which no reasonable person, observing the principle of neutrality, questions whether it should be dealt with.

Taking the second step, even if there were no consensus in favour of the government's actions (and one should perhaps expect this when working out sustainable development, as would be the case with the violent majority), it would still be justified and necessary. Of course, a government which had to act against a majority destroying nature would be placed in Achterberg's dilemma in the same way as a government confronting the bloodthirsty crowd in my analogy: either it may do nothing for fear of the expected opposition, or it does not succeed in its efforts because the opposition turns out to be too large, which makes it advisable for the government to chum up with the opposition and then appeal for something like an overlapping consensus. ('You would not think it fair if you were beaten up by people who just happened to be in the majority; so be a sport and fight against an opponent who at least has a chance of defying you.') However, that would only be (to go along with Rawls and Achterberg) 'a mere *modus vivendi*', that does not testify to loyalty towards shared moral or political principles.

I have now reached Achterberg's fourth step, the amendment of Rawls' theory of justice with a third principle. Rawls emphatically places himself in the history of liberal thinking. However, he never (at least not in *A Theory of Justice*) refers to the central doctrines of classic liberals such as Locke and Mill. According to Locke, one may only take ownership of natural resources if that does not have a negative effect on the position of others (Locke's proviso: there must be 'enough and as good left in common for others'). According to Mill, actions which are harmful to others are forbidden. The theories of Locke and Mill are not included in Rawls' list of alternative conceptions of justice either (*A Theory of Justice*, p. 124). Why not? Most probably for a very simple reason: these two theories are hidden in the first principle of justice ('Each person is to have an equal right to the most extensive total system of equal basic liberties compatible with a similar system of liberty for all'). This is immediately clear in Mill's harm principle. But Locke's proviso also can easily be derived from that first principle: if I, using the accidental circumstance that my birth preceded that of others, worsen the position of others by appropriating natural resources, I will have deprived them of the possibility of making use of these resources (and *a fortiori*: of worsening my position by their acts of appropriation). Achterberg ruptures the structure of Rawls' thoughts by adding his principle to the two others, as a third principle – which does not take away the usefulness of attaching that principle to the first, as a special case of it. All in all it can then be considered as a redefinition of Locke's proviso. There is no significant difference between 'There must be enough and as good left in common for others' (Locke's proviso) and 'We are not allowed to hand over the world which we have used and exploited, to our future generations in a (much) worse state than the one in which we received it' (Achterberg's transmission principle). Thus the transmission principle is present in Rawls' first principle of justice, that is, one must not obstruct anyone's freedom, including that of future generations.

My conclusion up to now, commenting on Achterberg's first four steps, is that environmental ethics does not find itself in an area of tension between neutrality and perfectionism, as the subtitle of Achterberg's paper suggests. It is possible to include sustainable development in liberal thinking in a less laborious way, by paying renewed attention to Locke's proviso as well as to Mill's harm principle, both of them heroes of liberalism. By treating nature as we do at the moment, we are acting in defiance of both principles – to be able to see this, the idea of an overlapping consensus is not necessary.

Finally, the fifth step of Achterberg's paper: the necessity for public support. In order to discuss this I can once more use my analogy of a murderous and oppressive majority. In a sense, my analogy applies to the relationship between the present and future generations. The latter cannot take a stand against the way in which we are destroying their life chances; their problem is not smaller than the one of the oppressed minority in my analogy. Is the government which takes action against such a majority in need of public support? In actual fact it may well be so, since it is difficult to take a stand against violent gangs. When the majority is oppressing the minority, public support will almost certainly be lacking. However, from a moral point of view public support will not be necessary: the government has the right and the duty to get the gangs under control.

If the problem of the environmental crisis can in fact be compared with my murderous majority, then rigorous measures would be necessary, but most probably barely feasible (we would find ourselves in a kind of Yugoslavia). However, fortunately there are differences. The environmental crisis is not only to the detriment of future generations, but also to that of the present one: we can say that we are terrorizing ourselves. We can also relate Locke's proviso and Mill's harm principle to ourselves: we are sawing off the legs of our own chairs. Why is it that the insight that we are acting against Locke's proviso and that we are harming ourselves and others is having so little effect in the case of the environmental crisis? This is because the harm which our treatment of nature is causing to both ourselves and to others is the result not of the actions of each of us individually, but of the combined actions of all of us, so that no-one feels particularly responsible for it (the effect that each individual car has on the environmental problem is negligibly small, and hence the disadvantages to each car user do not counterbalance the advantages of having a car). However, precisely that state of affairs can get through to everyone. In proportion as this occurs, we may hope that everyone will support political measures giving shape to collective responsibility. These measures imply force. This force can be taken to mean a special form of 'self-commitment': everyone accepts measures which force him to do what he would actually like to do, but for which he himself is insufficiently motivated.

These ideas can in a much more direct and simple way do justice to Achterberg's preoccupations, which I share with him, in a much more direct and simple way. In a more direct way, in that the necessity of sustainable development immediately follows from the principles of liberal democracy; in a more simple way, in that the necessity of it can be indicated without touching on the problem of neutrality.

In my argumentation I have kept within the limits of classical liberal anthropocentrism. Is that an advantage or a disadvantage? At any rate it moves away from the ideas of many who reflect on the environmental crisis. Achterberg would also like to combine a perfectionist view of nature's own value with liberal-democratic viewpoints, through the idea of an overlapping consensus. For that matter, I have no problem in agreeing with Achterberg's thesis that nature is entitled to the recognition of its independence and of its value, which exceeds the anthropocentric point of view. However, I am not certain that this thesis is backed by an 'overlapping consensus'. Nor do I see the point of a discussion as to whether the majority of for instance the Dutch population recognises the autonomous value of nature. It reminds me of the Swiss discussing the question as to whether women should be allowed to vote or not: that that question is discussed demonstrates that women are not taken very seriously. If nature has autonomous value, its recognition should not be dependent on a majority decision. Seen in this way, the advantage of my paper is that it remains within an anthropocentric point of view. That people should abide by Locke's proviso and Mill's harm principle, is not to be founded upon a majority decision or upon an overlapping consensus. This increases the chance that Locke's and Mill's arguments are listened to – which then leads to increasing the chance that anthropocentrism is not taken for granted. For us to respect nature's own value, is in fact a more or less natural extension of our respect for each other. If in order to stimulate respect for nature's own value I use an anthropocentric argument (nature intact is to the benefit of all mankind), this is purely a question of tactics. The statement 'We serve our interests most if we concentrate less on our own interests and give nature's integrity more of a chance' forms a step towards the disinterested view that there is nothing better than to become enveloped by a nature which exceeds us on all sides.

Achterberg's question was 'Can liberal democracy survive the environmental crisis?'. This is a somewhat strange question, since liberal democracy is actually no more than a means to a different end. It may be better to pose this question: Can we ourselves survive the environmental crisis? However, the substitution of the second question for the first suggests that we may leave liberal democracy behind us, as long as we ourselves survive. This may lead to something like a green dictatorship. This is why I will abide by this question: Can liberal democracy help us to survive the environmental crisis? We should at any rate not ask whether the environmental crisis is going to survive liberal democracy. If we were not to survive the environmental crisis, this is not liberal democracy's fault but our own.

Chapter 13

LIBERAL NEUTRALITY AND THE JUSTIFICATION OF ENVIRONMENTAL CONSERVATION

Bert Musschenga

1. TYPES OF PROBLEMS

There was a time when only a handful of people realized how serious the problems facing the environment are. Only a few prophets warned of the approaching calamity. Theirs was the fate of all prophets, since there were initially few who saw the seriousness of their message. This has changed now. The omens of the approaching disaster, such as the hole in the ozone layer and the greenhouse effect, are being forced upon everyone. Local disasters, such as the dying forests, are already being observed. Everyone now realizes that something must happen: things cannot go on like this. So one of the preconditions for a solution to the environmental problem has now been met: the presence of sufficient awareness of the problem. The following questions are now relevant for an ethical reflection on the environmental crisis:

a. There is still too little agreement about both the seriousness of the problems – especially the problems of which the effects cannot as yet be felt – and the best approach to them. The approach to environmental problems is a classic example of 'dealing in uncertainties'. A rational choice between alternatives is almost impossible because our knowledge is inadequate, and on some points it may be absolutely limited. I call this the uncertainty problem.

b. Everyone realizes that a radical approach to environmental problems not only costs a lot of money, but also requires a change in lifestyle. The necessary measures and adaptations in behaviour will be perceived as a decline in welfare by many. The question is whether people are willing to take such sacrifices. I call this the motivation problem.

c. In the previous point it was presumed that measures would be taken. The uncertainty is as to whether people will be willing to conform themselves to them. However one can also question whether there will be sufficient agreement about effective measures on a governmental level. Will those parties that agree with measures which lead to a considerable limitation of (car) mobility not immediately be punished electorally? Is a democracy capable of generating agreement about optimal measures to protect public goods? I call this the democracy problem.

d. Political measures always lead – definitely if they are fixed as laws – to the limitation of some people's freedom of action. A characteristic of a liberal democracy is what J. Feinberg calls the 'presumption in favour of liberty'. This presumption implies that every limitation of individual freedom of action must be justified by an appeal to the 'liberty limiting principles'. I call this the justification problem.

Naturally these problems are linked with each other. However it is only possible to analyse their connection when they are distinguished from each other. A measure cannot be justified if its effectiveness is controversial. Doubts about effectiveness are continually misused to disguise unwillingness to conform with measures that imply sacrifices. Measures which ask too much of people will not be effective because of this. No one will agree wholeheartedly with a measure if he feels that it cannot be justified. The inability to take effective decisions has a lot to do with a lack of agreement about the effectiveness and justification of policy options. The motivation problem and the democracy problem are mentioned in Achterberg's article, but they are not discussed systematically.[1] He is concerned with the preconditions for public agreement about constraints on, and restrictions of, freedom of individuals and groups, especially economic freedom; and thus about the possibility of public justification of this. Narrowing things down, we can ask: can measures to protect the environment be justified within a liberal morality?

2. TWO MEANINGS OF NEUTRALITY

Characteristic of liberal, ethical justification is the idea of public justification. It must be possible to justify measures to everyone, independent of their social or ideological background.[2] I believe that this requirement for public justification corresponds with the liberal requirement of neutrality.

The demand for liberal neutrality has two meanings or aspects which are often insufficiently distinguished. The first demand is that for fundamental neutrality. This demand is not related to specific measures as much as it is to the principles of the basic institutions of the democratic, political order. In justification of this, one should not refer to the values and beliefs which are only subscribed to by supporters of one or a few of the ideologies which are present in society. An appeal can only be made to the values and beliefs which are common to the supporters of different ideologies. According to Rawls, the public defence of principles and institutions is of great importance for the stability and the unity of a society. It is because of this demand for public justification that Rawls keeps emphasizing that his theory of 'justice as fairness' is a political and not metaphysical theory of justice.[3]

The second meaning of neutrality is that a measure should not favour one of the rival conceptions of the good above the others. Here I am speaking about political neutrality. In the weak interpretation of the demand for political neutrality, it is impermissible to aim at favouring one conception ('neutrality in aim'); the strong interpretation also discards measures if they appear to favour a conception in practise, even though this was not aimed at ('neutrality in effect'[4]). I agree with Achterberg that the strong interpretation is untenable, partly because the effect of measures is never totally predictable. The weak interpretation of political neutrality – called 'neutrality in justification' by Achterberg – is not the same as fundamental neutrality.

What is the relationship between fundamental neutrality and political neutrality? According to Rawls, fundamental neutrality implies political neutrality.[5] In his theory, fundamental neutrality is embodied in the construction of a hypothetical original situation, in which rational individuals chose the principles for their co-operation and coexistence behind a veil of ignorance. One of these principles would then be the principle of political neutrality. I will come back to the question as to whether fundamental neutrality indeed implies political neutrality later. I myself dare to doubt this.

Achterberg is primarily interested in fundamental neutrality. He defends the supplementing of Rawls' two principles of justice with a third principle, namely that of sustainability, which can also be seen as a principle of interspecific and intergenerational justice. His question is whether such a principle can be justified neutrally. The rawlsian idea of an overlapping consensus plays a role here.

3. INHERENT AND INTRINSIC VALUES

The justification of environmental conservation can only be called liberal – in the sense of fundamentally neutral – if it refers to public values and ideologies. In the literature one can find two justifications in which an appeal is made to non-public values and ideologies. In the first type of justification it is stated that all natural entities that have intrinsic value (for example because they have a good of their own, i.e., things can go better or worse for that entity) belong to the moral community, and have rights because of this quality. The notion of 'intrinsic value' is controversial, because it is based on metaphysical presumptions which are not shared by all ideologies. In the second type of justification, life in harmony with nature is seen as an essential part of a good life for human beings. The wellbeing of both nature and humanity are essentially linked with one another. Impoverishment of nature through the extinction of species leads to the spiritual impoverishment of humanity. This idea of living in harmony with nature can be worked out in several different ways. One of these is for example the anthroposophic, biodynamic way of living. This is why one could speak of a partially inclusive concept of good, which is comparable with that which Achterberg calls a 'binding framework'. In practice, the metaphysical notion of intrinsic values, and the evaluative notion of life in harmony with nature will often be linked to one another. However they must be distinguished from one another.

In my view, living in harmony with nature is compatible with a weak form of anthropocentrism. The proposition that the enjoyment of trees, plants, animals and ecosystems is a necessary part of a spiritually rich human life does not imply the discarding of anthropocentrism. The enjoyment of nonhuman nature is seen as a the satisfaction of a human desire. To be able to satisfy that desire not only now, but also in the future, it is necessary to keep the objects of desire, the natural entities, intact. Nature has inherent value in this approach. An object that has inherent value can only retain it if it stays intact. Here lies the difference from the concept of 'instrumental value'. Food only has instrumental value, a wilderness also has inherent value. The concept of 'inherent value' can be included in a subjective value theory, in which the value of something depends on it being the object of human desires.

It is only when the environmental vision recognizes the intrinsic values of nonhuman entities that it becomes non-anthropocentric. Even though the assignment – or recognition – and the articulation of intrinsic values is a human activity, there is no necessary relationship between intrinsic values and human desire. The concept of 'intrinsic values' presumes a non-subjective theory of values, that is, a theory in which the value of something is not exclusively determined by the fact that it is an object of human desire. The relevance of the distinction between inherent and intrinsic values as a basis for environmental conservation will be indicated in the following section.

4. LIBERAL MORALITY AND THE JUSTIFICATION OF ENVIRONMENTAL CONSERVATION

Once again I shall make a distinction, this time between:

(i)   justifications in which environmental conservation is seen as a demand of justice, thus as an obligation, arising from a liberal conception of political justice, and

(ii) justifications which are compatible with liberal political morals.

I believe that two types of justification belong to the first category:

a.   the justification of environmental conservation as the protection of primary goods (i.e. a justification that remains within the existing framework of Rawls' theory); and

b.   the justification of environmental conservation as a demand of justice on the grounds of a transmission principle (as the third principle of justice; thus a justification in which Rawls' theory is further expanded).

I believe that a third type of justification belongs to the second category:

c.   the justification of environmental conservation as the protection of valuable ways of living (i.e. a justification in which Rawls' theory is exceeded).

The justification of environmental conservation must not be made dependent on just one type of justification. It is better to develop a range of justifications, in which the cogency is determined by the values and beliefs of the group which has been targeted. I shall now examine how far these three justifications are adequate and will then investigate their relationship with liberal morality.

a. The environment a primary good?

Rawls believes primary goods to be things which rational people want, whatever their aims in life may be. In their plan of life, people can aim towards many very different ultimate ends. However in order to achieve them they all require specific primary goods, whether natural or social.[6] Natural goods include such qualities as health, vigour, intelligence and imagination. Social goods include rights and freedom, possibilities and abilities, income and wealth.[7] In as far as society can influence primary natural goods, they too have a social aspect. Health care can be seen as a primary social good which aims to get rid of or correct shortcomings in the primary natural good 'health'.

Can one characterize environmental conservation to be a primary social good using the same type of reasoning? I believe that this is possible up to a point. A clean environment and sufficient natural resources are preconditions for the realization of every kind of plan for life. A polluted environment is disadvantageous for health, while the exhaustion of natural resources leads to a strongly limited range of options for the construction of life plans. It is not difficult to indicate the limitations of this type of justification. Many forms of environmental degradation, such as the extinction of certain species, have very little influence on the goods which are required for the realization of any type of life plan. The avoidance of future environmental degradation which is the result of present day human behaviour also falls outside the range of justification of environmental conservation as a primary social good. The interests of future generations do not have a place here. This justification of environmental conservation is too partial to be adequate. However it does remain within the scope of a liberal, political, ethical theory. This is because this justification indicates only preconditions for the realization of life plans, and it does not indicate the contents of specific life plans.

b. Sustainability as a requirement of justice

Achterberg proposed to add a third principle of justice to those of Rawls and calls it the transmission principle. It seems to me that this is a principle of intergenerational justice. I rather doubt whether the range of such a principle covers for example the conservation of species which are irrelevant to human welfare. However I will not discuss the relationship between this principle and the interspecific justification here.

The question is not whether the expansion of a political concept of justification to include a principle of transmission is necessary or desirable, but whether it can be justified within the scope of Rawls' theory. In that theory rational people deliberate behind the veil of ignorance. They have been deprived of all sorts of specific information about themselves and their society. They have been provided with general information about the nature of human beings and the nature of the human society. Hence they know that there is a partial convergence and partial conflict of interests. This partial convergence makes co-operation possible and useful. The principles which they are going to agree to will avoid or regulate the possible conflicts about individual claims to a share of society's natural resources and about the division of the fruits of the co-operation. Rawls describes the attitude of the people with respect to one another as 'mutual disinterestedness'.[8] That is, it is of no interest to them to realize the interests of the others. The fact that humans are slightly altruistic is included in the general information about the nature of human beings, that is that they are concerned with the wellbeing of a limited close circle (family, friends and other people that are close to them). Thus they worry about the wellbeing of the future generation to some extent.

Is it possible to expand Rawls' theory of justice to such an extent that environmental conservation and sustainability come to fall within it as requirements of both intergenerational and interspecific justification? I do not believe that this is possible. It is true that Rawls himself provides openings to extend his theory, for example to include the relationships between states. This expansion can very easily be defended using the arguments of 'circumstances of justice'. Methods of mass communication and high speed transport act to gradually fade the borders between countries. Seen from an economic point of view, countries are becoming dependent on one another to a large extent. One could defend the argument that the welfare of people and that of nature are also inextricably linked to one another. However this independence is somewhat onesided. Humanity needs nature for food and other natural resources, while nature would most probably be better off without the presence of humans. Achterberg too agrees that there is no real reciprocity between humanity and nature. Another problem is nature's representation behind the veil of ignorance. One could suggest that nature's interests could be represented by people as trustees. However one then comes into conflict with the idea of 'mutual disinterestedness'. Rawls wants to base his theory of justification on presumptions of human motivation which are as minimal and realistic as possible. Concern about nature's wellbeing goes much further than a realistic approach permits. Achterberg is correct to conclude that Rawls' justification of his two principles of justice cannot be used as justification of the transmission principle. So what then? Achterberg says that Rawls' justification of his two principles should be supplemented; but what does 'supplemented' mean here? Does it mean the development of the theory retaining unity and coherence or the addition of a totally different type of justification? I believe that it is not possible to justify a transmission principle which can be added to Rawls' existing theory without any problems.

There is another problem too. Let us consider that the interests of non-human nature in the 'original position' are to be represented by people. The question is, which entities would be eligible for representation? A criterion for representation could be the presence of intrinsic value. As has already been mentioned, those entities have intrinsic value, for which it is possible to speak of wellbeing and no wellbeing. Achterberg mentions that a non-neutral element of the concept of political justice creeps in when using the term 'intrinsic value'. In referring to what I have already mentioned in section 3, I would argue that the belief in the intrinsic value of at least part of non-human nature can be seen as a metaphysical belief rather then a perfectionist one. According to Achterberg, its introduction into a Dutch context should not be a problem, because the beginning of a consensus on the belief already exists. However I doubt this. There may be consensus on the fact that nature's value cannot only be seen from an instrumental viewpoint, but it's a big leap to go from 'not instrumental' to 'intrinsic'. The justification of environmental conservation, in which the intrinsic value of part of nonhuman nature is indicated, is not neutral as in fundamental neutrality, and hence it cannot fulfil the requirement of general acceptability.

Until now it has not been possible to justify the whole range of measures that can be grouped together as environmental conservation, as requirements for a liberal political morality. The first justification turned out to be inadequate while the second cannot be publicly defended.

c. Environmental conservation as the protection of valuable life

If a transmission principle had been successfully justified by referring to reasons which were compatible with a liberal morality, then it would have been possible to reject all those lifestyles which are nature-unfriendly, as not compatible with the liberal conception of justice: thus on non-perfectionist grounds. Hence nature-unfriendly lifestyles would not be rejected because they are less valuable than nature-friendly ones. The grounds for justification would then be that they are not compatible with the conception of justice. At the most one would be able to speak of indirect perfectionism, because nature-unfriendly lifestyles are to be dealt with and discouraged on the grounds of justice. However the 'neutrality in aim' would not be damaged.

As I have already mentioned, I do not agree with Achterberg when he proposes that an overlapping consensus between different conceptions of a good life already exists about the desirability of environmental conservation, at a level which is broad enough to justify the whole range of protective measures. It would be possible to attempt to enlarge the sensitivity for nature values by means of environmental education, for example. And that must definitely occur to a greater extent than is the case at present. However is it not possible for the government to carry out far-reaching measures in the mean time, to safeguard the diversity of species, without violating the principle of political neutrality?

There are different ways of achieving such a justification, but I will only elaborate on one of these. I spoke of my doubts about the proposition that political neutrality implies fundamental neutrality in section 2. The requirement of fundamental neutrality means that the political conception of justice should be defensible in public, thus in the presence of supporters of different views of the good life. In justifying this, non-personal values only may be referred to – values which are a part of the overlapping consensus which everyone can subscribe to. An example of such a value is health. Goods that are necessary to achieve or maintain such values can be called fundamental values. Hence health care can be said to be of fundamental importance to the public. Following de Marneffe, a society's constitution could be called legitimate if it protects every person's fundamental interests.[9] De Marneffe speaks of constitutional neutrality. Well, if the government issues laws which favour or handicap specific conceptions of the good life without damaging people's fundamental interests, then constitutional neutrality will not have been harmed. Constitutional neutrality does not imply legislative neutrality. De Marneffe uses the example of the ban on the production and use of drugs. Recreational use of drugs cannot be called a fundamental interest. De Marneffe concludes that political neutrality does not imply fundamental neutrality. It must be defended on moral grounds that are independent of this.

It is questionable whether this is possible. One could use the principle of autonomy. Violation of neutrality could then be seen as an assault on the principle of autonomy.[10] Along with Raz, I question whether each limitation of options for the choice of a life plan can be called an infringement of autonomy. It is not true that the preconditions for autonomy are only fulfilled if one can choose between a limitless range of options. Options are actually always limited. Everyone's ambitions are restricted by limits. Firstly this is due to limits to capacity and talent, secondly due to the absence of social conditions. Only a few of the people who can play the piano will be able to earn their living by doing so. This is because of a limit to the social need for pianists. Not everyone who wants to, or has the capacity to do so, will be able to acquire a place to learn surgery. However we do not say that that person has been unjustifiably frustrated in living a life according to his choices. He has had bad luck, and society cannot be held responsible for this. One can only speak of impermissible limitations when people are systematically prevented from being able to live a life which is both suitable for them and corresponds with their capacities. Up until recently this occurred to children in East Germany, whose parents stood up for their beliefs and did not want to become members of the communist party and its organizations. They were not given the chance to study, for example.

If a government fixes measures to protect the nature-friendly life style of some people, it concomitantly limits consumers' freedom of choice and the economic freedom of businesses. Can they rightly complain about this? There is still sufficient room for action for them. The question is, on which grounds a government should take such measures. If they do not take them, the fundamental interests of the nature lovers will not really be damaged. To justify its environmental protection measures, a government would only be able to indicate the importance of the values which are held in a nature-friendly life style. For the justification to succeed, the government will have to indicate the importance which is attached to the values, even when one does not find nature-friendliness to be an essential part of the notion of a good life.

But isn't the problem the fact that not everyone subscribes to these values? I would like to go along with Nagel in differentiating between the importance or value which one attaches to something from an objective viewpoint, and the personal value attached to something.[11] Why shouldn't a manager, for whom the speed of decision-making is all-important, be able to appreciate the value of the contemplative life of a monk? Such a life style may not be compatible with the life plan which he has sketched for himself; but that is another matter. In this way agreement may be reached about the value of music, art etc., even though this is not become apparent in the actual preferences of all the members of the society. There are many values and the relative importance of each cannot be fixed, while it is also impossible to realize them all in one life. To summarize in one word: they are incommensurable. This theory of moral pluralism is defended by authors such as Berlin and Hampshire, as well as Raz and Nagel.[12]

5. CONCLUSIONS

I agree with Achterberg that the idea of liberal neutrality does not have to present impossible limitations for the justification of environmental conservation. However I cannot see how perfectionism – in the sense of Raz's perfectionistic pluralism – can be avoided if justification is adequate. I agree with Achterberg in this as well. We differ in our reasoning on the justification of environmental conservation. Achterberg attempts to extend Rawls' theory by adding a principle of sustainability, while I believe that justification of environmental conservation must exceed the theory.

NOTES

1. See Achterberg's contribution to this volume, 'Can Liberal Democracy Survive the Environmental Crisis?'
2. Jacobs, F.C.L.M., 1985.*Ten overstaan van allen,* doctoral thesis, University of Amsterdam.
3. Rawls, J., 1985. 'Justice as Fairness: Political not Metaphysical', in *Philosophy and Public Affairs,* **17**: 223-52.
4. For a distinction between the two, see article by P. Jones in Goodin, R.E. and A. Reeve (eds.) 1989. *Liberal Neutrality,* pp. 9-39. London/New York, Routledge.
5. According to Rawls, the idea of 'justice as fairness' can be seen as a procedural neutrality (in my own terminology, fundamental neutrality). '...and... also hopes to satisfy the neutrality of aim in the sense that basic institutions and public policy are not designed to favor any particular comprehensive doctrine.' (Rawls 1988. 'The Priority of Right and Ideas of the Good', in *Philosophy and Public Affairs,* **22**: 251-77. Quotation on p. 263.)
6. Rawls, J. 1971, p. 92. Oxford, Clarendon Press.
7. Rawls, 1971 p. 62.
8. Rawls, 1971 pp. 127-30.
9. Marneffe, P. de,1990. 'Liberalism, Liberty and Neutrality', in *Philosophy and Public Affairs,* **22**: 253-75, especially p.258.
10. Raz, J. 1986. *The Morality of Freedom,* p.411 ff. Oxford, Clarendon Press.
11. Nagel, T. 1987. *The View from Nowhere.* Oxford, Oxford University Press. See pp. 171-5, especially p. 172: 'Each person has reasons stemming from the perspective of his own life which, though they can be publicly recognized, do not in general provide reasons for others and do not correspond to reasons that the interests of others provide for him.'
12. Berlin, I., 1969. 'Two Concepts of Liberty', in *The Four Essays on Liberty,* pp.118-73. Oxford, Oxford University Press. More recently, Hampshire, S., 1989, in *Innocence and Experience,* Cambridge, Mass., Harvard University Press.

Chapter 14

MARKET FORCES AS CAUSES OF ENVIRONMENTAL DEGRADATION

Hans Opschoor

1. BACKGROUND

Until recently the question of the relationship between economic order and environmental degradation was at least empirically relevant. Nowadays it seems as if this relevance has disappeared into the black hole of outdatedness, along with socialism in central and eastern Europe. However, appearances deceive. The liberation theologist and economist Hinckelammert suggested that the present 'social market economy' could shake off its social makeup now that its rival, the plan economy, has disappeared from the scene. This gives reason to fear that the environmental lessons which are only just being in our capitalist society will soon be forgotten. In the light of this, the following essay will deal with three topics:

a. Institutional causes of environmental pressure

When we speak of the environment and nature, there are good reasons to consider a number of 'inherent risks' which are concealed within the market economy. Vermeersch (1990) speaks of the social background to the environmental issue in terms of a 'scientific-technological-capitalist (STC) system', with autonomous dynamics, which sooner or later will exceed the natural carrying capacity of social activities. I do not totally agree with the suggestion of unavoidability as far as the dynamics are concerned. However the metaphor of the STC system rightly indicates that we are dealing with structural forces, which we should understand properly. My analysis of the political economic facets of these in particular are given below.

b. Humankind-nature images and the economic process

Even though economic factors can be regarded as being relatively autonomous in explanations of the direction in which society is developing – an autonomy which is definitely not advanced only by the left –, it is clear that norms, values and 'world images' play an important role in individual and social choices. The question is, whether and how far the economic process is influenced, as far as its exploitation of the environment is concerned, from this level of values etc.

c. Faith in growth and faith in the market

I believe that a number of the elements alluded to above are slowly developing into an ideology which could block the discussion of the social roots of the environmental crisis, and which could hence block finding an adequate solution to that problem.

This chapter will be organized as follows. In section 3, I will examine why a market driven economic process tends to neglect the limits set by the physical environment from a technical and ethical viewpoint. I will do so using a short historical sketch of the development of the market economy (section 2). As an economist, I feel called upon to proceed by next indicating several directions in which solutions could be found in terms of sustainable institutions and instruments (section 4), before going into a couple of factors of a more ideological nature. Examples of these are humankind-nature images or world images (section 5), and economism, which has more or less turned into a religion (section 6).

2. FROM 'COMMERCIAL SOCIETY' TO SOCIAL MARKET ECONOMY.

Historically, industrial capitalism has been the product of two processes: (i) technical and scientific development which resulted from the rise of applied sciences since (especially) Bacon, and (ii) the 'commercial society' which has developed and expanded (Smith), since the fifteenth century. The present environmental crisis has been explained by environmental philosophers by tracking its historical roots back to the Enlightenment, rationalism and empiricism (i.e. process (i)). Environmental philosophy has hardly made the connection between environmental degradation and the development of the 'commercial society'; so this is done in sections 2 and 3. I do not aim there to express some kind of judgement about the relevance of the different processes, which I have discussed side by side elsewhere (Opschoor 1989), but I will come back to this in sections 4 and 5.

The economic, political roots of present-day capitalism can be traced back to the feudal Middle Ages. Population growth enhanced the development of towns as centres of trade and traditional industry. Agriculture increasingly produced for the 'market'. During the Middle Ages this developed into a system of international trade relationships (for example, via the annual markets). Trade became still more important from the sixteenth century onwards. Exchange at markets, international division of labour, and increases in productivity were essential aspects of the new mode of production (i.e. societal system) which developed around the end of the Middle Ages. Partly because of exchange on the market, and because of the role of money, the newly created form of society is called 'commercial capitalism'. During and after the sixteenth century, this commercial capitalism expanded under the leadership of western Europe, up until the Second World War: colonialism, imperialism, and greatly expanded world trade in the post-colonial age. In this way more and more people, and a larger expanse of the world were brought into the ambit of a single economic system.

A new phase developed out of commercial capitalism during the nineteenth century: industrial capitalism. That system is and was characterized by unequal, rather than homogenous development: that is, a northern, strongly industrialized and technically advanced centre, and a periphery of countries which primarily supply raw materials to the centre and which have been left behind (see Terhal 1988, amongst others). Widespread and growing markets were created and serviced due to international trade. For the industrial countries, world trade was also a mechanism to supply themselves with natural resources and raw materials against prices which were as low as possible, the materials already having been used up in their own part of the world, or only extractable against much higher costs, or never having occurred there.

Parallel to these actual developments, reflection about the 'commercial society' also developed and ultimately gave rise to economic science. The main stream of this science strongly legitimized the market economy and even declared it to be the best conceivable form of society. In what follows we will firstly stop to consider this conceptual development and the alleged advantages of the market mechanism. After this we will consider its effect on environmental pressure. In section 5, we will look at the ideological aspects which can be seen behind the actual developments of the economic theory.

The political economy of capitalism

Classical economic science as it was developed from 1789 onwards (the year in which Adam Smith, the founder of modern economics, published *An Inquiry into the Nature and Causes of the Wealth of Nations*), has been preoccupied with how the wealth or welfare of a country could be made as large as possible.

Where does welfare or wealth come from? For Smith's predecessors from Plato onwards, but in particular for his direct predecessors, the so-called Physiocrats of the eighteenth century, the land (or, in other words, nature) was the source. Smith emphasized the importance of human work in the creation of wealth. Given the possibilities of the physical environment of a country, its wealth is dependent on the amount of labour and the skill or productivity of the labourers. Smith saw productivity grow as the production process of a society became more specialized and the division of labour developed further. He predicted that specialization would continue as the economy grew. He perceived hardly, if at all, that growth could encounter physical limits. The fact that he lived at a time when the great 'empty' continents such as America were just beginning to be exploited on a large scale most probably plays a role here.

Characteristic of the classical economists, including Marx, is that they determine the value of goods according to the amount of labour involved in their production ('labour embodied'), or which can be obtained in exchange for these goods ('labour commanded'). This is known as the 'labour theory of value'. To Smith wealth was the product of nature and labour, but put more precisely, it is labour which adds value to what is available in nature (which will always remain available, thought Smith). Without labour, nature is, as it were, worthless. Classical economics mainly limits itself to a study of the value of labour, its enlargement and the sharing of labour.

The labour value would also explain the level of market prices. Smith thought – in his days a very new, even demystifying notion – that prices were the result of an ideal, typical process of supply and demand, which he referred to as 'natural', and of technical and economical progress. In the end the price at which exchange took place would tend towards the production costs, at a level equal to the value of labour embodied in the product. When exchange takes place via a transfer of money, that is, when trade takes place, Smith speaks of a 'commercial society'. Smith believes this to be a desirable type of social organization for societies aiming to increase their wealth and welfare. If everyone aims to achieve their own interests via the market, then the market mechanism will transform this into a situation in which the largest number of people have the greatest wealth. Or: *however egoistic or bad someone's motives are, the market mechanism will guide him 'as if by an invisible hand' towards behaviour which maximizes the general interest.* Smith believed that society should be organized in such a way that market forces can fulfil their co-ordinating and guiding roles to a maximum extent. The government should avoid interfering with social affairs as much as possible.

Before going any further, it is important to emphasize once again the innovative element of Smith's theory. The market which he spoke of did not actually exist: it was an image originating in Enlightenment doctrine, which was projected against the restricting wings of the then existing Mercantilist system, an economic system characterized by rules, social control, an ordered economic process etc. One was not free to do as one wished, for example because of control by the guilds, and one was not free to go where one pleased because of tolls. Smith set the free market against this: *laissez faire, laissez passer.* People participate in the free market process as individuals and they are seen as essentially equal individuals. They must not be so familiar with one another that they could influence the outcome of the market process via mutual agreements. The actual rise of the 'commercial society' can thus be seen as the realization of the Enlightenment's vision: the struggle to introduce the market was a successful attempt at the realization of an artifact, in an over-regulated society: one can therefore speak of liberation.[1]

The neoclassical revision: market conformity

Since Smith's days much has changed in economic science. For example, the labour theory of value has disappeared. However the idea of the market as the optimal regulation mechanism has remained, as has its justification: the invisible hand. We have begun to see that there are situations in which the market process can lead to socially undesirable outcomes, and that governmental action is necessary in such situations. This is because the market can sometimes be more inefficient than other regulatory mechanisms, or because its effects do not fulfil the criteria for justification (Haveman 1976). In such instances one speaks of 'market imperfections' or 'market failure'.

Old style market imperfections.

In principle all those situations in which the actions of one influence the welfare of another, without the other being able to influence the decisions sufficiently, fall within the category of 'market imperfections'. This is the situation of 'external effects': one is not confronted with the complete effects of a decision or action, because part of the latter will affect others. One can speak of economic inefficiency here.

A second category of circumstances in which the market fails on grounds of efficiency, is that of the so-called 'collective goods', such as public health or safety. The provision of collective goods must as a rule be determined on a different level to that of decentralized decision making via markets, namely that of society as a whole, or the government. Finally, governmental regulation of market processes on the grounds of efficiency can be defended where knowledge is insufficient or because economic mobility is insufficient for one reason or other.

Governmental action can also be defensible on the grounds of equity, as is the case when the result of the market mechanism leaves something to be desired as far as the division of incomes or job opportunities is concerned. This includes collective control of the division of natural resources across generations, in order to protect future generations' rights to these resources.

The above can also be expressed as follows. A pure market process contains three inherent limitations:

(i)   Demand is registered, and honoured according to the level at which it is expressed in terms of purchasing power.

(ii) Supply is only elicited in as far as it is rewarded.

(iii) Values are only respected in as far as prices or rewards are attached.

Therefore the market mechanism tends towards a negligence of the individual requirements of the poor, and of the collective requirements of everyone. Furthermore, where no property or use rights have been established, price formation will not occur, and so the interests of both nature and future generations will be ignored when left to the market.

Mainly because of their social effects, market imperfections have led to a large amount of regulation of market forces. Thus we have seen governments arise which forbade the development of cartels, banned child labour, etc. In this way a society was formed in which the sharpest edges of the market mechanism had been removed. A mixed economic order was created in which the so-called 'budget mechanism' (decision making concerning the incomes and expenditures of the state) functioned besides the market mechanism. This mixture was called the 'social market economy'. In this, the government must take care of the efficiency and the justice of the economic process, and if necessary, it must direct the market process, add to it, demarcate its domain and/or neutralize or compensate its adverse effects.

It is questionable whether the government is able to make use of sufficient instruments within the social market economy to be able to act out its traditional role as guardian of efficiency and justice. However I am not going to expand on this.

New style market imperfections: unsustainability and biological deterioration.

The environmental crisis raises the question as to whether the government should confine itself its traditional role in the case of efficiency and justice. Because of the long term effects and the uncertainties which are inherent in environmental change, and because of the issue of equity between present and future generations, the government has a role in guarding not only the sustainability of economic growth, but also the diversity of the natural environment as something which must be transmitted to future generations. What barriers will the government come across in carrying out its task concerning these new imperfections and which mandates, institutes and instruments will it require? Sections 3 and 4 will deal with these questions respectively.

3. TENDENCIES TOWARDS UNSUSTAINABILITY: ANALYSIS

In order to indicate the government's role in the case of these 'new style market imperfections' a diagnosis is necessary of the tendencies that are inherent in a market economy with respect to its relations with the natural environment. This will be elaborated below by referring to four tendencies which I believe contain a structural inclination to neglect, especially, the aspects sustainability and justice towards other generations and species: (a) accumulation push factors (b) distance between decision makers and the environmental effects of their behaviour, (c) cost shifting tendencies in the social market economy, and (d) neglect of the environment in social and political considerations. Figure 14.1 depicts their effect on the economic process.

(a) Accumulation

Since 1850 – more or less the beginning of the industrial age in a number of west European countries including the Netherlands – there has been expo-

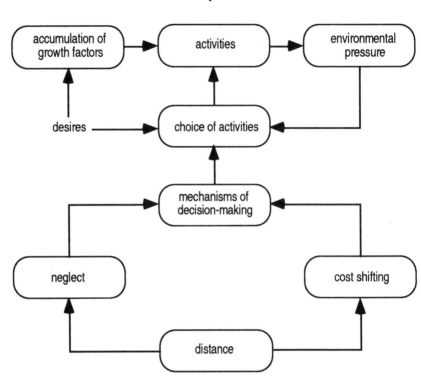

Figure 14.1. The economic process and environmental degradation

nential economic growth. It is undeniable that this growth has been paired with increasing pressure on the environment. The question is whether this can be explained on the grounds of factors within the economic structure and within the economic process itself. I believe that this is the case.

Firstly, our form of society implies that all the actors within the economic process are aiming for growth: I will illustrate this below for individuals, companies and states. Secondly, impulses for endless expansion emanate from the mutually linked system of economy and economic ideology; this will be discussed later (in section 5). Finally, the economic process exerts a 'push' in the direction of economic growth via technological development; this will be dealt with in this section.

Individuals within our society tend to display behaviour in which they prefer more (incomes, consumption, welfare) rather than less. In our utilitarian, materialistic society, 'more' is synonymous with 'better'. In fact, material consumption prevails above 'sustainable welfare'. Hence there is broad public support for economic growth. As long as poverty and inequality exist, whether in our own society or in a universal relation, this public support for growth will remain.

Companies are characterized by the aim for growth for other reasons. In a decentralized economic order like the market economy, they are confronted with the necessity to keep themselves from going bankrupt in a situation which is determined by competition and innovation. Hence the striving for growth in the market share and for control of the market can be explained, as can the urge towards innovation. This then leads once more to a reinforced stimulus to make a profit and to expand.

Governments also prefer growth, especially when there is an emancipating neglected group, such as labour in the previous century. A government which is aiming towards continuity (of the prevailing social order and/or of itself), should control tensions within society. A means of doing so is by accommodating the material demands of those groups which could increase the tension. This costs money; and money is found or reallocated most easily in a context of economic growth. In this way the division of incomes and welfare can be made less unequal, without this being to the detriment of the dominant group. A large amount of the aim towards growth of social democrats, Christian democrats and liberalism can be explained in political, economic terms in this way.

Another driving force behind economic growth is to be found in technological development, which itself can again be explained using characteristics of the economic process in a market economy, such as the push towards innovation. Technological development means that increasingly less labour is needed in order to make the same number of products. This results in structural unemployment. When one regards mass unemployment as undesirable, as is the case in our society, there is but one solution: expansion of the production capacity and increase in consumption so that the working population can remain employed as much as possible. Thus the Dutch Scientific Committee for Governmental Policy's report 'Room for Growth', argues that a more or less compulsory growth in consumption of at least 3% per annum and a production growth of 4% is necessary for this reason.

(b) Distance

The key word 'distance' covers several aspects of decentralized decision making all leading to undesired environmental degradation. The first is: a lack of communication between decision-makers whose actual interests are related to one another (the Prisoner's Dilemma). The second is the effects of distance in time between a decision or activity and its environmental effects. The final one is the effect of distance in space between an activity and the environmental repercussions related to it. I will deal with each of these situations.

Prisoners' Dilemma. Many environmental problems can be analysed as resulting from a situation in which one party's conditions are dependent on what another party decides or does, without it being able to exert influence on that other party, and without it being possible to make agreements. Why should a cod fisherman be the only one to abide by a fishing quota? Why should one country take the lead with a stringent environmental policy, if other countries refrain from doing so and hence achieve an industrial and competitive advantage with respect to that one country? Individual environmentally friendly behaviour in the public interest tends to be punished rather than rewarded. Consequently, nature and the environment, especially future environmental quality are easily sacrificed. Only when all those involved gain the insight that it is to everyone's advantage to avoid a long term undesired situation for everyone, or when there is an authority which is capable of effectively limiting people's individual behaviour in respect of the public interest, can this tragedy, this dilemma be broken. Van Asperen (1986) has summarized this as follows: In the case of several groups which find themselves to be in a prisoners' dilemma or tragedy situation a central authority or government at a sufficiently high level is necessary to collect information and determine a collective strategy, trace evaders and punish them.

Distance in time. Many environmental problems manifest themselves at a considerably later date than the moment that they are caused, because they are spread out in the environment in both time and space and they cause sequential changes in physical environmental parameters. An example of this is the threatened rise in sea level, which is the result of, amongst other things, continually increasing fossil fuel combustion for more than a century. This distance plays a potentially large role in individual and social process decision making on behaviour.

Structural short-sightedness (Pigou speaks of a 'defective telescopic faculty') in human perception makes us chronically devalue the importance of future interests and values, as far as their effect on decision making today is concerned. Economists call this euphemistically: 'time preference'. One apparently attaches more value to events in the present than in the future. Economists express this preference as a percentage interest or 'discount rate'. In this way the future meaning of a development is reduced, and this is dangerous in the case of non-reversible situations, or developments which are much more expensive to reverse then the costs now required to avoid the development.

Distance in space. Besides the distance in time between the cause of an environmental change and its manifestation, there is also the factor that many problems manifest themselves elsewhere than where they have been caused. Here again it is important that the causers of the environmental problem are others than those which experience the effects. An extreme example of this is the transfer of the environmental effects of economic activity across borders.

International division of labour and the world trade which is linked to it lead to the creation of activity patterns and trade flows which are in the interests of one country but which may lead to adverse environmental consequences elsewhere. This may lead to serious damage to the environment as the basis for future economic activities or as the place in which people must live. The world market does not indicate this environmental damage as a loss, and does not include it in the cost price of, for example, meat or wood which is exported from economically weak Third World countries to the North. In such a situation in which there is no conscious direction and regulation, world trade can easily reach a situation in which the benefits of trade are reaped by the North, while the environmental costs pile up in the South. Internationalization of the world economy means that environmental degradation for the benefit of consumption and material welfare shifts from one specific region to another. International division of labour facilitates drawing our curtains somewhere near our borders, so that the environmental degradation which is related to specific production and trade links is only visible to us in as far as it takes place in our own homes.

(c) Cost shifting

The regulation of economic traffic via the market mechanism has large potential advantages in terms of efficiency and increases in welfare. However, one of the principle disadvantages is that the cost minimization which is implied leads to individuals and enterprises transferring as large an amount as possible of the negative total consequences of their decisions and behaviour onto society, thus onto others. In the 1950s the Swiss economist Kapp drew attention to this tendency; he spoke of 'cost shifting' as a typical phenomenon of entrepreneurial production. We must realize that the tendency towards cost shifting is always present when this tendency is rewarded by increased security or incomes and/or a better competitive position.

(d) Neglect

Cost shifting has a counterpart in situations in which it is not the market mechanism but the government which takes decisions concerning the course of the economic process. The term *neglect* seems suitable to describe such intervention.

Environmental problems can be seen as the effects of conflicting interests within a society. These may be conflicts between regions, or, more frequently, conflicts between economic sectors. If such sectors clash it is usually the strongest one which wins. Short term interests which are expressed in terms of purchasing power, stand strong, even in the political debate. This leads to a resulting tendency towards neglect of environmental considerations, even within the political world.

We have seen that environmental interests are neglected when they manifest themselves over time. This neglect is still worse when interests which will no longer affect the present day decision makers and their voters are at stake. *A fortiori*, this applies to environmental changes which have no known value to humanity, such as the threat of extinction to certain species of animals and plants. Future generations and especially other forms of life have neither voting rights nor purchasing power. They cannot present their stakes in natural resources and diversity on either the present day market or the political arena.

4. INSTITUTIONAL CHANGES AND SUSTAINABLE DEVELOPMENT

Market failure correction

The failures of a system based on the market mechanism, described above, warrant governmental regulation of economic processes, an environmentally conscious demarcation of the scope for market forces. Over the past twenty years a range of instruments for environment and nature policy has been developed. One can ask oneself whether this set of instruments is sufficient to realize the correction of new market failures. I believe that it is not, and the fact that environmental pressure continues to increase, strengthens this position.

I shall now sketch some directions derived from the above analysis of the environmentally relevant elements of the economic system in which one can search for the instruments and institutions that are necessary to safeguard the sustainability of economic processes (see also Opschoor (1989) and

Opschoor & Van der Ploeg (1990)). One can ask oneself how the economic engine can be regulated and fed in such a way that neither transfer of environmental degradation nor neglect of sustainability interests take place, and that the tendency towards accumulation is sufficiently controlled or slowed down.

Neglect

It is possible in principle to prevent neglect to a certain extent by letting economic sectors aim towards diversity and sustainability 'from within'. For example, one could expect that industry and agriculture have a long term interest in their basis of natural resources remaining intact. However if the environmental interests are totally different to the self-interest of companies, organizations, sectors and departments, then such an attempt to integrate would appear to be less likely to succeed.

So the most important answer to neglect is: develop and practise counterforce or countervailing power. This sometimes originates spontaneously and it then expresses itself via the market process (for example via consumer boycotts of aerosols containing CFCs). However, countervailing power has to be exercised more often from outside the economic process.

Neglect of environmental issues may be the result of the 'Prisoners' Dilemma'. One can only solve the dilemma by international co-operation or integration. Much of the present day international environmental negotiation is concerned with searching for arguments for voluntary co-operation on the grounds of self-interest: one searches for 'positive sum game' situations, for example in the cases of acidification and prevention of the greenhouse effect. However, one fears that eventually the possibilities of creating 'positive sum game' situations will have been exhausted. Before that time there must be a sufficiently well developed system of internationally approved rules and institutions for international environmental policy to be able to break down this barrier (see Opschoor & Schrijver 1990).

Cost shifting

Cost shifting can be prevented or counteracted in two ways: (i) by inducing environmental degraders to make their own behaviour ecologically viable from 'within', and (ii) by changing external conditions so that the degraders are motivated to make their behaviour more environmentally friendly out of self-interest. The first approach implies a strategy based on 'voluntary internalization' of environmental values. The second approach relies on what

I would call 'institutionalized internalization'. In an economic order which is based on competition, it appears to be easier to combat transfer by altering the external conditions: institutionalized internalization. This would render cost shifting more expensive than what it would cost the polluter to avoid the environmental effects himself (the Brundtland Commission speaks of 'merging economics and environment in decision making' – WCED 1987). This can take different forms.

Let us firstly consider the banning of a specific environmental effect, such as the discharge of cadmium, whereby violation is linked with a heavy penalty. This leads to legislation which in fact changes the laws on ownership and use, with respect to environmental goods. It is no longer possible to exploit everything freely. Another path which can be followed is to hold those that harm the environment legally responsible for the environmental damage which the activities have caused. A third way is to tax environmentally unfriendly or non-sustainable activities to such an extent that cost shifting becomes unattractive (for example, a levy on water pollution which is more expensive than the price of the construction of a purification plant). A counterpart of the levy on pollution is selling (temporary) permits to pollute.

The alternatives given all involve changes in rights and obligations. These changes must allow and generate sufficient financial, economic, or legal countervailing power to prevent or nullify cost shifting behaviour. In reality this is far from being the case yet.

Distance

I have indicated above that there appear to be three forms of 'distance' or segregation between the cause of an environmental effect and the experience of its results. I will now restrict myself to distance in time.

Bridging of the distance in time requires an active government which has a policy on the protection of natural resources, ecosystems, species and so forth. Decisions on important activities, both private and public, should satisfy the demands of a minimum protection against short-sightedness. This means, for example, that the habit of discounting advantages of measures which will manifest themselves in the future must be restrained. The employment of special, adapted discount rates for develoments which may result in irreversible changes to nature and the environment have been considered. One can also think of fixing absolute preconditions which would safeguard against unacceptable damage to nature and the environment. Environmental Impact Assessments could be made applicable to many more activities than is currently the case. In the Netherlands, physical constraints such as standards and zoning, and Environmental Impact Assessments are seen as the main ways in which the significance of nature and the environment can manifest itself. This appears better than it actually is. In those cases where these physical constraints have insufficient judicial and policy status, they can rapidly be overruled. Up to now, for example, opinions about the level of the collective financial burden and the financial deficit have always been more important then the necessity of sustainable or ecologically suitable behaviour in the Netherlands. It has been suggested that our legal system should make room for an Ombudsman type of organization, whose task would be to see whether social developments comply with criteria for justice with respect to future generations (Hilhorst 1987): this authority could perhaps also concern itself with the interests of plant and animal species, as well. In reality even such an authority would be only a weak defence of future interests. Instead, a system of internationally accepted standards on sustainability and diversity should be established, by which countries should abide and which governments could impose on the economic process.

Accumulation

This point in particular makes clear how profound an ecological reformation of the economic system would have to be, if we wish to make structural and preventative environmental policy possible.

In the end, control of the urge to grow means a decrease in uncertainties and inequalities, and in competition between companies and countries. In a world made up of individual countries or blocks of countries, an 'external' urge to grow can only be controlled by intensive co-ordination of the economic development within the individual countries or blocks. The urge to grow as triggered by differences in welfare requires the establishment of more equality between groups or classes within countries, and more equality between countries. This requires both national and international policy which is capable of thoroughly correcting the results of economic processes, by redistributing welfare, and where necessary of intervening in these processes in order to ensure that more desirable effects are created. The pursuit of sustainability is aided by a just, more co-operative, international economic order.

The urge to grow 'from within' is the logical result of the decentralized way of making decisions on production, investment etc. Society may wish to influence the level of activity, or volume of production of sectors which are very important for social or ecological reasons: intensive livestock farming and transportation are topical examples in the Netherlands. It must be possible to control or curb heavily polluting activities, while in contrast to this clean activities are stimulated. Such 'volume oriented policies', aimed at stimulating growth or curbing it in the various sectors of the economy, are however far from popular in a market economy.

Patterns of production and consumption

In the above, I have made an appeal for influencing the course of economic processes in the direction of a sustainable, i.e. ecologically viable, interaction with nature and the environment, by means of the fixing of limits and conditions. Without elaborating on the idea in detail, I suggest that this means that it should be possible to direct the development of science and technology, and consumption and production patterns. I will discuss only the last point briefly.

An effective environmental policy will express itself in raising prices of products which now lead to high pressure on the environment. Products whose pressure on the environment is low will suffer less, and so will become relatively less expensive. This in itself will lead to a shift in the patterns of consumption, because people react to differences in prices. This tendency will most probably be strengthened by an increase in environmental awareness.

These are two mechanisms which arise more or less spontaneously: they are built into the system. The question is whether these mechanisms will be sufficiently powerful. It must be remembered that the average world citizen in 2050 will absolutely not be able to consume the same flow of goods as the present day European. This means that serious attention must be given to the development of patterns of consumption (as well as the accompanying production patterns) which will be ecologically viable in the next century, assuming a more just distribution of welfare than is the case at present. Such patterns – if they exist – must be developed, and society must be willing to adopt them. There is a good chance that they exist but that they are not very attractive to people who find the present excess of consumer items pleasant and desirable. These patterns of material consumption will be plainer, perhaps less varied, but generally more environmentally friendly. There is every reason to work out the ideas of a 'economy of sufficiency' (as proposed by Dutch economists such as Goudzwaard & De Lange (1986)), certainly seen from an environmental perspective. This chapter should clarify that the realization of such an economy of sufficiency would at least require that technical and economic processes be subjected to social and political decisions and control, as far as the direction and speed of these processes are concerned.

Plan or market?

Environmental problems which result from cost shifting, accumulation, distance and neglect are closely related to the social regulatory mechanism, and especially the role of the market in this. The social market economy is a form of society which typically leads to environmental problems. Do other systems display this defect to a lesser extent?

In theory a whole range of economic systems exist, varying from a completely decentralized society without a government to one in which the entire economic life is meticulously planned and centrally directed. These two extremes are known as the market economy and the plan economy respectively. In reality neither of these extremes exists. There is always a mixture, either with more 'market' (as in the social market economy) or more 'plan', as was the case earlier this century in Eastern Europe.

Should the social market economy be replaced by a plan economy because of the environmental problems? That is not very plausible. First of all, a plan economy as such is not the type of society to guarantee sustainability and diversity. This depends on the direction in which it is guided. The actual plan economies were not so very encouraging as far as this is concerned. However there is also a second, more practical aspect. Plan economies are inflexible, administratively inefficient and bureaucratic. This may give rise to very specific environmental problems. Examples are wastage of water, land, wood and other raw materials. The system did not provide sufficient incentives for those who had to realize the plans in factories or on the farm far away from the planning agency. Finally one can pose the question as to whether such centralized societies work anyway. At present we see that most existing plan economies are being transformed into market economies. 'Abolition' of the market could thus be a measure which is worse than the symptoms in certain respects.

In the coming decades the environmental problem will definitely lead to further canalization or correction of the market mechanism. However it is improbable (and not necessary either) that this mechanism will be totally abolished. There are large advantages linked to market forces, because they stimulate creativity and produce efficiency, provided that sufficient checks are placed on their use. However more plan elements must be included in the mixed economic order. This involves more 'volume oriented policy', as has already been mentioned, more systematic fixing of standards with respect to environmental quality, and a socially directed management of our natural resources. There must also be more programmed and centrally financed stimulation of clean technology and nature development.

5. HUMANITY-NATURE IMAGES AND THE ECONOMIC PROCESS

A number of central elements in western ideology can be seen as relevant to the understanding of the present environmental problem as a consequence of society-environmental interactions in the dominant social system: (i) anthropocentrism; (ii) the belief in progress; (iii) embracing of the market mechanism; and (iv) materialistic/utilitarian ethics. Below, the role which each of these elements plays in the economic process will be discussed, with most attention being paid to elements (i) and (ii). In the following section (iii) and (iv) will be dealt with as factors related to one another, which taken together, lead to a very powerful reinforcement of the existing social and economic order.

Anthropocentrism

Nature was and still is seen as subordinate and of service to humanity (anthropocentrism). Nature is thus only of importance to the extent that it can satisfy human needs. It is especially modern western European culture since the Enlightenment which has promulgated this ideology, leading to the threatened collapse of the environment. This anthropocentrism has become legitimized, which has led to society sometimes feeling justified in causing the extinction of plant and animal species, for human benefit.

   This is reflected in a functional approach to nature and the environment in the decision making and the behaviour of the economic actors. The value of elements and processes in nature and the environment is determined through their economic meaning. In its most blunt form, this reduces the value of trees and woods to the selling price of chopped wood, and a more enlightened form of this vision entails that the value of the wood is equal to the sum of the values which people ascribe to the wood: its actual and potential visitors and users. The value of the panda is at the most the value which members and contributors of the World Wide Fund for Nature are prepared to give for its conservation plus what the panda is worth in terms of the revenues which it would attract through zoos. It is evident that a number of categories of values (or at least 'interests' or 'stakes') are thus excluded.

Belief in progress

At the end of the Middle Ages an experimental science was created of which the aim was to learn to use the laws of nature to the benefit of humanity. People felt that they had been called upon to change, improve, the world. Following on from seventeenth century rationalism and eighteenth century Enlightenment, and fed by the results of empirical science, the ideology which Goudzwaard (1976) called the 'belief in progress' came into being. This can be described as a view of the world in which the ongoing development of 'reason' through science and technology is expected to lead humanity towards an ever brighter future.

This belief in progress stands in the way of an uninhibited analysis of the role of the economy and technology as causes of the environmental crisis. It soothes anxiety about the negative effects of economic growth on the environment and nature, since up to now things have only got better. If there is such a thing as an environmental crisis then this can be solved by science, economics and technology. In reality this belief is expressed in many neoclassical economic analyses of environmental problems and the exploitation of raw materials: it is presumed that there are infinite possibilities for substituting one resource by another, that continually more satisfaction of needs can be distilled from nature's unlimited capacities by means of innovation, and that disappearing 'environmental capital' and natural riches can be replaced by produced capital. This attitude is reflected in economic progress, in a readiness to take risks as far as changes in the environment are concerned, and in non-monetary valued elements being regarded as of little importance. In reality, this attitude in particular often leads to cost shifting and neglect.

6. BELIEF IN THE MARKET AND IN GROWTH

Maximization of utility and the belief in growth

As far as demand is concerned, the actual decisions taken in the free market are thought to be determined by given individual preferences, a materialistically and individualistically orientated motivation system and a utilitarian, hedonistic orientated ethic. According to current neoclassical economics, the individual and his wellbeing are thought to be of central importance, and this wellbeing is dependent on the 'utility' derived from consumption. In practice this means that only the effects of a specific action on the material wellbeing of the consumer are taken into account. Thus only what individuals find important – weighing individuals according to their purchasing power – is socially relevant in a market economy. This Utilitarianism – the modern variation of a much older hedonism – was elaborated philosophically by Bentham in the nineteenth century. Economic science embraced this doctrine after 1870, when it became one of the main tenets of neoclassical economics. The consequences of this are that norms and values are reduced to entities which are quantifiable, can be expressed numerically, and can be added or subtracted. All the effects of social activity are thus taken to be translatable into one single dimension. This dimension gradually became more emphatically: money. In this way the existence of a hierarchy of norms and values which are not always convertible is denied. This is replaced a by one dimensional morality. Abiding by this belief, human activity does not take account of primary values such as 'respect for life' and 'responsibility', but mainly bases itself on the result of the sum of homogenized desires and the associated costs to those directly involved.

Moreover, what was regarded as useful and good gradually began to be identified with material wealth and welfare to a greater extent. Thus the preference for more utility developed into the pursuit of growth in production and consumption. Here we find one of the ideological roots of the process of material economic growth (see above). At the same time we find a source of the idea that the fortunes of a society can most easily be measured by using material production, consumption or material welfare: the gross national product as the Golden Calf.

Having reached this point Achterhuis (1988) digs a bit deeper. Our societal order is one which creates and incites scarcity. The ideology of the infinity of human needs (satisfied to a continually greater extent by economic activity) stands opposed to a reality of ever more rapid expansion of wants relative to the possibilities of satisfying them – the 'means'. It is evident that this type of dynamics turns the process of accumulation into a process of hopeless but ever accelerating growth, with increasing environmental pressure as a consequence.

Belief in the market

Adam Smith expanded the ideology of the Enlightenment to include society itself: he described the economic process, driven by the market mechanism as a (pseudo) 'natural' process. He believed he had proved that a free market can drive the economy better than any other institutional arrangement of economic decision making. Exchange via the market ensures that society maximizes its wellbeing. These are some elements of the classical creed.

In the industrialized, 'commercial society', Smith's central proposition about the blessings of the market developed into an ideology to justify the capitalistic design of society. According to some, this analysis degenerated into a conservative total vision legitimizing the status quo; this equalization of 'what is' and 'what ought' can also, fairly justifiably, be called a totalitarian view of the economy. Van Leeuwen (1984) sees little more than 'middle class religion' in the economic science which is thus orientated.

Present day economic science is busy meticulously researching the way that markets work, and the situations in which they maximize individuals' satisfaction of needs, given their incomes and preferences. Economic science – at least the neoclassical main stream – has thus developed itself into a theory which confirms the system and legitimizes the market mechanism. This ensures that a debate about desirable environmental policy instruments rapidly obtains an ideological character, which may make the controllability of the environmental problem more difficult.

The view that the free market always realizes the greatest good for the greatest number of people, as if it were guided by an 'invisible hand', has become the ideology of pragmatic conservatism in the north. In this ideology, the results of the market process are not seen as indicators of the performance of a specific regulatory mechanism, in order to evaluate it critically in comparison with other possible mechanisms. Quite the opposite, the reliance on market forces as such actually becomes normative to a great extent. Whether something is 'economically possible' (i.e. if, expressed in money, the benefits exceed the costs) is thought to determine decisions to be made. If a specific regulation is thought to be in conformity with the market, this is considered to be a guarantee of its social usefulness.

7. CONCLUSIONS

The environmental issue is (amongst other things) an economic, political issue. It forces society to question its actual aims and to consider which measures can be taken, or which strategies must be followed, to realize its ultimate aims. If the aim is sustainable development, then we need 'a process of change in which the exploitation of resources, the direction of investments, the orientation of technological development, and institutional change... enhance both current and future potential to meet human needs and aspirations' (WCED 1987).

All together, this requires at the least a large amount of effort and sacrifices. It also includes an appeal for a far-reaching process of transformation of the economic system, aimed at bringing society back to a safe and hopefully comfortable place within the ecological carrying capacity. This means that the flaws which are inherent in the current social organizations, conventions and control mechanisms, must be removed or controlled. This also means reorientation, directing the economy and technology towards other aims, to real aims such as sustainability rather than short term profit, and diversity rather than undirected, continually accelerating expansion. I have briefly indicated the directions in which alternative instruments and institutions may be found.

This therapy is also lacking if it is not supplemented from a critique of present views on the relationship between humanity and nature, especially when these affect nature and the environment through the economy. I have not suggested any kinds of solution as far as the latter is concerned, but it has become clear that many ideological elements have an effect which is indeed relevant to the environment. Most environmental policies are too involved with a purely technocratic and instrumental approach to the environmental crisis, using superficial analyses and diagnoses, and are insufficiently aware of institutional and ideological aspects as discussed in this chapter. This is perhaps understandable: if more attention were paid to these aspects, the environmental problem would immediately become much more of a politically discriminating issue – which, if the analysis of this chapter is appropriate, it should be!

NOTES

1. I owe this to B. Goudzwaard. See his *Kapitalisme en vooruitgang*.

REFERENCES

Achterhuis, H., 1988. *Het rijk van de schaarste*. Baarn, Ambo.
Asperen, T. van, 1986. 'Milieu en overheid', in Achterberg, W. and W. Zweers (eds.) *Milieufilosofie tussen theorie en praktijk*, pp. 175-95. Utrecht, Ekologische Uitgeverij.
Goudzwaard, B. 1976. *Kapitalisme en vooruitgang*. Assen, Van Gorcum.
Goudzwaard, B. and H.M. de Lange, 1986. *Genoeg van teveel/genoeg van te weinig: wissels om in de economie*. Baarn, Ten Have.
Haveman, R.H. 1976. *The Economics of the Public Sector*. New York, Wiley.
Hilhorst, M.T. 1987. *Verantwoordelijk voor toekomstige generaties?* Kampen, Kok.
Leeuwen, A.Th. 1984. *De nacht van heet kapitaal*. Nijmegen, SUN.
Opschoor, J.B. 1989. *Na ons geen zondvloed: voorwaarden voor een duurzaam milieugebruik*. Kampen, Kok/Agora.

Opschoor, J.B. and S.W.F. van der Ploeg, 1990. 'Duurzaamheid en kwaliteit: hoofddoelstellingen van milieubeleid' in Commissie Lange Termijnplanning (CLTM), *Het milieu: denkbeelden voor de 21ste eeuw*, pp. 17-41. Zeist, Kerckebosch.

Opschoor, J.B. and N.J. Schrijver 1990. 'Actieve internationale milieupolitiek in de jaren negentig', in *Beleid en Maatschappij*: **XVII**, 3.

Terhal, P.H.J.J. 1988. *World Inequality and Evolutionary Convergence*. Doctoral thesis, Erasmus University, Rotterdam.

Vermeersch, E. 1990. 'Weg van het WTK-complex: onze toekomstige samenleving' in CLTM, *Het milieu: denkbeelden voor de 21ste eeuw*. Zeist, Kerckebosch.

WCED (World Commission for Environment and Development) 1987. *Our Common Future*. Oxford, Oxford University Press.

WRR (Wetenschappelijke Raad voor het Regeringsbeleid) 1987. *Ruimte voor groei*. Staatsuitgeverij, Gravenhage.

Chapter 15

THE LIE OF SUSTAINABILITY

Hans Achterhuis

In the newspaper dated 2nd January, 1981, I read an article in which minister Ginjaar claimed that the Netherlands would no longer have toxic waste dumps in ten years time. I found it such a remarkable statement that I noted it in my diary, and copied it with more astonishment each year. The time has almost come.

This letter, which was sent in to the leading Dutch newspaper *de Volkskrant* on 15 December 1990 by Mrs J. Pilgram, had a central position in an invitation to commemorate the tenth birthday of the environmental group 'The Netherlands Without Toxic Waste'. This took place on 7th March, 1991 in the Pulchri Studio in The Hague. I have referred to it to warn emphatically against aims such as sustainability which are lightly professed in theory without looking at all at practical realization. For politics continually appears to formulate this type of aim in theory, while in reality society is in fact departing from it more and more rapidly.

What lies behind this contradiction? Which social forces prevent us from achieving such aims as sustainable use of the land and a clean soil? Why are we, as a society, continually drifting further away from the goals which we profess to want to achieve? This type of fundamental question should precede the umpteenth repetition, expressed in new words it's true, of a policy aimed at sustainability. In this article I shall attempt to dig still deeper than Opschoor does in his article to answer this sort of question. Perhaps a number of principles lie under the final social assumption dug up by him of an 'economics which has almost become a religious belief'. Perhaps on the grounds of these exposed foundations we might conclude that Opschoor has finished off his account too rapidly and easily, despite his in depth analysis.

Before exploring two of these foundations, I would like to return to the meeting on 7th March in The Hague, to show that the inconsistency between words and deeds of which environmental policy is a testimony is not coincidental but structural. In the introduction to this meeting Lucas Reijnders claimed that this inconsistency has always been present in the past. Ginjaar's statement is not a solitary example at all. The Secretary for State for the Environment, Kruisinga, had promised the same ten years earlier. In presenting a bill concerning soil pollution, he gave an assurance that the Netherlands would be clean within ten years. So minister Ginjaar had been warned. He knew what he was saying, and he realized that his promise had to come true.

As it turns out, seldom has a promise been more false. The estimates of soil pollution in the Netherlands increase each year. This is not the place to trouble the reader with large numbers of empirical details:[1] however, the official figures for 1988 tear Ginjaar's promise to shreds. In that year the number of polluted areas was estimated at 525,000, while the number of toxic waste sites to be cleaned was around 100,000. These estimates have not taken into account the continuous flow of pollution which occurs in the air, in polluted riverbeds and lake bottoms, in soil pollution caused by fertilizers and pesticides, from leaking sewage systems and oil tanks and from the dispersal which takes place at existing toxic waste sites.[2]

At the commemoration of the tenth birthday of 'The Netherlands Without Toxic Waste', minister Alders, the present Minister for the Environment, was sensible enough not to make the promises which his predecessors had done before him. In fact he had absolutely no reply to Reijnders' conclusion, which was substantiated with a large number of facts: 'Ground policy as it is being implemented today is not making the ground cleaner but more polluted.' Thus even in the future, policy which is being sold as 'sustainable development', the motto which has been derived from the Brundtland Report, will in fact lead us further away from actual sustainability. It appears that we are facing here a phenomenon which is much more fundamental and structural than the short term perspective of parliamentary politics or the lack of political will shown by a coincidental governmental coalition.

1. A MORE FUNDAMENTAL ANALYSIS

That sustainability is inconsistent with modern economic society was comprehensively argued by the philosopher Hannah Arendt more than thirty years ago. In her important study *The Human Condition* she writes 'Under modern conditions, not destruction but conservation spells ruin, because the very durability of conserved objects is the greatest impediment to the turnover process [of the economy], whose constant gain in speed is the only constancy left wherever it has taken hold'.[3]

According to Arendt the capitalist economic process of production and consumption cannot function without continual growth and acceleration. In the modern economy, which has gradually taken shape since the sixteenth century, things are consumed and destroyed and the stability of the world is continually being undermined to a greater extent. This process 'can continue only provided that no consideration about durability and stability is permitted to interfere, only as long as all artefacts, all end products of the production process, are fed back into it at an ever-increasing speed'.

Arendt's analysis in 1958 had nothing to do with the environmental question. It was purely based on a lucid estimation of the actual characteristics of the modern economy. At that time even Arendt, despite the theoretical accuracy of her analysis, could hardly imagine that the economic process could irreversibly destroy nature. 'The world' which she talks about, is the human artifice which is an enclave within nature. To her sustainability is concerned with the permanence of that world which is being damaged, and not with the sustainable carrying capacity of nature. Arendt as a matter of fact presumed that nature as the encompassing whole of the human world was in fact stable and sustainable. Not until 1975, faced with the symptoms of the environmental crisis becoming continually more clear, did she recognize that the modern economy was destroying and consuming not only the human world, but also nature.

Starting from her fundamental analysis of the economic process, however, she is not quickly tempted to look for a solution to the social impasse of the environmental crisis. She realizes that the fixing of a limit – and who does not call for 'limits to growth' within different fields of policy? – would lead to the 'immediate downfall of our type of economy'. Of course the fact that the threatening environmental dangers were beginning to be realized was a 'first ray of hope' to her in a development which was leading into an abyss. However she emphasizes that 'as far as I can see, no-one has yet come up with a measure against this economy which has run amok, which would not lead to a more serious disaster'.[4]

It seems to me that this last statement still applies almost twenty years later. Solutions and ways out of our present predicament still do not appear to be on hand, besides the kind written by or voiced by politicians that I considered in the beginning of this article. It seems barely possible to stop the social flight forward towards the abyss. As has already been suggested, no attempt is going to be made to come up with the umpteenth solution here. An indication – an actual analysis is impossible within this short scope – of two fundamental presuppositions of our economy, can at the most point towards a direction in which solutions can be searched for.

2. THE EMBEDDING OF THE ECONOMY

Opschoor has no doubts about the 'tendency to unsustainability' of our economic system. Left to itself the economy will lead us ever further away from the ideal of sustainability. This is why it must be embedded within the framework of environmental values.

I am not sure whether Opschoor is directly referring to Polanyi, the great economic historian, when he uses the term 'embedding'. In his classic study *The Great Transformation*, Polanyi describes the disembedding of our modern economy. The main characteristic of the modern market economy is that it breaks away from all cultural, religious and social frameworks. In modern times, the economy becomes an autonomous sector of human existence which – as Marx rightly said – begins to control and determine the other sectors to an increasing extent.

Polanyi describes the enormous human suffering which accompanied this process in the nineteenth century. He also indicates that this unique occurrence, this 'earthquake' which knocked western society free from the General Human Pattern, as Jan Romein described the universal condition of humanity, will end disastrously for both man and nature. Within a purely economic process, in which people are purely a labour force and nature is purely a resource, both realities threaten to be destroyed. If their cultural and social protection were to disappear totally, humanity and nature as we know and experience them would be totally ruined. As is the case with Arendt, Polanyi too is quite unaware of an environmental problem, which hardly manifested itself in the 1940s when he was writing his book. However, he did not doubt that such a crisis could occur in a pure market economy. 'Nature would be reduced to its elements, neighbourhoods and landscapes defiled, rivers polluted, military safety jeopardized, the power to produce food and raw materials destroyed.'[5]

Thanks to social counter movements, the West has never lived in a pure market economy. This is not to deny that the disembedding of the economy, the expansion of its domination over other social sectors, no longer continues. Given the power of this process, which has already taken place for centuries, Opschoor's appeal for 'embedding' seems too simple to me. He uses the beautiful image of the social process as a motor which can be adjusted to maximal speed or maximal efficiency, and of the economy as the vehicle which can be steered in this way. This image however already suggests the embedding, which, if we follow Polanyi and also Opschoor to a certain extent, has not existed for centuries. In other words 'the economic motor', which needs to be fed and regulated, may no longer exist at all in modern times. The blind logic of a barely steerable and controllable process appears to have taken the place of a motor, which in the tradition used to be embedded.

This sounds rather defeatist. It appears to deny the fact that our government, as Opschoor so rightly shows, certainly has a number of elements of control at its disposal, and that we luckily do not live in a pure market economy. However, I would rather speak of adjustive than of controlling mechanisms. I am not underestimating the importance of this adjustment, but I do not think that steering in a radically different direction will occur, although this is actually what should happen. Tellegen is right in saying that 'a society directed towards sustainability must move in the opposite direction'[6] from where we are going presently. To him this opposite direction means that we must 'dramatically limit the domain of the economy, by which I mean all those institutions that have a role in the market process'. I find it questionable whether our present economy and politics can provide the instruments for this. A more fundamental analysis of the relationship between economy and society than economic science itself appears to be capable of is required here.

Another point needs to be made. The social counter movements in the West have partially decreased the market economy's powers to destroy both humanity and nature. However at present these powers seem to be expanding rapidly in the Third World. Paradoxically, the Brundtland Report, which reduces human society to economic categories, may actually contribute markedly to this process in the long run.

Both humanity and nature are reduced to resources in this report. As we know, a resource always serves something else and it has no value in itself. According to Polanyi, where humanity and nature lose their traditional cultural and social protection, they run the danger of eventually only being used as resources to stimulate the economic process. 'Doing more with less',[7] one of the main slogans of *Our Common Future*, could, after a shortlived profit, lead to long term accelerated destruction of both humanity and nature.

3. THE FOUNDATION OF SCARCITY

The above refers the reader to Polanyi's work for an in-depth analysis of the economic historical issues which I have mentioned briefly. For my second short comment on Opschoor's article, I have permitted myself to use my own work. The phenomenon of growth and the belief in progress which are mentioned by Opschoor gain an extra dimension in the light of the concept of 'scarcity' which I have developed.

By 'scarcity' I mean the situation which Opschoor describes with the help of the well known 'Prisoner's Dilemma'. I believe that we are confronted here with a much more general situation in modern society than Opschoor suggests by means of his specific examples. Scarcity is perhaps best described by the seventeenth century English philosopher Thomas Hobbes as an overall societal power struggle, 'a war of each against each.' We find the fear of this struggle in the works of a large number of philosophers of the seventeenth and eighteenth centuries. Starting from this fear the feelings of anxiety, envy and competition that Hobbes is talking about, the phenomena of growth and progress appear in a totally different light from what we are used to. Economic growth and progress can be seen as the main answers to the fear of scarcity that arose in the seventeenth century. At the end of this century John Locke stated that the struggle for scarce resources could be avoided by producing more and by expansion in 'empty spaces'. Instead of the march forward towards a shining future, we may actually be participating in a flight forward because of fear of scarcity.

The deeply suppressed, negative feelings which hide behind growth, expansion and progress make it nearly impossible to stop this flight forwards and fix limits to economic growth. As postmodern people we no longer rush forward through the dark tunnel of scarcity because we still believe that a shining future is waiting for us at the exit, as Keynes still believed in the 1930s. No, it is mainly anxiety which is pushing us forward as individuals and society. 'Standing still means going backwards', we tell each other as we keep on running. The tunnel is becoming continually deeper, environmental scarcity is looming large in nature, which we are destroying and consuming, but to reverse or turn into another direction seems barely possible.

I totally agree with Opschoor that the belief in progress 'stands in the way of an unbiased analysis of the role of the economy'. If we do not come to realize that this belief is built to a great extent on a foundation of the fear of scarcity, we will never understand its continued existence. An unbiased analysis of the role of economy must therefore also expose this foundation.

NOTES

1. For this see *Op weg naar een schone bodem*. Utrecht, Nederland Gifvrij, 1991.
2. Op.cit., p. 20.
3. Arendt, H. 1958. *The Human Condition*, p.253. Chicago & London.
4. Arendt, H., 1989. *Zur Zeit*, p.186. Munchen.
5. Polanyi, M. 1957. *The Great Transformation*, p.73. Boston.
6. Tellegen, E., 1990. Over milieu en beschaving, in *Beleid en Maatschappij*, 1990/3, p.145.
7. The World Commission on Environment and Development, 1989. *Our Common Future* (The Brundtland Report), p.206. Oxford/New York.

Chapter 16

AN ECONOMIC THEORY OF NATURAL RESOURCES

Jan van der Straaten

1. INTRODUCTION

At the end of the sixties and the beginning of the seventies a general unease about the situation of our natural environment arose. Continuing industrialization, which started after the Second World War, affected the quality of water and air in a negative way. In this period economists were active in the social debate; they tried to find solutions for the increasing number of environmental problems. Unfortunately, this attention to environmental problems ebbed away in the course of the seventies and the eighties. In the second part of the eighties, however, there was an abrupt change in the social debate about environmental problems in nearly all the countries of Europe.

This development raised an important question in the field of economic theory. Over twenty years ago many articles and books had been written about environmental economics and a complete system of environmental laws was introduced in many industrialized countries in Europe. But in spite of all these efforts in the field of economic theories and economic policies, the quality of the environment and nature is worse than ever before. The obvious question is, what causes this bad situation? How is it possible that nature and the environment came to be in such a deplorable state?

Marxists of an orthodox character did not hesitate about the answer to this complex question. They were of the opinion that the central paradigms of Marxist theory were capable of solving these problems too (see among others Knut Krusewitz, 1978 and Ken Coates, 1979). The class struggle was the ultimate solution to the alienation of nature and the environment which was experienced by the labour class. Efforts to develop a useful environmental economic theory based on neomarxist starting points cannot, however, be judged as successful (See Immler, 1989; Dietz and Van der Straaten, 1990).

Non-Marxists do not generally have such a pronounced opinion on these problems. The development of an economic theory began at a much earlier stage. Opschoor, for instance, argues thus: 'The way in which and the tempo at which society creeps through this space (that is, the ecological space) is not just determined by norms and values (the "ideology") alone, but also by the way society makes arrangements about collective decision making in the field of economic processes (the "institutions")' (Opschoor, 1989). This statement is true; but the question is whether this approach gives sufficient attention to economic theory itself and the role of the state in economic theory and economic policy. In my opinion, attention should not be focused on the market process. The conflict between different economic groups in society will not become clear in this approach. This will be demonstrated below.

2. NATURE AND THE ENVIRONMENT IN CLASSICAL THEORIES

Classical economists believe that the value of a good is determined by the quantity of labour which was necessary to produce a good. This is called the Labour Theory of Value. The starting point in this theory is a constant quantity and quality of nature (Ricardo, 1823/1975). Production and consumption do not have a negative effect upon the quantity and quality of natural resources (see among others Dietz and Van der Straaten, 1990).

However, classical economists depart from the Law of Diminishing Returns as well (for exceptions, see Dietz and Van der Straaten, 1991). According to this law, the production of goods will decrease in the course of time, in spite of an increasing input of production factors. Malthus' theories about population (1798/1966) and J.S. Mill's theories about the Steady State (1886) are derived from this Law of Diminishing Returns. In this view natural resources are the key factors in the production process. One may therefore argue that classical economists have laid the foundation for the theoretical insight that in production three production factors are used, namely, labour, capital and natural resources.

3. NATURAL RESOURCES IN NEOCLASSICAL THEORIES

Neoclassical economists consider the market process of greater importance than classical economists generally do. This is because of the change which took place during the Industrial Revolution, which was characterized by a totally different use of natural resources. During the Industrial Revolution a conversion took place from flow entities to stock entities in the use of natural resources. As a result, an increase in the production of goods could be realized. Stock entities such as coal and iron ore became the new cornerstones of welfare.

This production, on a large scale and concentrated in place and time, needed an outflow to the world market. It speaks for itself that economists in this period increasingly concentrated their analysis on the market process. This development also changed the way in which economists looked at the importance of natural resources. Neoclassical economists saw with their very own eyes that there was an abundance of natural resources. This abundance resulted in a stream of inventions, especially in the field of physics. This technological development gave new impulses to industrial growth processes (Marshall, 1925, p. 180). So the importance of the production factor natural resources was moved to the background.

Neoclassical economists did not recognize the problems, because in this period the phenomenon was hardly noticeable. The volume of stock entities was extremely large in proportion to the use of these resources and so they were seen as inexhaustible. The disruption of ecocycles occurred only locally and on a small scale; global disruptions were not at issue. Such development led to a situation where economists did not discuss the problem of natural resources between 1870 and 1960. Only a few individuals issued warnings about these problems (King, 1919; Fabricant, 1947; see also Martinez Allier and Schluepmann, 1987). This neglect of environmental problems was found not only in neoclassical circles. Marxists had the same limited outlook on environmental problems (Ullrich, 1979).

In the neoclassical approach, however, there is an initiative which can help to analyse and solve the problem. Pigou developed the concept of the external diseconomy and elaborated this in the direction of environmental problems (Pigou, 1920/1952). The negative effect is caused by the fact that market parties have a negative influence on the welfare of non-market parties. It is called external because it is found outside the market, which is in the core of the theory. As a result of this phenomenon, social cost price is not the same as private cost price, and so an optimal allocation of production factors is disturbed.

According to Pigou, the solution can only be found through actions of the state, as an economic actor which should serve the common good. The state can realize this by making an inventory of negative external effects together with the related costs. These costs are transferred by the state to the polluting industries. By doing this, social cost price is the same as private cost price again, and an optimal allocation of production factors is restored. For many years this approach played only a theoretical role; no attention was given to this concept until environmental problems were seen as a severe social and economic problem (Blaug, 1978).

4. Recent Theories about Natural Resources

It is obvious that economists, when confronted with environmental problems, started to use the concept of the negative external effect. Mishan, for instance, used this concept for the core of his criticism on the neglect of environmental problems (Mishan, 1967). In the Netherlands Hueting in particular tried to use this concept for an analysis of environmental issues. This approach, however, presented a number of problems in the field of quantification of costs and benefits of environmental measures (see also Opschoor, 1974). These imply that preferences regarding a sound natural environment could not be calculated. But in this situation it is also true that the prices of goods and services which are produced at the expense of the environment are not a real reflection of what is sacrificed.

The response of economists to this problem has been quite varied. The majority act as if it does not exist, a view which suggests that economics only deals with the interests of labour and capital. The importance of the production factor natural resources will only be seen in the case that it is traded on a market, as is the case with oil and natural gas. Thus economic parameters are only those elements which have a meaning in the context of the market process, such as employment, the deficit of the state, the price level, the level of production, the balance of payment, and so on. Environment and nature are, for these economists, something like the Third World, the community centre and public health. One cannot avoid doing something about them; but if economic situations become worse there is only one solution: reduce the budget. This approach is very popular in the present economic policy in many countries of Europe (See e.g. Rutten, 1989 and Van der Straaten, 1992).

Many environmental economists do not realize that this approach is connected with the lack of a generally accepted economic theory regarding natural resources. If an optimal point of pollution cannot be determined with the help of the price mechanism, other steering mechanisms should be developed. Such a steering mechanism is of great importance. If one does not have such a steering mechanism at one's disposal, no economic statements about the allocation of the production factor natural resources are possible.

Goudzwaard (1970) and Daly (1973 and 1977) have chosen to argue these problems within the realm of economic policy. This approach has the advantage that in economic policy every subjective starting point can be introduced without serious problems. This approach prevents the researcher from being blamed for introducing subjective elements into the economic theory itself. In this approach the theory itself remains free of values and norms. This approach could hardly be defended when there is such a long and strong tradition in distinguishing three production factors: labour, capital and natural resources. One cannot avoid giving the production factor natural resources an equal position in economic analysis.

5. THE ENVIRONMENTAL POLICY OF THE NETHERLANDS

Economic actors do not, via the prices of products, receive the desired incentives to change their behaviour in accordance with environmental possibilities. There is a need for state environmental policy to realize this behaviour. Economists recognize this as a traditional economic problem: the policy of the state should correct the externalities. Opschoor argues in this respect: 'Economic processes should be submitted again to socially relevant criteria... With these current portrayals of mankind and ideologies regarding the market and economic growth are at stake.' (Opschoor, 1989)

When introducing impulses other than the current price impulses, there are some fundamental problems. In neoclassical approaches one generally has the starting point that 'good' information leads to 'good' actions of the government without any real problem. There is a picture of a government which makes a rational decision based on the responsibility for the common good. It seems that this approach neglects the fact that the government, as all other human organizations, is subject to the abuse of power, and that therefore the government can damage the environment considerably (Hueting, 1980).

The question is how economists deal with this problem of power when environmental measures are introduced. Marxist approaches are hardly useful to analyse environmental problems. The production factor labour has as much, or as little, interest in a sound environment as the production factor capital. We must give full attention to the misuse of power in the state itself, as far as damage to nature and the environment is at stake. We have the starting point that in the state and in the state machinery several vested interest groups were able to establish their position (Van der Straaten, 1989).

Elsewhere I have analysed the policy of the Dutch state regarding acid rain during the last ten years. (Van der Straaten, 1990). It became clear that a conscious policy was being realized, through which problems regarding acid rain were foreseen and inevitable. This is not caused by the absence of effective instruments, but by the non-use of effective instruments. The relative protection of the agrarian sector and the oil refineries against strict environmental measures is a consequence of the importance given to current economic variables such as the export position, the balance of payments, the state deficit and the withdrawal of the national state from economic life.

The structural economic policy regarding traffic, agriculture and an expanding production has been realized in such a way that environmental policy did not get the slightest chance of realizing even a minor part of its goals. General policy regarding 'the economy' combined with generally accepted economic ideas in this segment of society about the necessity of an ever expanding production will wipe out all interests of the production factor natural resources, which is not given an independent place in economic policy. The Ministry of the Environment may have an environmental policy, but its articulation may not go so far as to actually affect traditional economic aims. So one can conclude that in environmental and economic policy, neoclassical starting points are really dominant. Therefore there is no reason to confront production and consumption processes with 'socially relevant criteria', which could be something other than economic criteria. In the first place, it is important that in environmental and economic policy relevant economic criteria should be included. Such an approach can be realized without any real problem. It is not necessary that current 'ideologies and portrayals of mankind regarding the market and economic growth should be at stake'. Economic theory and economic policy should be confronted with relevant economic principles regarding the production factor natural resources.

When we examine a country like the United States, in which the price mechanism functions really well, we see, contrary to the situation in the Netherlands, an adequate environmental policy based on economic criteria. In the recent Clean Air Act Amendments we see that measures are taken which could not be dreamt of by the most radical environmental groups in the Netherlands (Anonymous, 19 October 1990). This is a very peculiar situation, as the losses caused by acid rain in the Netherlands are relatively much higher than in the United States.

6. AN ALTERNATIVE MODEL

The use of natural resources originated in the social system. In the current economic way of thinking all relevant information about the quantity and quality of natural resources reaches the economic actors by the price mechanism. But, as was argued previously, the price mechanism does not work adequately when these problems have to be dealt with.

As a starting point for the working of the model we take sustainable development, as this is a normal economic way of thinking. In this sense the model may work if a certain number of limiting conditions are fulfilled. In the first place it is of great importance that the deterioration of nature and the environment be brought to an end; the exhaustion of natural resources should be stopped as well. In principle it is possible to stop the extraction of materials from the stocks and no longer to use them in the social system. But, it is impossible to do this in the short run. The start of this process is possibly to diminish the use of these materials. This is true for raw materials and energy resources as well.

Such a change in production processes would lead to a decrease of the use of ores and fossil energy resources. Nowadays quite a number of countries in the Third World are largely dependent on the export of these materials such as iron ore, copper, and oil. If one takes sustainable development as a starting point for these countries too, a kind of recycling fund, to facilitate a conversion of their production processes too, will be required.

A workable model for natural resource use should be based on ecological criteria. Therefore it is necessary to split up the model into two parts (see Figure 16.1): one part describing the social system and the other part describing the natural system. There is a connection between these subsystems caused by the flows of resources and pollution between them. The ecological processes are described by using the ecocycles employed in the production and consumption processes used in society. The sun is the ultimate source of energy in this model. This model is based on the method usual for production and consumption from the beginning of the Industrial Revolution. This will inevitably lead to an open system, in which disruption of ecocycles and exhaustion of resources are everyday practice.

Ways of closing this open system are investigated. In the model we distinguish stock and flow entities. The first term is used for all raw materials and energy sources of which only a limited supply is found in the earth's crust. They are used in society, while the residuals are emitted in the ecocycles, which will be disturbed by materials alien to them. Exhaustion of stock resources is the other side of the coin.

The emission of materials originated in the flow system cannot cause these serious problems. Such materials are normal in ecocycles; without the emission of these substances new life cannot be created. However, overloading of ecocycles on a regional scale is possible. In principle this disruption can be neutralized by stopping the emissions. Consequently, the total discharge of substances foreign to the environment would decrease. Moreo-

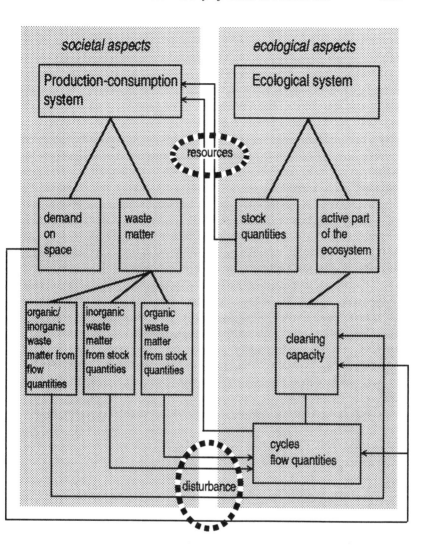

Figure 16.1. Global Interactions between the Economic System and the
Ecological System

ver, the exhaustion of fossil resources would be slackened. Technological
development can play a very important role in this process of conversion. The
current economic instruments can be used to realize this policy. With the help

of charges, subsidies, controls and commands, the desired development can be influenced by the government. Subsidies should be given from collective funds to adapt technological development to save the environment. When charges of materials from the stocks are at stake, the functioning of the ecosystem itself is the norm which should be used. These norms are sought to quantify the level of discharge which is possible from an ecological point of view. Such an environmental policy can be put in place using current economic instruments. In this view every level of pollution can be subjected to every normal economic instrument. The price mechanism can play an important role in this case. But the working of this mechanism is completely different from the situation in traditional neoclassical theory, in which the negative external effect has to be quantified by authorities. The government should internalize these social costs by the implementation of an environmental policy. But in our model the norms originate in the ecological system with the aim of reaching sustainable development. In this approach prices are an instrument to realize the ecologically desired ends formulated before.

Finally we should deal again with economic policy itself. The process sketched previously would have a considerable impact upon the economic balance of power in the production process. The conversion process would cause an economic development different from what would be the case in a situation of unhindered economic development. The economic policy aimed at a realization of a sound sustainable development would be attacked by all those powerful economic groups which would lose some of their economic power. Their present powerful situation has been brought about by the historical development of society based on the disruption of nature and the environment. This is true for the production factor labour as well as for the production factor capital. Both factors have achieved their social position by damaging nature and the environment. The conflicting interests between capital and labour could be set aside by tackling the third production factor. So, the 'solution' of the so-called social question was only made possible by introducing a new problem: the ecological question. The production factor natural resources has hardly any power in the state and the state machinery. The environmental movement can be seen as the only countervailing power of any importance which could defend the position of the production factor natural resources.

From an economic point of view, it is very important that the interests of labour and capital do not steer collective decision making in the direction of a socially unacceptable economic development. To achieve sound sustainable development it is not necessary to develop a new value system or a image of humanity. The problem is a traditional economic one, which was sketched by Pigou many years ago. Pigou's 'solution', namely, the internalization of externalities by quantifying them, does not work, however. Nevertheless, the restricted possibilities of the natural environment, for use in production and consumption processes, should be distributed among the various sectors of the economy of a country. This ecological space is considerably smaller than the space being used nowadays. This means that there is a traditional problem of distribution: scarce means have to be distributed among a great number of applicants. Labour and capital have long had an extremely strong position in the state and the state machinery. In the next century the social target will be to diminish this position in favour of the position of the production factor natural resources. This can only be done through a normal process of collective decision making.

This struggle can be compared to a certain degree with the 'social question' in the last century. One gets the impression that the problem of the sustainable development of our economy is as unmanageable as the social question. This means that it will take a long time before everything is arranged in this respect. We are still at the beginning of a process of conversion of production and consumption in the direction of sustainable development. Such a conversion is a traditional economic problem. So, economists have a lot of work to do.

REFERENCES

Anonymous. Clean Air Act Amendments, *Wall Street Journal,* 19 October 1990.
Blaug, M. 1978. *Economic Theory in Retrospect.* Cambridge, Cambridge University Press UP.
Coates, Ken, 1979. *Socialism and the Environment.* Nottingham.
Daly, Herman E., 1973. *Towards a Steady-State Economy.* San Francisco, W.H. Freeman.
Daly, Herman E., 1977. *Steady-State Economics.* San Francisco, W.H. Freeman.
Dietz, Frank and van der Straaten, Jan, 1990. 'Economic Analysis of Environmental Problems; A Critique of Marxist Approaches'. In Sylvia Brander und Otto Roloff (eds), *Politische Ökonomie des Umweltschutzes.* pp.147-71Transfer Verlag, Regensburg.
Dietz, Frank and van der Straaten, Jan 1991.'Economische Theorieën en de Inpasbaarheid van Ecologische Criteria' (Economic Theories and the Integration of Ecological Insights), *Tijdschrift voor Politieke Economie,* August. pp. 29-55.
Fabricant, S., 1947. In *Studies in Income and Wealth, Volume Ten,* Conference on Research in Income and Wealth, New York.
Goudzwaard, B. 1970. *Ongeprijsde Schaarste (Scarcity without a Price).* Kampen, Kok.

Hueting, R., 1980. *New Scarcity and Economic Growth.* Amsterdam, Elsevier.

Immler, Hans, 1989. *Vom Wert der Natur.* Opladen, Wesdeutscher Verlag.

King, W.J. 1919. *The Wealth and Income of the People of the United States.*

Krusewitz, Knut 1976. *Anmerkungen zum historisch-gesellschaftlichen Ursachen-Zusammenhang der Umweltkrise,* Blätter für deutsche und internationale Politik, Pahl Rugenstein Hefte nr. 28.

Malthus, T.R. 1789/1966. *An Essay on the Principle of Population.* Harmondsworth, Penguin.

Marshall, A. 1890/1925. *Principles of Economics.* London, MacMillan.

Martinez Allier, Juan and Schluepmann, Klaus 1987. *Ecological Economics.* New York, Basil Blackwell.

Mill, John Stuart 1886. *Principles of Political Economy,* London.

Mishan, E.J. 1967. *The Costs of Economic Growth.* London, Staples Press.

Opschoor, J.B. 1974. *Economische Waardering van Milieuverontreiniging (Economic Valuation of Environmental Disruption).* Assen, Van Gorcum.

Opschoor, J.B. 1989. *Na Ons geen Zondvloed (After Us no Deluge).* Kok, Kampen.

Pigou, A.C., 1920/1952. *The Economics of Welfare.* London, Macmillan.

Ricardo, David, 1923/1975. *The Principles of Political Economy and Taxation.* London, Everyman.

Rutten, F.W. 1989 'Op Weg naar Voltooiing van het Sociaal-economisch Herstel' (On the Way to Completion of Social-Economic Recovery), *ESB* 4 January: pp. 4-9.

Straaten, J. van der, 1988. 'Het Beleid van de Nederlandse Overheid ten aanzien van Zure Regen in de Jaren Negentig' (The Policy in the Netherlands regarding Acid Rain). In J. Glombowski, A. Keune and A. van Rooy (eds) *Kantelende Verhoudingen in de Jaren Negentig,* pp. 189-202. Den Haag, SDU.

Straaten, J. van der, 1990. *Zure Regen, Economische Theorie en het Nederlandse Beleid (Acid Rain, Economic Theory and the Dutch Policy).* Utrecht, Jan van Arkel.

Straaten, J. van der, 1992. 'The Dutch National Environmental Policy Plan: To Choose or to Lose'. *Environmental Politics* 1, Number 1: pp. 45-71.

Ullrich, Otto, 1979. *Weltniveau.* Berlin, Rotbuch Verlag.

Chapter 17

TECHNOLOGY AND THE ECOLOGICAL CRISIS

8 —

Koo van der Wal

The question I want to focus on in this contribution is that of the relationship between the environmental issue and technology. That such a relationship exists need hardly be said. But this is the case not only in our present day situation. As is well known, the degradation of the environment by humanity is not only a present day phenomenon; in the past, too, whenever humans caused extensive damage to their natural environment the use of technical equipment usually played an essential role. One only has to think of the deforestation of the Lebanese mountain range in the days of King Solomon, or the deforestation of mountain slopes in Palestine and Greece. By the way this does not mean to say that large scale historical damage to the environment should always be associated with technology. For example, damage beyond repair has been brought about in many places by long term overgrazing by herds of goats. But whatever the share of technology may have been in the manifestations of extensive environmental deterioration in history, the special relationship between the environmental crisis and modern technology in this day and age can hardly be doubted, if only because our present day environmental problems, as well as the population explosion, can be considered to be the unintended and unforeseen side effects of modern technological development.

If we may presume that there is indeed a special relationship between the present environmental crisis and modern technology, then the particular nature of this relationship comes into question. To answer that question a philosophical analysis and explanation of the phenomenon of technology is necessary. In other words, we need a philosophy of technology, and in particular a philosophy of the modern manifestations of technology. Here we are immediately confronted with a remarkable fact, namely that technology as an independent phenomenon has not become an object of philosophical thought until quite recently. As a philosophical theme in itself, reflection on technology only dates back to the last decades of the nineteenth century. And even in the twentieth century technology did not figure prominently in philosophical thinking for a long time, and maybe this is still true today, despite the growing insight that it is the determining factor of our society – that science and technology, as has been said, are the ideology of our time.[1]

1. MINIMAL AND MAXIMAL INTERPRETATIONS OF TECHNOLOGY

Surveying philosophical discussion on technology, one can say that it is taking place between two extremes, employing on the one side a minimum, and on the other side a maximum interpretation of technology. To my mind, the characterization of technology as applied science, which was particularly prevalent in the nineteenth century and is still common, is a minimal definition. In this view technology is hardly an independent phenomenon with characteristics of its own, and therefore not really very interesting. Here attention is mainly focused on the central phenomenon, that is to say science, and only secondarily and marginally on its applications. The applicability of science issues forth from science's own structure or, better, from the structure of a specific type of science: that which works according to the 'nomothetical' method. Once this scientific model has been given its explication in the philosophy of science, little more of interest is left to be said about application as a separate theme.

In fact in this view there is no such a thing as technology in the sense of an independent phenomenon with specific characteristics of its own, but only a multitude of concrete scientific applications, all of which are included in the name 'technology'. In short, in this view one only sees the trees, and no wood.

The other extreme in the discussion on technology is taken by those who see it as the way of thinking or living of a society, most usually of modern western society. Heidegger, one of the most prominent exponents of this position, even sees its roots stretching back to ancient culture.[2] He describes technology not only as 'the greatest and most impressive symbol of an entire era',[3] but as representing an entire way of life. It is the all-controlling force in the life of humanity, certainly of modern humanity, which permeates our way of thinking and perceiving and determines our attitude with respect to surrounding reality, our fellow humans and even ourselves.

In this view, then, technology is the determining factor of our time; it implies a frame of mind, a way of conceptualizing phenomena, and a theory about what it means to have knowledge of reality. Furthermore it includes a specific concept of reality, as ultimately material, as a reservoir of resources waiting for technical processing. Finally, it implies ideas concerning what life is actually about, and what can be considered to be a flourishing human existence. In short, it represents a way of thinking and living in which ontological, epistemological and ethical elements are included, if mainly implicitly.

It is clear that the image of technology presented here is rather different from the prevailing ones. While the definition of technology as an applied science stops at the many different forms of technology and is blind to the connections between them, the opposite seems to be the danger here: that in looking for the specific characteristics (the 'essence'[4]) of technology, the concrete, illustrative phenomena are overlooked and all that remains is a very abstract power. To go back to the metaphor on the previous page, it seems that now only the wood is being seen, and not the trees.

The question, then, is: is it possible to have a philosophical explanation of technology which remains in touch with the phenomena? Which, in other words, on the one hand remains recognizable to both the technologists and ourselves as users of technology, and does justice to our experiences of it through both production and consumption, and which, on the other hand, does not stop at these surface factors? Yet again, is there a perspective on technology which does not home in on the phenomena so closely that their wider context remains unnoticed, but which does not move away so far that every link with reality is lost? Philosophy is an attempt to gain insight into our human experiences: this is no different in the case of philosophical reflection on technology. Its starting point too must be the at level of experience in daily life, if it is to develop more insight into things from there. We must search for a position which makes it possible to see both the trees and the wood.

A philosophical analysis of technology which is sufficiently aware of the phenomena must, therefore, start from a concept of technology in a narrow sense. We have a great many definitions of technology[5] by now; maybe not as many as the 288 once counted by M. Terentius Varro and, in his footsteps, Augustine, in defining happiness, but quite a lot anyway. Generally speaking, two sorts can be distinguished, which I shall call broader and narrower. In a broader sense, technology can be understood to mean every form of methodical action, 'jede methodische, planvolle und zielgerichtete Verfahrensweise' (every methodical, planned and purposeful procedure), as Friedrich Rapp[6] defined it. In short, rational, goal-orientated action. But a concept of technology in a narrower sense can be distinguished as well, and this is basic to our further considerations. Here, we understand technology to mean those human actions whereby on the basis of knowledge about reality – in the case of modern technology this means on the basis of scientific knowledge of reality – natural resources (materials, energy, information) are manipulated so that they can be used to fulfil human needs and desires. In that context an arsenal of technical objects, tools and procedures are created which from then on lead an existence independent of the people who discovered and used them: this in contrast to, for example, the technique of a violinist, which is strictly personal.

Technology in this sense has a number of branches which each represent a special type of technique. In relation to this Ellul[7] speaks of 'principal subdivisions of modern technology' and lists three, namely:

(i)   the production of material goods;

(ii)   organization technology, i.e. all the methods involved in the creation and control of social relationships;

(iii)   humane techniques, which aim to control, or bring about, specific changes in the psychic and mental reality, that is in humanity's inner life.

Two further types of technology must be added to this list, namely biotechnology and information technology, both of which are also developing into 'principal subdivisions' of modern technology.

2. DESSAUER'S ANALYSIS OF TECHNOLOGY

Having outlined the scope of modern technology I shall pass on to further explanation through the works of Friedrich Dessauer.[8] I have chosen this starting point because Dessauer, a professor of biophysics and radiology,[9] approaches technology from within, from the position of technologists. In this way he has developed an image of technology which stays in close contact with the concrete phenomena and which is therefore easily recognizable, especially to technologists. His book *Streit um die Technik* ('Fight about Technology') (1956) was even written at the invitation of the Union of German Engineers (VDI), and the author Heinrich Stork, who was originally a chemist, also leans heavily on Dessauer in his book *Einleitung in die Philosophie der Technik* ('Introduction to the Philosophy of Technology') (1977).[10] So, he remains 'in touch' with the phenomena, one of the requirements of a philosophy of technology which we formulated earlier on. At the same time, however, he keeps sufficient distance from concrete phenomena to be able to see the wider relationships, what the various manifestations of technology have in common, and in doing so he meets the other requirement.

I shall highlight four of the main theses of Dessauer's analysis:

a. In order to examine technology, we must extricate it from other factors with which it usually is entwined, particularly science and economics. Dessauer too noticed that science, technology and economics form a complex, which leads a relatively autonomous existence within modern society. And he believes that, because of this, the special characteristics of technology can hardly be distinguished. Therefore, in order to get a good look at technology, one must search for it where it is still 'pure and uninvolved'. To Dessauer, technology in its pure form is technology as seen through the eyes of the creative engineers, the pioneers, who are not prompted by motives of prestige, profit, power or something similar, but by an idealistic motive specific to the technical domain, that is, a sincere interest in solving a technical problem. To Dessauer 'true' technologists are idealists, people motivated by noble commitments.

So, Dessauer believes that technology is based on scientific knowledge of reality, but that it also contains a typical dimension which becomes visible in the invention, and especially there. In other words, the characterization of technology as applied science is totally inadequate.

b. Despite its wide variety of manifestations, technology forms a single whole. This is not to deny that the concrete products of technology – stone tools, fireplaces, huts, clothes, weapons, medicines, vehicles etc. – were each in their own right concrete answers to concrete problems. However, to see clearly, as Dessauer himself puts it,

> that unity exists between a spade, a coat, a palace, a vehicle, a book, musical instruments, a penknife, an X-ray tube..., thus between very heterogeneous objects, that there is a real link, an inner relationship, a coherence of meaning, origin, aim, method, and even a common way of working, so that we are talking about something coherent, about one historical power, a factor which changes the world..., has been reserved for our age.[11]

Of the same kind are characterizations of technology as 'Einheitsgestalt', 'einheitliche Machtgestalt' (unitary/uniform configuration of power), etc.[12] According to Dessauer, this moment of unity of technology was first clearly seen by Ernst Kapp in his book *Grundlinien einer Philosophie der Technik* ('Fundamentals of a Philosophy of Technology') in 1877.[13] Such insight is required in order to develop a philosophy of technology, and at the same time this explains why technology was so late in becoming an independent theme of reflection within the field of philosophy. Once this has happened, it also makes sense to inquire after the essence and meaning of the phenomenon technology. For after all, says Dessauer, in general philosophizing means the posing of questions about essence and meaning with respect to the phenomena we observe, and therefore, in this case, with respect to technology.

c. Technical entities and procedures are subject to special technical standards which differ from other sorts of norms, e.g. those of an economic, aesthetical or other nature. Dessauer calls this specific type of normativity, to which technical phenomena *qua* technical phenomena are subject, the 'specific service value' ('spezifischer Dienstwert'). From a purely technical point of view different solutions to the same technical problem can be ranked according to their increasing level of success in solving the problem. In other words, from that point of view an ideal, 'best one way' solution to each problem exists,[14] and we do see that in practice a series of solutions converge towards a specific point, whether it concerns the bike, the car, a medicine for a specific ailment, or whatever. Dessauer here even introduces a platonic theory of a realm of already existing ideal types of solutions to each type of technological problem.[15] In other words, technical solutions are not randomly invented but ultimately just *found* by us. This theory also provides an explanation of the convergence just mentioned, and of the view of many technologists that the result could not have been any other than the one arrived at by way of experimenting. The technical quality of a technical object or a technical procedure is therefore determined by the closeness with which it approaches the ideal solution. What from a technical point of view may seem the best possible solution does not necessarily have to be that when other, non-technical (especially economic), norms are applied.

d. With his statement that technology has its own moral imperative Dessauer opposes a widely held view that technology is morally neutral because of its being just the total of means for achieving random goals; in other words, in that view technology is purely functional and therefore the moral quality of its usage depends on the purposes for which it is being used.[16] According to Dessauer technology, of its own accord, aims at realizing moral values.

In this context Heinrich Stork, who is much inspired by Dessauer here too, uses the comparison with law and medicine: law is orientated towards justice and its realization, not only externally and coincidentally, but by its very nature; while medicine, analogously, looks at health as an essential component of human wellbeing, both possessing their own specific moral imperative. And this can also be applied to technology.[17] To quote Dessauer himself:

> The idea of technology, its historical meaning, which is clearly recognizable to the non-biased eye, is the liberation of mankind and his offspring from the bondage and dependence which we find in the world of animals and plants,

the progress in the direction of the spirit...[18] In essence technology means precisely this: to provide man with the opportunity to escape from animal subordination to nature and to liberate himself from it in order to shape the *Umwelt* in a responsible way in agreement with the spiritual soul. Therefore technology means freedom in two respects: freedom from subordination and freedom to design one's own life, to shape the future.[19]

Thus, by its nature and 'idea', technology can be seen as serving the liberation of humanity from submission to nature, releasing it for self realization. In short, technology is anything but morally neutral.

3. SHORTCOMINGS OF DESSAUER'S POSITION

The above is an account of what I consider to be the most important elements of Dessauer's analysis of technology. It seems to me that it provides some valuable insights which any philosophical explanation of the phenomenon of technology has to reckon with. Of course this does not mean that going along with the tenor of those insights implies accepting the way they are substantiated; for instance, that Dessauer's platonic approach has to be taken on board along with the 'best one way' idea in technology. At the same time it becomes clear that an explanation of technology along Dessauer's lines leaves a number of aspects underexposed or obscure, some of which are of particular importance to reflection on the environmental issue. At the same time Dessauer's position appears to be based on premises which in the light of the ecological crisis must be considered highly contestable.

I have three main criticisms of his position:

a. Firstly Dessauer does not see that reality being finite may cause a problem for technology. In Dessauer's opinion, technology is characterized by having no limits in various respects. One of the ways in which he characterizes technology is that it is the intermediary between human needs, wants and desires on the one hand, and what nature provides in the form of raw materials, energy and laws on the other, which through the mediation of technology is shaped so as to satisfy these human needs and desires. According to Dessauer unlimitedness exists in both aspects:

> There is the realm without limits of the human wants, needs, wishes. It expands unceasingly, because every fulfilment arouses new desires. There is the realm of things provided by nature, materials, energies, laws (of nature). Here too we see no limit.[20]

In addition, one of Dessauer's favourite themes is that creation has not yet been completed, and that thanks to technology creation is a continuing process – or as the Dutch writer Andreas Burnier puts it, because of technology this is the eighth day of creation.[21] Our technical activity is leading to a 'continually growing legion of shapes' which, corresponding to human needs and wishes by way of some sort of *harmonia praestabilita*, are transported from a situation of potentiality to one of actuality.[22] In this way, technology is the expression of the dynamic character of creation, and man is the bearer of that process. This may explain the restlessness in his being – in this context Dessauer speaks of man as the 'bearer of restlessness' and as one who, given this restlessness, does not feel at home in the present universe.[23]

However, it remains to be seen whether nature is as limitless as Dessauer presumes and whether there is room to make space *ad libitum* for that great legion of new technical shapes without ousting existing ones from their places; and whether, in the words of Anaximander, in a finite world the arrival of the one does not necessarily mean the removal of the other, with things paying fines to each other for occupying the stage of reality for a while.

b. When Dessauer says that creation has not been finished yet, he says so from a human perspective. For technology is an expression of the fact that humanity does not accept reality as it actually is, but 'tackles it', changes and completes it, in short rebuilds it into an 'Umwelt' of its own design, easier to live in than the natural surroundings originally given. In that same train of thought Dessauer now characterizes 'all of technology as the extension of the Umwelt of mankind,' or as the 'building up of the house of mankind'.[24] The value, or even dignity ('Würde') of technology is achieved through it being a means to humanization. Its meaning is then formulated as follows: 'Technology has its uniform meaning in building a human world beyond what is provided by nature, aiming at man's spiritual existence, his destiny and his true humanization.'[25] It is clear that only 'human requirements, needs and wishes' are determinants for the direction in which creation will continue. In short, Dessauer's interpretation of technology is radically anthropocentric.

c. Finally, weak links in Dessauer's analysis are his expositions concerning the historical, social and cultural aspects of the phenomenon technology. It is not that no references to it can be found in his work, but they remain largely disconnected. E.g. for a cultural-historical dissertation on technology he refers to the third volume of Franz Schnabel's *Deutsche Geschichte im 19. Jahrhundert* ('German History in the Nineteenth Century'), bearing the title *Erfahrungswissenschaften und Technik* ('Empirical Sciences and Technology') (1930). In this book Schnabel characterizes the modern empirical sciences and technology, which are forming an increasingly close alliance, along with the constitutional state as the heritage of bourgeois society. Hence Schnabel recognizes technology as a cultural-historical phenomenon in its own right and examines it from the standpoint of the sociology of knowledge, the implications of which are not understood by Dessauer. As a social carrier of modern technology, a social class characterized as activist, pragmatic and goal-directed is indicated, people who think in categories of usefulness, security and computability, who want to rationally reorder and control reality, both materially and socially; who, in other words, think in terms of the 'makeability' of things. Their central socio-political category is that of the social contract, including a belief that society has to be built up from point zero in accordance with principles which have been agreed upon by all.

This makes it clear that modern technology is part of the so-called project of the Enlightenment, of the bourgeois view that things are the carrier of the process of modernization, and the corresponding social attitudes. Other elements of this idea of reality and corresponding attitude are: the refusal to recognize limits; the rejection of the premodern idea of an all-embracing and at the same time factual and normative order of nature in which everything has its natural place, in other words, the rejection of the idea of an objective teleology which is embedded in reality; combined with an attitude of antitraditionalism and 'meliorism', a belief therefore in unlimited improvability, progress and 'growth'; and at the same time an attitude of profligacy. I will come back to this later on.

So one aspect of technology which Dessauer touches on but hardly analyses is the social dimension of the phenomenon, technology as a social enterprise, and in particular as a social force. I have already quoted Dessauer's typifications of technology as being a unitary configuration of power etc., in short, of technology as the power that changes the face of the earth. Dessauer assigns this power to technical entities (objects and procedures) themselves: they are the carriers of that power. With this Dessauer touches on the question of an autonomous dynamic of technology.

4. TECHNOLOGY AS A SOCIAL PHENOMENON

Socio-philosophical analyses of the phenomenon of technology, such as those of Ellul, Gehlen, Schelsky, Jonas and others, start at this very point. To all these authors technology has become the all-controlling factor of modern society, penetrating its most remote corners and subjecting everything to its demands. Ellul[26] has developed the most articulated and most radical image in this regard; he distinguishes eight characteristics of what he calls 'le phénomène technique', i.e., technology in its modern form as the determining force of the whole socio-political order: autonomy, unity or rather indivisibility, universality, totalization, independent growth, automatic activity, causal progress and absence of finality, and acceleration.[27] This means that technology, wherever it manifests itself, works to conform to its own laws, which are then forced on everything non-technical; it means that these laws are the same everywhere and that the technological system, once it has absorbed everything, has the tendency to withdraw into itself; it means that it automatically proliferates, apparently entirely from within and immune to all interventions from without, at an ever increasing speed and fuelled on by causal forces only, in other words, without it being possible to indicate the meaning of it all.

One may leave aside the question whether Ellul's view of things does not tend to over-emphasize specific characteristics of the image of modern culture; the fact remains that his analyses are parallel to those of many others as regards technical categories and ways of thinking penetrating into all sorts of sectors which are by nature non-technical, such as science, art, religion, law, education, politics etc.[28] But assuming that his diagnosis of 'the technological phenomenon' and hence of our present-day societal situation is correct , then the crucial question is: How could technology, which in pre-modern societies too was always was a standard component of human existence, since technology is as old as mankind, become in modern times this social force, this dominating social phenomenon with these characteristics?

5. PRECONDITIONS OF THE LEVEL OF IDEAS FOR THE RISE OF MODERN TECHNOLOGY

To begin with, it is clear that a more or less satisfactory explanation for such a complex social phenomenon can only be found along pluricausal lines. That is, only the simultaneous occurrence and interlinking of a number of very diverse preconditions can make the coming about of modern technological society understandable. Several factors on the social level have already been indicated, such as the fact that in the modern era the bourgeoisie, with its pragmatic, calculating, utility-orientated attitude is becoming the leading class and is creating a favourable social climate for the development of modern technology. I will now concentrate on a very specific aspect of the issue: the sustaining ideas, which have played an essential role in the development of modern technology. After all, in this volume we want to focus on the philosophical aspects of the environment issue, and on technology in that context. Ideas constitute the material of philosophy. Its task is, on the one hand, to articulate these ideas, especially those that characterize an era, while on the other hand it has to weigh and assess those ideas as regards their validity. Now it is presumed that ideas function amongst other things as preconditions for the occurrence of social phenomena, in other words that they have real social influence and effects. So de Bonald's remark about the French Revolution also applies to technology, namely that philosophy's share in it should not be underestimated. One can indeed say that the French Revolution was not simply a social disturbance but that it derived its historical meaning from the ideas about man, society, and the nature and origin of authority on which it was based. Because of that ideological moment it became the social event that marked the beginning of a new era. Without it, it would have been no more than a temporary, albeit rather violent movement at the surface of social reality, which would have died down rapidly and without leaving many marks.

Something similar can also be said of technology in its present form: modern technology could not develop into the phenomenon which it has in fact become until a series of preconditions on the level of ideas had been fulfilled. These preconditions can be specified further as the fundamental ideas of the symbolic universe of modern times, the conceptual and referential framework in terms of which we interpret reality and our own place within it; a framework, too, for forming a picture of the good life, such as crystallized in Europe after the Middle Ages, initially within a relatively small circle of philosophers, scientists and literati, and became accepted by an increasing number of people from the eighteenth century onwards. So my argument is that only within the framework of interpretation and orientation characteristic of modern times can modern technology find a favourable environment for development and become the phenomenon we know.

Every symbolic universe comprises three main components: an ontology or conception of reality; an epistemology, that is a view or 'model' of (true) knowledge; and an ethic, a system of normative opinions about right behaviour, the good life and the meaning of human existence. We can characterise the ontology, epistemology and ethic of the modern age as follows:

(i)   Ontologically, reality is interpreted in terms of the mechanized world view.

(ii)   In an epistemological perspective, an operative, activistic model of knowledge gains the upper hand.

(iii) In an ethical sense a radical anthropocentrism comes to the fore.

I will look into this in more detail.

Re (i), a good way of making clear what the mechanistic world view[29] means, is to contrast it with a mythical or symbolic view of reality. Mythically 'the world is full of gods', whereas the mechanized world is 'disenchanted' reality, from which all godly or sacred elements have been eliminated. Schiller splendidly expressed the difference between these two images of reality in *Die Götter Griechenlands* ('the Gods of Greece'),[30] even though with him the mythical element appears to be strongly aestheticized: When the gods were still present in this world (which was then, and is for that reason still a 'beautiful world'), everything.– springs, brooks, trees, hills, reed, sun, wind – was a dwelling place of gods. Everything bore evidence of their presence:

> Alles wies den eingeweihten Blicken,
> Alles eines Gottes Spur.
> *(All things showed the traces of a deity*
> *to the initiated eyes.)*

How different, how dead reality now appears:

> Wo jetzt nur, wie unsre Weisen sagen,
> Seelenlos ein Feuerball sich dreht,
> Lenkte damals seinen goldnen Wagen
> Helios in stiller Majestät...
> Ausgestorben trauert das Gefilde,
> Keine Gottheit zeigt sich meinem Blick;
> Ach, von jenem lebenswarmen Bilde
> Blieb der Schatten nur zurück.
> *(Where now, as our sages say,*
> *only a ball of fire is revolving,*
> *there in those days Helios steered his golden carriage*
> *in silent majesty...*
> *The deserted field is mourning,*
> *no deity manifests itself to my eyes.*
> *Alas, from that lively and warm picture*
> *only a shadow is left.)*

In this desacralized nature everything works purely mechanically, like a clock, the great modern metaphor for reality, where God, if He still exists, becomes the great watchmaker:

> Fühllos selbst für ihres Künstlers Ehre,
> Gleich dem todten Schlag der Pendeluhr,
> Dient sie knechtisch dem Gesetz der Schwere –
> Die entgötterte Natur.

(Callous even about its maker's fame,
like the deathly stroke of a pendulum
it slavishly serves the law of gravitation –
desacralized nature.)

From this world, which from then on could cope without them, the gods, having become superfluous, returned back home, 'und alles Schöne, alles Hohe nahmen sie mit fort, alle Farben, alle Lebenstöne, und uns blieb nur das entseelte Wort' (*and they took with them all that was beautiful and sublime, all colours, all sounds of life, and we were left with lifeless language*).

This world, in which everything has turned inanimate and dead, was philosophically characterized as *res extensa* by Descartes. It is a reality with which man, being *res cogitans*, can feel absolutely no affinity, which appears infinitely strange to him – even Sartre's chestnut root as a pure *en-soi* is an echo of this. To quote Pascal, this universe, where eternal and impenetrable silence reigns, cannot but instil fear.[31] At the same time that world has nothing left for which we would want to respect it: it no longer refers to a transcendent reality, it no longer reveals traces of a deity to the initiated eye.[32] There is no objection to – on the contrary everything speaks in favour of – using this reality of mute, lifeless, meaningless things as the raw material for building a reality of our own design.

Re (ii), closely related to the conception of reality so outlined is a new epistemological model which can be characterized as technical-activistic. It takes the place of a long tradition in which knowing was seen as a form of observing, of looking with the spiritual eye. In this context Plato comes first to mind, and in fact all the Greeks, whose words specifying the activity or the object of knowing (*theoria, eidos* etc.) almost all had to do with looking, contemplating. This tradition can be traced through the Middle Ages in their phenomenology and idea of *Wesensschau* (intuition of essences). According to this contemplative theory of knowing, the knowledgeable subject is receptive to a reality which is in itself thought to be intelligible, that is, open to thinking. The philosophy of the Middle Ages expresses this in the adage 'verum et ens convertuntur', the true and the real are interchangeable concepts, related to one another and covering one another. Thus, here the criterion for truth is the correspondence between thinking and being.

In contrast to this, a non-contemplative, operational and instrumental model of knowledge has developed since the late Middle Ages. This is clear first in Nicolas of Cusa, and then in a long line of modern thinkers such as Bacon, Hobbes, Vico, Leibniz, Kant, Fichte, Hegel, Marx, Dilthey and others. Vico, evidently taking issue with the medieval adage mentioned above, formulated the fundamental thesis: 'verum et factum convertuntur', the true and the factual, in the sense of the *made*, are mutually involved with one another.[33]

Things are understandable, not because of the fact that they are and, therefore, are intelligible also, but because of the fact that they are made and makeable. Comprehensibility and producibility are related; we only really understand those things which we ourselves can produce.

Hence the truth of certain insights is not confirmed by their corresponding with what is known, but by our ability to (re)produce the object of knowledge: 'veri criterium est ipsum fecisse', the proof of truth is to have made the object of knowledge (Vico). Pre-eminently this applies to mathematics, already (or rather, again) seen by Nicolas of Cusa as the model of compelling knowledge. After all, mathematical entities are constructed by us, and having been made by us they are transparent to us. He believes the knowledge which God the Creator has about nature to be analogous with this. However, because we ourselves have not created nature, it remains to a large extent obscure to us. Vico again: 'What belongs to mathematics can be proved by us because we make it; if we could prove what belongs to the natural sciences, we should have to make it.' This same idea supplies him with the argument against the Cartesian mathematical-physical ideal of science: that it is the cultural and not the natural sciences that embody the model of human knowledge, because culture (languages, history etc.) is our own product, whereas nature has been created by God.

As has been said before, this operative model of knowledge is characteristic of the mainstream of modern western philosophy. The following passage in Kant's preface for the second edition of his *Critique of Pure Reason* is famous:

> When Galilei rolled balls of a weight chosen by himself down a slope, and when Torricelli demonstrated that air could carry a weight he had ascertained to be equal to that of a column of water known to him... then it dawned upon all natural researchers. They understood that reason only comprehends what it designs and creates itself.[34]

Or, formulated even more succinctly: 'Denn nur das, was wir selbst machen können, verstehen wir aus dem Grunde.'[35] (For we only understand thoroughly what we are able to make ourselves.) After all, Kant's fundamental idea is that of the 'schöpferische Vernunft', the autonomous-creative (not contemplative-receptive) reason, which produces the (phenomenal) reality of its own design. This is why Schelsky calls Kant 'the original philosopher of modern technology' in his well known article *Der Mensch in der wissenschaftlichen Zivilisation* ('Man in Scientific Civilization').[36]

Explicitly referring to mathematics, Hobbes, in his theory of polity, had already applied this same model of knowledge to social reality:

> Of arts, some are demonstrable, others indemonstrable; and demonstrable are those the construction of the subject whereof is the power of the artist himself, who, in his demonstration, does no more but deduce the consequence of his own operation... The creation of a body politic by arbitrary institutions of many men assembled together... is like a creation out of nothing by human will.[37]

In this Hobbes holds a point of view on political theory which is totally 'poietic': the state is a work of art – the metaphor of the clock is used even in this respect – created in order to solve a problem, namely that of peaceful coexistence. This same programme of 'political technology' (a term which originates from Hella Mandt) recurs over and over in the political philosophy of modern times, for example again in the works of Kant.[38]

The outcome of what has just been said is that, even quite some time before the rise of modern technology, a technical way of thinking and a technical theory of knowledge began to develop in western philosophy. When we combine this with what has already been said about the modern outlook on reality, we can formulate the following conclusion: where all of reality is considered to be the raw materials for our creating or recreating (and where this means that, for example, animals are machines that can be experimented on and manipulated at will), where furthermore our knowing relationship with that same reality is seen as a technical-productive one, the scene is set for modern technological development. In other words, modern philosophy has created a symbolic universe which has provided a very favourable medium for the technological phenomenon to develop.

Re (iii), finally, as far as the normative component of the modern framework of interpretation is concerned, this factor, because of its radical anthropocentrism, has favoured the rise of modern technology as much as the other two. It is true that western ethics have always focused on improvement of human wellbeing: the central ethical question in ancient and medieval philosophy, and to an important degree even in modern philosophy, is the question of 'happiness', of flourishing or good human existence.[39] In this sense, western ethics have always been anthropocentric and even 'egotistical': in that view every person is spurred by a desire for self fulfilment, rooted in human nature.[40] In premodern philosophy however, this desire is subject to two normative influences: on the one hand there is a social dimension in that humans are social by nature and happiness is thought to be realizable only in a social context, while on the other hand the natural teleology of human existence is placed in context in the order of nature as a whole.

In modern philosophy the social dimension of human existence loses its natural character. The natural situation is taken to be that of the pre-social individual, who only secondarily enters into relationships with others, for reasons of well understood self-interest.[41] The human individual now really becomes an egocentric being who on the social level neither knows nor recognizes natural relationships with others. After all, commitments arise only from their being recognized as such. As Kant succinctly puts it, 'Niemand ist obligirt ausser durch seine Einstimmung' (nobody is obliged unless by his own agreement).[42] In other words, commitments only exist where one commits oneself – another way of wording the principle of autonomy. At the same time, in modern philosophy humanity also emancipates itself from nature and its order – this has been philosophically expressed in Descartes' already mentioned duality of *res cogitans* and *res extensa* or Kant's *noumenal* and *phenomenal* worlds; two orders separated from one another by a radical ontological gap.[43] But these two orders are by no means of equal importance: in modern philosophy the individual, who has become autonomous, and the progressive realization of his liberty are at the core of nature and history. In other words, modern philosophy is thoroughly anthropocentric and even egocentric.

That means however, that in fact human behaviour, at least as regards nature, has become 'unlimited'. When we revert to the characterization of technology as the activity whereby we reconstruct reality into our 'Umwelt', then with regard to nature this reconstruction is not subject to any limits or measure based on moral principles. There are, at the most, only factual limits, namely those that are caused by the limits of human capacities with respect to nature. But in principle everything that is possible is allowed, and is perhaps even compulsory. In the modernistic view the only fundamental restriction on human behaviour is on the level of intra-human relationships, and it consists of others' liberty having to be respected. However, in this frame of reference nothing prevents technology from becoming modern humanity's weapon of conquest as far as nature is concerned. The modern image of the human is as the 'infinite desirer', the 'infinite consumer' and the 'infinite appropriator' (the typifications are Macpherson's).[44]

6. THE NECESSITY FOR A DIFFERENT FRAME OF REFERENCE

For a philosophical characterization of technology, and in order to keep in touch with the phenomena, we started above from a limited definition of technology and used the analysis of a philosophizing technologist. But even in that approach a number of characteristics of the phenomenon of modern technology remained beyond the horizon. So, by completing the image of modern technology, we have moved quite a way in the direction of what we had described as a maximum conception of technology, a conception in which technology is seen as the way of life and thought of modern society, the dominating force in the life of us present day humans, which determines our view of reality, our self perception and our attitude to reality.

Having investigated the role of philosophy in all this, we have seen that mainstream modern philosophy has worked out a framework of perception and orientation which has created very favourable preconditions for modern technology to develop into the dominant power in modern society. Again this is certainly not meant as a monocausal explanation for the rise of the technological society, but it does make clear that the set of fundamental philosophical ideas outlined above has played a significant role and has merged with social, economic and other factors into a unity of which it constitutes the ideological part. As an integrating part of the social system these philosophical ideas have in this way obtained the status of being self-evident, the greatest 'success' philosophical ideas can possibly achieve.

On the philosophical level these ideas are being increasingly contended. However, this does not prevent their influence in practice increasing rather than decreasing in various ways. We still see technological modes of thinking continuously and increasingly penetrating originally non-technical domains such as art, law, politics and science – the information technology revolution will certainly be a powerful new stimulus to this process. Policy drafts, for instance, convey that political and policy issues are frequently seen as problems for which a specific, optimal solution must be found, as though they were 'puzzles', technical problems so to speak. In line with this is the continuously and uncontrollably increasing number of new types of specialists who take charge of ever new parts of human existence. One may also think of the application of organization technology in fields that are by nature unsuited to a calculating attitude, such as science, art, law, education and even religion – the scientists and even the religious leaders are in danger of becoming managers first of all. At any rate they are forced to operate increasingly within institutional structures that have little to do with the specific nature of their specializations, but are primarily concerned with technical/organizational matters

Environmental problems too are basically the result of our way of dealing with technology. It is a widely held opinion that problems which have been caused by technology can and must be conquered by that same technology. This means, though, that the phenomenon of modern technology itself is not brought up for discussion. Only the excesses of technology are corrected by technological means. But, as the correction will always lag behind the emergence of the problem, which anyway often does not come to light until after a rather long incubation period, the correction will become more and more inadequate because of the ever increasing acceleration and scale of technology. And, most important, modern technology's inherent tendency to expand in scale and take over other domains can thus continue unchecked. In other words, if technology correcting technology is the only answer to the problems of modern society, that is nothing better than swimming against the tide. I am primarily talking about ecological questions now, but one may also think of the staggering increase in the numbers of people with mental problems. The so-called technology assessment too – the (laudable) purpose of which is to anticipate and investigate problems connected with new technologies before they are introduced instead of after, and to act accordingly – operates within this dominant frame of thought

7. OUTLINE OF A NEW FRAMEWORK

An answer to the problems caused by modern technology will therefore have to be found in a different, 'alternative' technology only. And here too one can distinguish between a rather limited definition of alternative technology and a broader one.[45] It can be described more specifically by means of characteristics such as smallness of scale, low energy consumption, emphasis on recycling of raw materials, traditional methods, diversity and so on. At the same time we see that in descriptions of alternative technology certain characteristics are often mentioned, such as decentralization, regional autonomy, non-alienating, not frustrating the creativity of the working people involved, or more positively, contributing to the self fulfilment of those involved, and harmonizing with prevailing culture and institutions. All of these characteristics are of a psychological, socio-political and ideological nature. In other words, alternative technology – many of its advocates understand this, if only intuitively – requires alternative lifestyles and hence a frame of thought and a set of values that are different from the dominant ones.

Frameworks of orientation, however, are not like clothes that can be put on and taken off at will. They have to do with beliefs and attitudes which constitute the core of our identity, and which are therefore part of our innermost being. But even though our view of, and our attitude towards things cannot be changed at will when it suits us and circumstances require us to do so, I still believe that there are reasons for assuming that such a change in attitude and lifestyle is coming up and that it may be adopted in wider circles. From a philosophical point of view we are interested most of all in such factors as work at the ideological level and appeal to human insight.

In this connection it is possible, to my mind, to differentiate between two types of consideration, one negative and one positive. As far as the first is concerned, it seems to me to be undeniable that the technological lifestyle poses an increasing threat to its own preconditions for existence, both physical and mental , and that ultimately it may even destroy them. This is most noticeable as far as the physical environment is concerned. In the public debate there is hardly any doubt about there being a crisis in this respect, although the extent of the threat does not seem to have sunk in yet, judging by most people's behaviour. This is even less the case as regards social reality, which relies on understanding between people, on trust and at least decency, and furthermore on a common cultural tradition which brings about recognition in the world, and on a social climate in which people feel at home; in short on the 'gentle forces' within human society being intact. Because of their nature, these do not lend themselves to a socio-technical approach in terms of counting, measuring or controlling, but on the one hand they create the preconditions for such a 'hard' organizational and managerial approach, and on the other hand they are increasingly eroded by it. This then leads to relationships between people becoming ever more impersonal, to an increasingly chilly atmosphere in our institutions which are being dominated more and more by 'business' viewpoints such as efficiency. The result is, not surprisingly, a sharp rise in the number of dropouts, people unfit for work and psychiatric patients, especially among people under 35. This is highly alarming, as people who have their entire future still ahead of them and given their age should be hardy, are cracking up before life has actually got going.

Perhaps such a sombre view of our era may awaken us to the situation. Some, such as Hans Jonas[46] with his 'heuristics of fear', are in fact counting on it. I myself believe that its effect will be very limited if we do not succeed in finding a positive counterpart to it, that is a new form of existence and lifestyle and a non-technological framework of interpretation and orientation. In that respect philosophy can see it as one of its tasks to contribute, by using all its means, to a breakthrough, to a new view of and attitude towards things. This should be in dialogue with art, literature, spiritual movements within and outside the existing religions and world views, and with social movements inspired by ideals, all of them mutually inspiring each other but with each one minding his own business. So the task of philosophy would be to work out ideas in the light of which we see reality and our place in it.

8. POSITIVE CHARACTERIZATION

What that positive counterpart to criticism of the dominant frame of perception in our society should be like has been a major subject of philosophical thinking in the last few decades, insofar as philosophy has been developing alternatives to the so-called project of Enlightenment and modernity. In fact such counter-projects have accompanied modern philosophy since its rise; one can think of names like Boehme, Rousseau, Herder, Schelling, Klages and Bergson, to mention just a few. This does not alter the fact that we have only the first beginnings of a new structure for defining and directing our thoughts and actions. Which, in turn, leads one to remember that the development and elaboration of the modernistic view of reality took approximately five centuries of intensive philosophical work and has not been completed by a long way. As a matter of fact, does not each philosophy remain a fragment, and was it not Kant who complained that he already had to finish off his work even though to his mind he had only just begun?

With all these reservations, I would like to sketch an outlook on and an attitude towards reality which is not already implicitly technological and so does not already contain the environmental crisis and thus have no means to counteract it. I would once more refer to the triptych of ontology, epistemology and ethics, although even this scheme may perhaps not be purely formal and neutral with respect to each possible framework, and may already be laden with presuppositions.

Ontologically, it would be a counter-design opposed to the image of a mechanized, dead and disenchanted reality, which does not have any meaning or sense in itself. Such a different understanding of reality, allowing for things to have their own contribution and meaning, has been formulated many times in modern literature and philosophy. In it 'things' are not purely seen as objects, as 'material' with which people can do as they please, but as entities having a voice and presentation of their own. We find it expressed by Rilke: in his poems on things, these things have an independent, fulfilled way of being which is violated by the interference of man, who manipulates them to suit his own purposes:

> Die Dinge singen hör ich so gern.
> Ihr rührt sie an: sie sind starr und stumm.
> Ihr bringt mir alle die dinge um.

(I love to hear the things singing.
You touch them: they are rigid and mute.
You are killing all things to me.)[47]

Analogous experiences of nature, as not just a collection of dead things surrounded by eternal and impenetrable silence but having a language of its own, have been expressed by many others, for example by the Dutch poet Guido Gezelle:

Als de ziele luistert
spreekt het al een taal dat leeft,
t'lijzigste gefluister
ook een taal en teeken heeft ...
(When the soul is listening
all that lives speaks a language,
the softest whispering
also has a sense and meaning...)

Or again: 'Mij spreekt de blomme een tale...' (*To me, flowers speak a language...*) Or when he writes about the 'sad melody' and the 'singing harmony' of the rustling reeds, etc.[48]

     As in Gezelle, the experience of nature speaking may lead to the realization that reality has a referential character, in other words that it is not purely opaque, but that it allows for transparency or, to quote Schiller, shows traces of an underlying dimension. In modern times it was Goethe first of all who continually articulated this 'symbolic' understanding of reality.[49] In his opinion, science and art have the task of making the idea within the phenomena visible, of learning to interpret the multitude of phenomena of the temporary reality as the expression of eternal godliness, in short to learn to see the world as 'der Gottheit lebendiges Kleid' (the deity's living robe).[50] With Goethe, science and art in this sense are closely related or even identical to religion: 'Wer Wissenschaft und Kunst besitzt, hat auch Religion.' (Who possesses science and art, possesses religion too.)[51] To him the 'pious', revering mentality with respect to the unnamable mystery which reveals itself in the world of phenomena is the source of inspiration for both science and art. Where this is lacking, as Goethe believes to be the case in Newton's physics or Holbach's *Système de la Nature*, and in the modern realism in art, one cannot speak of science and art in the true sense of the word, nor, for that matter, of religion worthy of that name. Along the same lines, Einstein considers natural science without religion to be crippled, and religion without natural science to be blind. He means religion in the sense of 'cosmic religiousness', namely the conviction and understanding that the order of the perceptible world, which forms the field of research in science, is rooted in a mysterious, cosmic order.

> Das Schönste, was wir erleben können, ist das Geheimnisvolle. Es ist das Grundgefühl, das an der Wiege von wahrer Kunst und Wissenschaft steht. Wer es nicht kennt und sich nicht mehr wundern, nicht mehr staunen kann, der ist sozusagen tot und sein Auge erloschen. Das Erlebnis des Geheimnisvollen – wenn auch mit Furcht gemischt – hat auch die Religion gezeugt. Das Wissen um die Existenz des für uns Undurchdringlichen, der Manifestationen tiefster Vernunft und leuchtendster Schönheit, die unserer Vernunft nur in ihren primitivsten Formen zugänglich sind, dies Wissen und Fühlen macht wahre Religiosität aus.
> *(The most beautiful thing we can experience is the mysterious. It is the basic emotion being the source of art and science. Whoever does not know it, and has become incapable of wonder and astonishment, is so-to-say dead and blind. The experience of mystery – though mixed with fear – has brought forth religion. The awareness of the existence of things unfathomable to us, of the manifestations of the most profound reason and the brightest beauty, which are accessible to our reason only in their most primitive forms, – this knowledge and this feeling constitutes true religiousness.)*[52]

It is not necessary to emphasize that this concept of science is totally different to that of organized research in its present day form, where nature is indeed placed on the rack and research results are wrung out of it one after the other. There – with some honourable exceptions – it has fully become 'religiöser Alltag' (religious midweek), to put it in Max Weber's words. There reality is approached as being totally prosaic. However, it is certain that the image of reality of science so understood and practised does not cover the experience of reality of modern times just like that: on the contrary. Perhaps we should ask ourselves whether the image of reality held by Goethe, Gezelle, Rilke, Einstein and many others, in which nature far transcends humanity and has its own miraculous order, does not give a far more adequate account of our experience than the mechanistic world view does.

Towards nature seen as the embodiment of an ideal order, as 'the deity's living robe', an attitude of exploitation and destruction is hardly imaginable. Where things have their own 'self' – which is undeniably the way we experience animals and plants, and landscapes, mountains and the sea as well – they are for that very reason in a way 'unimpeachable' and appeal to be spared. In this way it is possible to develop a form of reverence for nature too.

In this connection Kant's comment is remarkable: 'Two things fill the heart with ever new and increasing admiration and respect the more and more persistently they are considered: the stars above me and the moral law within me'.[53] With the 'philosopher of technology' and of the constitution of the world of experience through creative reason, the latter is not at all surprising. Indeed, it corresponds very well with the view of a mechanized reality from which all meaning has disappeared into an 'extra-natural' moral order. But that the stars as part of the world of phenomena can of their own accord instil admiration and respect is certainly remarkable and can hardly be seen other than as an erratic experience that does not allow itself to be categorized within the dominant framework.[54]

Speaking in terms of ideal types, the radical opposite to a totally prosaic and desacralized view of reality is that of myth, where nothing is contingent but everything the expression of the numinous ('full of gods'), where all things are the embodiment of a sacred order and part of a universal community of life. Even though the modern understanding of reality has become largely profane, this does not mean that every form of mythic experience of reality is lost.[55] Paul Rodenko has spoken of the mythical dimension in the work of the Dutch poet Gerrit Achterberg. The central figure in many of his poems, the dead beloved, is clearly credited with a value beyond her actual individuality, especially in the later poems. In the words of Rodenko, she becomes the 'representative of the numinous'.[56] The struggle for her survival is in essence the struggle for the survival of godliness in this world. Existence is not just a matter of temporality and contingency.

Not only with Achterberg, but with every poet, the meaning of words is not purely their semantic meaning, but 'reality as seen in its sacred perspective'.[57] One of the outstanding characteristics of Achterberg's poetry is that the most ordinary, 'profane' things (a regurgitating cow, cartography etc.) are given a double meaning and become references to a 'second reality'. We find something similar in another Dutch poet, Nijhoff, for instance in his wellknown 'Ik ging naar Bommel om brug te zien' (I went to Bommel to see the bridge), or in 'Het uur u' ('the hour thou'), where a very different order suddenly shines through the normal one when on the appearance of a foreigner the gas and the water in the pipes under the street, the most commonplace things imaginable, begin to sing and people, at least the adults, are struck by a silent panic. In contrast to the belief widely accepted in our culture in the contingency of reality, here, by using what is ordinary as the particular tool for the job, the sense of the extra-ordinary (and of the nature of language beyond the conventional) is evoked. We even find the mythical topos of the 'natural place' of things in Achterberg's work: 'Everything arrives wherever it should be'.[58]

9. Rehabilitation of Suppressed Forms of Experience

Of course it is possible to write this off as a product of poetical imagination, as an expression of subjective emotion saying nothing about 'reality itself' but only about us and our reaction to reality. Here we are resuming the very old philosophical debate on the status of art (of the whole of human 'qualitative' experience, for that matter), especially the question of its truth value and its capacities for unlocking reality. With that we touch upon the epistemological side of the issue we are exploring. I assume that a radical 'emotivist' interpretation of art, as implied in Descartes' differentiation between primary and secondary qualities, and as again defended by the logical empiricism of Ayer and others in this century, is untenable. Then it is possible to defend the thesis that the sciences, which anyway do not form a single unit from a methodological viewpoint, do not possess the monopoly on the interpretation of reality, but that there are a number of types of experience that imply just as many independent approaches to reality. What we are talking about here is authentic forms of experience which are impossible to give up, and which will therefore continually assert themselves, but for which there is no place in the models of scientific knowledge except in a modified form that robs them of their essential characteristics. E.g. colours and sounds do not appear as such in science, except in the form of electromagnetic waves or air vibrations or physiological processes. Likewise, the validity of moral norms and the existence of divine powers are put between brackets in the moral and religious sciences. They appear there as just mental or social phenomena, as the fact that certain individuals or groups adhere to specific moral or religious convictions and practices, which are then described or explained from the perspective of the spectator. Science, over the whole breadth, takes up this outsider position. Because it refrains from participation, it never leaves the immediate, primary experience intact. Essentially it does not recognize the emotions aroused by a piece of music, nor a phenomenon such as spring which is described by many poets, nor nature as an all-including community of which people know themselves to be part. It does not recognize the inner experience of conscientious conviction, nor the 'you' that becomes accessible in relationships of trust or friendship, nor the sense of being an uninterchangeable 'I'.

What we are seeking is the outline of an alternative framework for thought and perception to oppose the dominant framework which is at least implicitly technological. I shall not consider here whether this dominant framework of thought can perhaps on a fundamental level be interpreted in a non-technological, 'contemplative' way.[59] Whatever the answer, at any rate it presents itself as an 'operative' epistemological model with Vico's adage that the truth of a statement is shown by the capacity it creates for producing the object or changing it in a particular direction as its test of veracity. In such a model of knowledge, with such a key to reality all those experiences of reality, must in fact become 'speechless' which by their nature cannot be laid on this bed of Procrustes.

The purport of what has just been said is that we actually have a broad spectrum of experience that is not open to operative interpretation. It would be possible to write the history of philosophy of the last century from the angle of the rehabilitation of forms of experience that have been suppressed by the dominant model. The names of Dilthey, Bergson, Cassirer, Buber, Heidegger, Jaspers and Wittgenstein and many others come to mind in this connection: for example, Dilthey spoke of language and myth as independent organs for understanding reality, next to science. And Cassirer developed his philosophy of the symbolic forms (myth and religion, language, art, history and science), as mutually irreducible forms by which the mind organizes and articulates our experience.

At the same time Cassirer is a good example of how much one can be in the grasp of the dominant model: to him science continues to hold a privileged position in interpreting reality.[60] Moreover, and perhaps even more important, his entire philosophy remains in the tradition of Kantian transcendental philosophy, so that the symbolic forms with which the mind is equipped still function as the principles by means of which reality in the different fields of experience is constituted. The mind, therefore, remains the active principle which determines how reality is to appear. This leads to the remarkable paradox that myth, religion, art and science, which ultimately, at any rate, are orientated towards the idea of an objective order, are nevertheless framed in a 'subjective' manner here: in the end the objective order proves to be dictated by ourselves, through our the design of our spirit. This transcendental philosophy is still based on the modernistic pattern of the production of reality by the subject and it is therefore the epistemological and metaphysical counterpart of the autonomy of the subject on a moral level. Both originate from the same modernistic roots and are very foreign to the mythical, religious or aesthetic understanding of reality. It is then an interesting 'inconsequent' turn in Cassirer's thinking that philosophy as the self-reflection of reason in its reality-constituting activities is no longer seen as activistic but as contemplative: it does not establish any type of reality of experience itself, but simply observes the symbolic activities of the spirit; in other words it is the observer of the spirit's activities.

Taking all this into account, Cassirer's rehabilitation of myth, art etc. is only a very partial rehabilitation. In a variation on Kant's words, it is true that he limits 'knowing' and restricts the sole right of science to the interpretation of reality and creates room for other forms of understanding it. However, in doing so he remains in the grip of a 'technological' concept of reality and knowledge which is fundamentally at odds with several of the ways of experiencing reality that he has already analysed. Hence rehabilitation must go further: the aesthetic, moral and spiritual experience must be released from the grasp of a technological way of thinking. At the same time mere juxtaposition will not suffice. It can be argued that a technological approach to things cannot hold out on its own, but presupposes, at least implicitly, a pre-technological frame of reference to which technological activity is orientated, both conceptually and normatively. This leads us to a second claim for the new framework besides that of the necessity of rehabilitation of forms of experience that have been suppressed by the dominant model of knowledge: that the primary place should be accorded to non-technological forms of the experience of reality, that is to say, forms not mediated by science.

How that is to be worked out further will be one of philosophy's most important tasks. We live in a situation of far-reaching modernization and rationalization, behind which we cannot go back, and cannot want to go back either. As far as the latter is concerned, it is often claimed that the process of modernization has produced solutions to a number of big problems of the past, such as starvation, epidemics, floods and the like. On a social level we can mention such benefits of the process of modernization as the idea and practice of the constitutional state and of democracy, and of the dignity, equality and fundamental rights of all human beings. In short, we would not want these achievements to be relinquished should the form of life and thinking within which they have been developed be radically reformed. Philosophizing on how to safeguard those achievements within a new framework has not actually begun yet. I am convinced though that for a number of reasons, including the environmental issue, we will have to start thinking about such a reform.

Needless to say that, apart from what we would consider desirable, a simple restoration of life styles and patterns of thought such as mythical or classical-religious ones is out of the question. We cannot get rid of the shadows of modernization and secularization. What I am claiming is that motives of mythical, symbolical, spiritual and other nature are not unknown to us, given the work of modern artists and philosophers and given the response to their work; further, that the expressions and experiences of recognition have for a while been drowned out by the outward successes of a technological culture; but also that, now that the euphoria over these successes is ebbing away, new opportunities for recognizing these suppressed dimensions of existence have come about.) p241

So, the gods will not return as if nothing has happened and the meaning of reality will not simply become transparent again. This means that metaphysical or religious positions, which give a simple and massive explanation of the order and sense of reality, have become implausible. However, this is not in conflict with the realization that reality speaks a language, a language certainly of *chiffres*,[61] of mysterious signs, but nevertheless a language.

10. WELTOFFENHEIT (RECEPTIVENESS TO THE WORLD)

This leads to the third aspect of a new framework of meaning, namely the ethical one, about which I will say a few words in rounding off, although this aspect has repeatedly been touched upon indirectly in what I have said before. When the insight dawns that things speak their own language and that by nature they are carriers of meaning, then we can no longer see ourselves as the unique referent for meaning and as the measure of things. An activistic attitude, in which a reality which is without either value or meaning is converted into a meaningful order by our doing only, is no longer adequate. Quite the opposite, an attitude of receptivity towards things is necessary once again, an attitude which lets things be what they are and allows them to speak their own language. I say, 'once again', because here too we are talking about the resumption of something which has actually never gone away, but which has only been obscured.

Perhaps one can say that humanity's ability to adopt such an attitude is exactly what is characteristic of it. While everything in nature falls under the law of self-maintenance, which means that all other things are considered from the perspective of the satisfaction of one's own needs, we possess the ability to transcend this self-centred relationship with reality. Naturally we too are creatures with 'needs' who, in order to be able to live and to live reasonably well, make use of things in our sphere of influence and subject them to our own aims. However this does not exhaust our mode of being: we are also capable of a certain 'unselfishness' and thus of not assessing things just for their usefulness, but also allowing them to be as they are.

Technology, one can say, is the ever more sophisticated way of subordinating reality to oneself. It reforms the world more and more into a human 'Umwelt', as we have seen with Dessauer. To that extent it does with new means what all organisms do, each one in its own way. If we characterize humans through their 'Weltoffenheit', their receptiveness to the world, as Max Scheler does, then that means that things are not only seen according to their usefulness for human purposes, but also that, because of his nature, we are capable of being receptive to these things as they are in themselves. In that sense true self-development as human beings does not mean that we subject everything to our own order: on the contrary, we are gradually being overcome by the uneasy feeling that we are sinking deeper and deeper into a crisis of identity and meaning the more we are confronted with only ourselves in a reality which is being recreated technologically (for example in biotechnology and information technology). This, therefore, is an indication of the opposite, of the paradoxical fact – one could call it the paradox of self-development – that we will not find, or rather refind ourselves until we are prepared to lose ourselves in the other, wonderful, reality around us.

11. CONCLUSION

The question which has been central to these considerations is that of the nature of the relationship between the environmental crisis and technology. To prevent an *a priori* conclusion of a certain kind we started with a limited definition of 'technology', that of the technologist Dessauer. Yet, while searching in the domain of ideas for the preconditions for the development of the phenomenon of modern technology, we have gradually shifted in the direction of the conclusion that in our western culture the dominant way of looking at and dealing with reality is largely characterized by a technological viewpoint. The conclusion which we attained was that on a philosophical level, that is on the level of the basic ideas by which we characterize reality and our relationship with it, our culture bore the marks of technology long before modern technology as a social phenomenon emerged. The assertion was that the framework of orientation and interpretation which has been worked out by mainstream philosophy has created very favourable preconditions for the development of modern technology as a determining force in our society.

Within this philosophical pattern of thought and the practices related to it, there is no fundamental objection, at the most a pragmatic one, to nature being continuously transformed in order to satisfy human desires and demands which, in this perspective, are insatiable. This does not mean that what is being done in the environmental crisis to gain control, in particular by applying all sorts of environmental technology, is senseless. Not in the least. However, it does mean that it will be absolutely inadequate when correcting measures of this kind only are taken. The environment will be striving against the stream as long as the stream of our thinking, experiencing and basic attitudes does not change its course.

We have it in common with all life, and it is also the pitch to which technology is tuned, that we have the ability to convert our surroundings to our own 'Umwelt'. If what I have said earlier is true – that we are characterized not so much by this as by our ability to recognize everything else in its being different – then we can conclude that a solution to the environmental crisis will not appear until we succeed in being truly 'humane' again.

Notes

1. Habermas, J., 1968. 'Technik und Wissenschaft als "Ideologie"', in the compilation under the same title. pp. 48-103. Frankfurt, Suhrkamp.

2. Heidegger, M., 1962. *Die Technik und die Kehre*. Pfullingen, Neske.

3. Lilje, Hanns, 1928. *Das technische Zeitalter*, p.54. Berlin, Furche.

4. Heidegger, *op.cit.*, e.g. p. 5 .

5. For a survey of definitions of technology see e.g. van der Pot, J.H.J. 1985.*Die Bewertung des technischen Fortschritts*. Part II, p.1206 ff. Assen/Maastricht, Van Gorcum.

6. Rapp, Friedrich, 1979.'Technik als Mythos'. In H. Poser (ed.), *Philosophie und Mythos*. Berlin, De Gruyter. Quoted by V.d. Pot, *op.cit.*, p. 1206. See also the definitions of Sombart, Timm and Ellul in V.d. Pot, p. 1207.

7. Ellul, J., 1964. *The Technological Society*, p. 22. New York, Vintage Books, . Compare Schelsky, H., 1965. 'Der Mensch in der wissenschaftlichen Zivilisation', in the same, *Auf der Suche nach Wirklichheit.Gesammelte Aufsätze*. p. 444 ff. Düsseldorf, Diederichs.

8. In particular, in Dessauer, Friedrich, 1928. *Philosophie der Technik*. Bonn, Cohen. Also, 1952, with X. van Hornstein, *Seele im Bannkreis der Technik*. Olten/Freiburg, Walten; and 1959, *Streit um die Technik*. Freiburg, Herder.

9. At Frankfurt (1921-33), Istanbul (1934-37), Freiburg in Switzerland (1937-53) and as from 1946 at Frankfurt again.

10. Stork, Heinrich, 1977. Darmstadt, Wissenschaftliche Buchgesellschaft.

11. *Streit um die Technik*, p. 18

12. *op.cit.*, p. 44, 17; comp. e.g. 13, 55.

13. Lilje too (*op.cit.*, p. 36) says that Kapp's book is 'der erste Versuch einer Philosophie der Technik' (the first attempt at a philosophy of technology).

14. *Philosophie der Technik*, p. 19 ff.; *Streit*, p. 79

15. *Philosophie der Technik,* p. 50 ff.; *Streit,* p. 82 ff.

16. See Ed. Spranger, *1950* (1925) *Lebensformen.* Tübingen, Neomarius (1925), p. 362 ff. Other representatives of this view are W. Stern, W. Sombart, F.L. Polak and many others.

17. *Op.cit.,* p. 19 ff.; comp. 22, 93.

18. *Seele im Bannkreis der Technik,* p. 54.

19. *Streit,* p. 100.

20. *Op.cit.,*p. 78

21. Burnier, Andreas, *1990.De achtste scheppingsdag (the eighth day of creation),* in the compilation under the same title, p.55 ff. Amsterdam, Meulenhoff.

22. *Streit,* p. 83 ff.

23. *Streit,* p. 84 ff.

24. *Streit,* p. 99.

25. *Streit,* p. 96.

26. See with regard to Ellul and Jonas the extensive and thorough essay by Weyembergh, Maurice, 1989, 'La critique de l'utopie et de la technique chez J. Ellul et H. Jonas', in the special issue on conservatism and technology (ed. Johan Stuy), *Tijdschrift voor de studie van de Verlichting en van het vrije denken,* **17,**1-2: p. 63-131.

27. Ellul, J., *op.cit.,* pp. 79-147 and Ellul, J, 1977, *Système technicien.* p.137 ff. Paris, Calman-Lévy, Paris, 1977.

28. See e.g. V.d. Pot, *op.cit.,* chapters 54 (p.220 ff.) and 64 (p. 246 ff.).

29. Of course the expression derives from the title of E.J. Dijksterhuis' well-known book *De mechanisering van het wereldbeeld (Mechanization of the world-picture).* Amsterdam 1950.

30. *Schillers Werke.* 1983, Nationalausgabe, Weimar, Böhlaus, Bd. II, 1, p.363 ff.

31. Pascal, F., *Pensées* (ed. Brunschvicg), many editions, fragment 206.

32. For mediaeval symbolism (also called exemplarism), where everything is seen as telling of the traces of God, see. Huizinga, J., 1949. 'Herfsttij der Middeleeuwen'(Waning of the Middle Ages), in *Verzamelde werken* (complete works). Part 3, in particular chapter 15, p. 245 ff.: 'het symbolisme uitgebloeid' (symbolism wilted).Haarlem, Tjeenk Willink.

See also, de Vos, H., 1970. *Beknopte geschiedenis van het begrip natuur,* p.19 ff. Groningen, Wolters-Noordhoff: 'Examplarism/ symbolism has not been able to hold out, neither scientifically, nor philosophically. And yet it may have contained more truth than was believed later on.'

33. For a description of this development see Löwith, Karl, 1986. 'Vico Grundsatz: verum et factum convertuntur (seine theologische Prämisse und deren säkulare Konsequenzen)', in: *Sämtliche Schriften,* **9,** pp. 195-227. Stuttgart, Metzler.

34. Kant, *Werke in zwölf Bänden,* 1956, ed. W. Weischedel. Part III, p.23.Wiesbaden, Insel.

35. Letter to Plückner dated 26 January 1796, quoted by Löwith, *op.cit.,* p. 27, note 14.

36. Schelsky 1965 (see note 7), p. 448.

37. The letter or recommendation accompanying the 'Six Lessons to the Professors

of the Mathematics'. In Hobbes, T.,*Works,* ed. Molesworth, vol. II, p. 93, and *Elements of Law,* II, 1, respectively, both quoted by Löwith, *op.cit.,* p. 24 ff.

38. Mandt, H. 1976. 'Historisch-politische Traditionselemente im politischen Denken Kants', in Zwi Batscha (ed.), *Materialien zu Kants Rechtsphilosophie,* p. 317 ff. Frankfurt am Main, Suhrkamp, .

39. In Aristotle practical philosophy (ethics in a wider sense) is defined as 'he peri ta anthropina philosophia', the (part of) philosophy that has to do with human relations, *Nicomachean Ethics,* 1181 b 15.

40. Norman, R., 1984. *The Moral Philosophers.* Oxford, Oxford University Press, p. 43, 56-67 ff.

41. See for instance Spinoza, *Tractatus Politicus* V, 2: 'For people are not born as social beings but made that way' (Homines enim civiles non nascuntur sed fiunt). And therefore individuals as well as states are enemies by nature, II,14; III, 13; VII, 24 etc.

42. Kant, E., *Reflexionen zur Moralphilosophie* 6645.

43. Pascal, *Pensées,* fr. 793, speaks of the 'infinite distance (distance infinie) between bodies and spirits' which symbolizes the 'infinitely more infinite distance' (distance infiniment plus infinie) between the spirits and christian love, that is to say between the natural and the supernatural order. That infinite distance between the spiritual and material domains of reality is, at the same time, also one from an evaluative point of view: 'All bodies, the firmament, the stars, the earth and its kingdoms (in short: nature, VdW) are not equal to the least among the spirits.' In other words: in comparison with the world of the spirit (where man is domiciled according to his true nature) the world of nature has no value.

44. Macpherson, C.B., 1973. *Democratic Theory: Essays in Retrieval,* p.24 ff. Oxford, Clarendon. See e.g. quotation Hobbes, *Leviathan,* Pelican edition, 1971, p. 160 ff

45. A list of definitions and characterizations can be found in V.d. Pot, *op.cit.,* chapter 217 (p. 920 ff.).

46. Jonas, Hans, 1979. *Das Prinzip Verantwortung. Versuch einer Ethik für die technologische Zivilisation.* p.8, 63 ff etc. Frankfurt, Insel, Frankfurt.

47. The end of the poem 'Ich fürchte mich so vor der Menschen Wort', in Rilke, Rainer Maria, *Sämtliche Werke.* Bd. III, p. 257, Wiesbaden.

48. Guido Gezelle, *Gedichten* (poems), publ. by E.J.M. Laudy-Arnolds, 1953. p.94, 99, 18 respectively. Utrecht/Antwerp, Spectrum.

49 .See e.g. 'Alles ist ja nur symbolisch zu nehmen, und überall steckt... noch etwas anderes dahinter.' (All things have to be taken... symbolically, and behind everything something else is hidden.) To Chancellor Von Müller, 8.6.1821, in Goethe, 1961, *Gedenksausgabe der Werke, Briefe und Gespräche,* ed. Ernst Beutler. Zürich/ Stuttgart, Artemis. Vol. 2, Bd. 23, p. 129.

50. *Faust* I, 509.

51. Zahme Xenien, Aus dem Nachlass, *op.cit.,* Bd. 2, p. 404.

52. Einstein, A., 1956. *Mein Weltbild* (ed. by C. Seelig). p.9 ff.Frankfurt a.M.. Compare 17, 18 etc. Also Goethe: 'Zum Erstaunen bin ich da'(I exist for the sake of wondering), 'Gott und Welt' (Parabase), *op.cit.,* Bd. 1, p. 516.

53. Kant, Kritik der praktischen Vernunft, *op.cit.,* Bd. VII, p. 300.

54. More telling than long philosophical dissertations is the question which Pfänder, prompted by disbelief, once put to Husserl on watching a sunset during a walk, namely whether this natural phenomenon also should be seen as having been constituted by him.

55. Hübner, Kurt, 1985. *Die Wahrheit des Mythos* (the truth of myth), p.293-414. München, Beck.The presence of the mythical in modern art, religion and politics is discussed. And, to give another example, Gerhard Herrmann (introduction to Mörike, Eduard, 1957 *Erzählungen und Gedichte*, p.5. München, Goldmann) speaks of the aspect of the 'Naturhaft-Mythische' in Mörikes work (p. 5).

56. Achterberg, Gerritt, 1976.*Voorbij de laatste stad,* (beyond the last city), compiled and introduced by Paul Rodenko. p.23. Amsterdam, Bakker.

57. *Op.cit.,* p. 34

58. *Op.cit.,* p. 134

59. On this question see Maarten Coolen's contribution to this book.

60. Cassirer, J., 1962 (1944) *Essay on Man,* New Haven/London, Yale University Press. The opening sentence of chapter XI, 'Science', reads: 'Science is the last step in man's mental development and it may be regarded as the highest and most characteristic attainment of human culture' (p. 207; many passages in the *Philosophie der symbolischen Formen* are in the same vein).

61. It seems to me that in this respect Karl Jaspers' conception of *chiffres* deserves renewed attention. See e.g. Jaspers, Karl, 1956. *Philosophie.* Berlin, Springer, part III passim; 1947,*Von der Wahrheit,* München, Piper, p. 108 ff., 632 ff., 1022 ff. etc.; and 1970, *Chiffren der Transzendenz.* München, Piper, München.

It is remarkable that Kant presents his interpretation of aesthetical judgements as the 'wahre Auslegung der Chiffernschrift,... wodurch die Natur in ihren schönen Formen figürlich zu uns spricht' (!) (true interpretation of chiffre-script,... through which Nature, in its beautiful forms figuratively speaks to us). *Kritik der Urteilskraft,* § 42, *op.cit.,* Bd. X, p. 398.

Chapter 18

THE TECHNOLOGICAL UNIVERSE

Pieter Tijmes

For Codine

1. SUMMARY AND INTRODUCTION

In this essay I shall consider two approaches to reality, following Jan Hendrik van den Berg: the quasi-phenomenological approach focusing on reality in its changeability, and the scientific approach focusing on reality in its unchangeable regularity. These two approaches result not only in different types of knowledge of reality but also in different types of behaviour. That is the reason why I prefer to speak of two different language games and forms of life (sections 2 & 3). The scientific language game has proved dominant in our culture (section 4). This dominant position is manifest in the way the twins, science and technology, have changed the face of society into a technological monopoly (section 5). Characteristic of this monopoly is its alliance with economics (section 6). This alliance of technological and economic activities constrains environmental policy so that it is unlikely to achieve its aim of the preservation of nature (section 7). Finally, I discuss the relation of the two language games to the environmental crisis (section 8). The point of this article is that many of the problems we are confronted with in the technological universe have their origin in the dominance of the scientific interaction with reality.

2. FIRST AND SECOND STRUCTURE

The Dutch psychiatrist Jan Hendrik van den Berg has formulated the so-called metabletic theory – popular with the general public judging from the considerable number of reprints and translations of his books, but bypassed and sometimes despised by the academic community. His metabletic theory focuses attention on discoveries – especially simultaneous discoveries – and tries to connect them into a coherent whole. He ultimately demonstrates why specific reformations and innovations in science, politics, arts, religion, etc. have taken place in a specific period of time – or, a little pedantically, not earlier and not later. Unfortunately his wild hunt for cross-references and his highly imaginative collages of synchronic phenomena have harmed his reputation. His arguments often sound too beautiful to be true. Nevertheless his books are a source of inspiration and critical reading of them is very fruitful.

In this essay I should like to discuss the phenomenologically inspired point of view articulated and worked out in his first book *Metabletica*. Here he makes a distinction between reality 'in its first and in its second structure'. Reality in its first structure can be known if the phenomena are approached with an open mind and if the context and the relationships of the phenomena are not disturbed. Reality in its first structure turns out to be malleable, flexible and changeable. It changes according to the mood of the observer. This mood, for example, may give the furniture in a room an angry look. Another mood may bathe it in a cheerful light. The pieces radiate reliability, intimacy, security, joy, happiness, etc. In other words, reality is 'willing', it is waiting for our intention. Dependent on our intention things have a different colour, a different size, a different face. This changeable appearance depends on our presence. When we look for mushrooms, we ask nature to show mushrooms and we do not see butterflies or insects. Conversely, when we hunt for butterflies, we miss the mushrooms. Thus reality continually displays itself in different appearances. The tree surgeon, the timber merchant, the burglar being chased, the boy who is fond of climbing, all approach the trees in the wood from a particular and selective viewpoint. Photographically a specific tree in the wood may have only one image, but for each of the four persons just mentioned it may look different: it may have different qualities.

The merit of phenomenological anthropology is to draw attention to the changeable aspect of reality. In a certain sense it was a reaction to the scientific approach to reality.[1] Science has to do with reality 'in its second structure'. It is not so much interested in the day-to-day realism where phenomena offer themselves, as in the constant and fixed qualities of things. The glory of science consists in the knowledge of laws. Its primary concern is not the capriciousness, but the fixedness of reality. In this respect quasi-phenomenology and science represent different language games, which do not necessarily contradict each other. People can participate in both language games alternately but not at the same time.

A few remarks on Van den Berg's position in the field of phenomenologists. It is undeniable that Van den Berg is a representative of the 'phenomenological movement' (Spiegelberg), but because of the way he speaks about reality in its first structure, he moves away from phenomenology and chooses his own direction. According to Van den Berg, the phenomenologist describes things as they *appear* to him. Being asked whether the described things actually exist in the described way, the phenomenologist will answer that such a question is not his concern. He has put the reality or non-reality of the phenomena in brackets. Van den Berg rejects this 'non-committal' attitude. According to him, the phenomenologist can tell nice stories without proclaiming whether they are true or not. Van den Berg then comes along with his so-called principle of reality: the phenomena are not deceptive appearances, but reality, reality in the first structure of day-to-day realism. This is an interesting principle, which of course does not authorize Van den Berg to proclaim in consequence that all the phenomena people are talking about should be adequate knowledge of reality in the first structure. In that case his choice is just as non-committal as that of his colleagues, the phenomenologists he is opposing. Here one must be able to decide whether it is a question of dreams, fantasies or adequate knowledge. When I take something that looks like a rabbit for a rabbit, I am mistaken. Thus speaking about reality in the first structure I cannot omit the words 'to be mistaken'. I use the term quasi-phenomenology to characterize Van den Berg's position. The examples illustrating the everyday language game are from different and not only from strictly phenomenological origins. I deliberately avoid his own term 'metabletical', because I am only using his theory to distinguish between the everyday and the scientific language game.

3. TAKING PART IN TWO REALITIES

There is a tension between the willing reality in the first structure and the constant reality in the second structure. In his four metabletical meditations, under the title of *Things*, Van den Berg juggles with the realities of the first and second structures in a very amusing way. In his first meditation he throws a wooden rail from the balcony into the garden. When it has reached the ground he sees that the rail has become smaller. From seeing this he concludes that the size of things changes when they move. Or more provocatively, that the material nature of things changes when they move. This does not compete with the fact that the rail *in its second structure* does not change. His story about the last five kilometres of a tiresome walking tour in Italy is very funny. These five kilometres were the longest he has ever walked.

> It looked as if the hundred metre bollards were set apart so that their distance exceeded the hundred metres and moreover progressively became still

longer. From then on I learned to say, that the distances were longer, in full reality. What is more real for knowing the distance than a walking tour? Thus in reality we knew how long the way from Lugano to Bellinzona was. Another ambience would result in another distance. The painful feet, the pressing backpack, the heat, the hunger, the thirst and the tiredness were the factors that made the distance long. Others factors might have shortened the distance. Specific factors are always involved. If a lot of conditions have been fulfilled, the road has a fixed length. In that case the walker is not allowed to be tired or exhausted, cheerful or worried, hungry or satisfied, lonely or accompanied by others. That is the case for nobody. The conclusion is that the road has a constant length, only if nobody walks along it. (p. 17)

As Van den Berg speaks about reality in its different structures, the underlying rules or principles of the respective language games are different. The ideal of knowledge is not the same in each case: in the scientific language game the aim is general valid knowledge, in the quasi-phenomenological game it is a question of concrete and specific knowledge of reality. The difference depends on the role of the subject in the process of acquiring knowledge. In the quasi-phenomenological view the subject is 'in the world' and cannot be detached from it. Subject and reality are coexistent. This relation between subject and reality may also be described by the term 'participation'. The subject is engaged in doing things. These things are waiting for his action and are clustered round the subject as a giver of meanings. When somebody enters his study, the desk is waiting for him to take his place, the ballpoint is sitting on the desk to be written with, the dictionary is ready to be consulted, etc. Contending that the subject knows himself to be separate from these objects and that he keeps them under control after objectifying them, is a rather artificial construction.

In the scientific view, on the other hand, an attempt is made to describe reality without taking notice of the role of the subject. The regularities, the laws, are valid regardless of the subject. Or, to quote Van den Berg: the subject is nobody. Taking into account the conditions under which the respective language games flourish, one is far from coming to the conclusion that the valid statements exclude each other.

Artists are the outstanding representatives of the quasi-phenomenological language game. Scientists pre-eminently speak the scientific language. Both enrich their languages with their articulations. The book *Things* can be regarded as a philosophical satire, taking into account that we – as artists or as scientists – speak both languages and are able to shift quickly from the one into the other. The interpretations generated within these two games inevitably lead to conflicts, especially when one set of interpretations is presented as the standard of universal validity. Nobody will venture to claim that articulations of reality by a 'poet' and a 'scientist' are in contradiction. They are incommensurable.

Van den Berg's distinction between the reality in the first and in the second structure and their reciprocal relation is not a generally accepted point of view. Normally, it is asserted that reality *as such* is unchangeably fixed, but that it is subjectively coloured and transformed into the so-called 'reality of the first structure'. According to this view the scientific approach tells how reality actually is, and delivers the material of nobody as a starting point for colouring and distorting by the subject. In other words: reality as such has no sunny, gloomy or depressive manifestation, but people can be sunny, gloomy or depressive so that reality may be coloured by their moods. They project their moods on reality, but they do not observe reality in its specific manifestation. In my opinion, however, this explanation of 'changeable reality in the first structure' on the basis of the projection-theory has many difficulties, whereas Van den Berg's phenomenological explanation is more elegant and spiritual.[2]

4. OUR CULTURAL PREFERENCES

In modernity the scientific language game has gained ground at the expense of the quasi-phenomenological game. Knowledge is for the greater part knowledge of reality in the second structure. This knowledge is objective and an aura of rationality has been attributed to it. The knowledge of the quasi-phenomenological source has been deprecated as subjective or even irrational. One glance at the curriculum of schoolchildren is enough to recognize the cultural preference for the scientific language game. From their childhood on people are trained to objectify, to manipulate and to influence the world. Of course education is necessary to accommodate children to their technological environment so that they can make their own way. In this context the Dutch anthropologist Van Baal speaks of the most refined training of the mind to which children have ever been exposed in the history of civilization. The two language games have turned out to be in a permanent political and social struggle, in which knowledge of reality in the second structure actually represents the higher value. Theoretically both language games can assert their own rights, but in fact the scientific language has driven out the other.[3]

For the history of science it is of the utmost importance that on the threshold of modernity scientists and craftsmen have found each other as partners. The result of this alliance is that science and technology in their contemporary state presuppose each other. One needs the other, with the result that they are interdependent. Now, science and technology aim at controlling and manipulating the world. Under modern conditions knowledge of reality in its second structure has become the higher value, and is sought because of its social and political benefit. Consequently science and technology have been manoeuvred into the dominant position of the colonizing life form. The implication is that modern people also have changed, especially in their attitude towards each other and towards things, and it is difficult for them to understand that another way of dealing with reality is possible. They look, for example, at traditional societies as *underdeveloped* or *developing* societies.

5. Utopia as Technological Universe

The beginning of technology might be interpreted in an instrumental-anthropological way. According to this interpretation, technical instruments are extensions of the human body.[4] They are used in order to replace, reinforce, or unburden human organs. A spade, an axe, an arrow are examples of the human necessity to compensate for organic 'deficiency' (Gehlen). In this sense technology is a universal cultural phenomenon. The impact of modern technological artifacts, however, – products, processes, procedures – cannot be investigated if these artifacts are interpreted as extensions of the human body. The main concern of the modern engineer or technologist is neither to replace, nor to reinforce, nor to unburden a leg, an ear or a nose. It is also one-sided to claim that the engineer meets the people's needs. Equally valid is the claim that he creates fulfilments that still have to arouse needs. Often the existing ensemble of technological products, processes and procedures is the starting point for new technological designs. The technological ensemble thus generates new problems and new challenges. When the challenges have been accepted and the problems solved, new problems and new challenges will appear by combining other elements of the technological ensemble. An end to this process is not in the foreseeable future. Technology does not aim at perfect mediation between needs and possibilities. The dynamics of technology has no fixed reference point, either in human aims and ambitions or in self-evident possibilities recognizable to humans. On the contrary, technological development reveals the flexibility, the unnaturalness and the artificiality of human aspirations and desires.[5]

Modern science and technology not only explore and manipulate the world, but also create, maybe inadvertently, a new world. The practical consequence is that humanity has exchanged dependency upon the natural environment for dependency upon the technological environment. We hardly have a relationship with the realities and elements of the natural environment any more, but have surrounded ourselves with instruments and artificial objects belonging to our technological environment. Our chances and possibilities of survival are now determined by our access to these artefacts. In short, we live in a technological universe, where the language of the modern *Homo faber* is spoken: the *Homo technologicus* who observes as the scientist, but has the designing attitude of the engineer, who creates, conserves and maintains.

In this universe, knowledge resulting from perception of reality in the second structure has acquired the sole exhibition rights. The structure of scientific and technological reality is known, if the fixed qualities of that reality are known. These constants are valid regardless of the subject and they are not tied to a specific place or time. On the other hand, according to Merleau-Ponty, the human body is an *a priori* for knowledge of reality in the first structure. The consistency of the perception with the human body has been eliminated in the knowledge of reality in the second structure. In the *experienced* space (first structure) we talk of 'here and there', 'near and far away', 'left and right', 'present and absent', etc. In the *constructed* space (second structure) all points are equal. This space is only a 'form', in which all spatial configurations can be described. The technological world, designed and organized on the basis of this knowledge, tends to be a placeless world, or at least unrelated to a specific place: a utopia in the etymological meaning of the word. It tends to be also unrelated to a specific time: uchronic, so to say. This technological environment has by definition not been tailored to concrete individuals, because its building blocks – the knowledge components of reality in its second structure – *originally* lack this arrangement.

It is unpredictable what new products will be on the market within seven years. The reason lies in the fascinating fact that technological artefacts are often designed on the basis of possibilities which are generated technologically. This hectic development has not been integrated in the framework of people's lives and culture, but is a culture of its own. What is possible must be tried out. In this case people have to accommodate to the 'blessings' of the technological universe. Of course one can also reverse the process: adjust the products to the people. Thanks to the nature of the scientific and technological language game we can at least understand why this latter policy – adjusting the products to the people – is not always self-evident. In short, the knowledge of reality in its second structure is subjectless, bodyless, utopian and uchronic.

The universal validity of such knowledge of reality makes it quite absurd to talk about German physics or Japanese technology. Technological artefacts are not tied to nationalities, they are of course transnational. They can flourish anywhere, on the condition that one agrees to distance oneself in a certain sense from one's own cultural past. In this respect the planetary technological culture is universal, whereas the world of technique prior to the eighteenth century was local.[6] An interesting paradox is that on the one hand this new culture undoubtedly enhances human possibilities, but that on the other hand all these possibilities go in the same direction, precluding others. Technological pluralism means that cultural plurality is reduced to uniformity. In modern architecture of new estates or houses, of hospitals, air-ports or hotels all over the world, the differences are only marginal. 'Local colour' is a phenomenon of the past. Taken with a pinch of salt, the Hilton Hotel and the Holiday Inn are the symbols of planetary *uniformity* of culture. That Rousseau in his *Emile* made similar complaints may be seen as a corroboration as well as an undermining of the correctness of the observation. The cars, the ships, etc. of different makes and nationalities may be an additional example of the tendency to uniformity, which is not anticipated by Rousseau.

This modern culture presupposes particular human relationships and forms of life, opposed to the traditional way of living. Anyone who can breathe the modern air is open to technological progress, the supposed 'guarantor' of prosperity, welfare and happiness. The development paving the way for it is often propagated by those who know that embracing technology is embracing a foreign culture. The route of western modernization has to be travelled by the developing countries at increasing speed, neglecting the costs of modernity.

To catch sight of the characteristic traits of the technological universe one must try to look at it with the eyes of someone belonging to a non-modern culture. Denying moderation and frontiers is one of the most characteristic features of this universe. As already mentioned, science and technology possess a power to reshape reality. On the one hand they transform reality and on the other they implement new customs appropriate to the transformed situation. This universe imposes a new uniform interpretation of, and a compelling interaction with, the newly created reality. In the technological universe it is a matter not only of new artefacts, but also of new relationships between people. This ambience stimulates people to still more abstract, audacious and bold ventures. Most spectacular are the technological manipulations of what is most private and personal, the human body. Without any doubt people today look differently at their bodies. A statement from a Dutch newspaper:

Hans Peters himself remains fairly cool about it, but what occurred to him sounds spectacular: he has the heart of a woman who is still alive, as far as he knows... The fact that he has got the heart of another human being still alive, has no special meaning for him.

The woman in question has had a lung transplant. In order to increase the chance of success she has also received a new heart, so that her own heart could be passed on. Thus human organs show the tendency to circulate as capital on the markets. This universe is one of unlimited possibilities. Most obvious is that this culture does not accept limits for scientific manipulation and exploration. Limits are seen as challenges, and challenges are to be met and overcome. Technological possibilities are to be explored and tried out. In the light of our essay it speaks for itself, because in the scientific and technological approach nature has been deliberately stripped of cultural meanings. Nature has been neutralized. Nature, the human body included, has been made disinterested, indifferent, immune, by the scientific approach and technological manipulation. This homogenizing is the quintessence of the technological approach.

6. THE ALLIANCE OF SCIENCE WITH ECONOMICS

Economic interaction with reality has many points in common with scientific and technological intervention in reality. The modern economy also alienates goods from their cultural meaning. They are homogenized in an economic sense: when goods are brought to the market, they are transformed into commodities. The traditional dwelling place of a family is transformed into property to be sold on the market. The traditional attachment to the *patrimonium* has more or less evaporated. Rendering services has been economized and is paid for. Even in families, money has become a means to co-ordinate the action of children; they are rewarded with a dime for doing the shopping. On the market people offer their working power. The reduction of people to labourers (wanted or superfluous) on the market leads and has led to much social misery. This recognition that the most inhuman exploitation is possible within an economic society does not necessarily lead to the glorification of a non-economic or traditional society. It is a fact however that in feudal relationships poverty was softened, because the lord was responsible for his subordinates. So of course the conservative powers not only resisted science and technology, but also modern economic ideas. They understood quite well what was at stake in their world. The promotion of economic activities in the sixteenth and seventeenth century in Western Europe did not respect the limits, the frontiers, and the privileges characteristic of these times. The circulation of commodities, labour and capital can flourish only in an unambiguous, uniform, limitless world.

Technology and the economy are closely related with each other in the technological universe. Technological products, processes and procedures have to make a contribution to economic circulation. What cannot be absorbed in it will have less opportunity to be developed. Aid for the handicapped will not be developed until they have purchasing power. This special modern condition of the production process is often regarded as an advantage, when one states that market mechanisms give us the best information about scarcity relations and provide us with incentives to save costs in production methods.[7]

The technological universe becomes increasingly less flexible and mobile in a new sense. People become more and more dependent on the corset of technological artefacts. A selective use of the assortment of artefacts and facilities is often not possible, because they are interdependent. Anyone who wants to move in this universe needs its means of transport, of communication, etc. Moreover these are so comfortable that they easily cause habituation or even addiction.

The technological universe is not only people's artefacts; behaviour has also been technologically regulated. The educational system at Dutch universities dances attendance on education technology. This technology will be introduced with the argument that nowadays the transfer of knowledge is not effective enough and too expensive. Education has become business. Management techniques keep the communication in factories and companies smooth and fluent. There is a conviction that these investments are rewarding. On the other hand Illich has made the point that the application of technological means is often counterproductive. The more communication techniques march forward, the more people forget how to talk to each other: doctors cannot talk any more to their patients, husbands to their wives, children to their parents. In other words, the concentration of professional competence contributes to the patronizing of ordinary people. During a press conference Mr Van Gent, a released hostage from Iraq, said, 'I felt fine in Iraq, I did a lot of things. This lasted until we heard the messages of psychologists from Holland saying that you could come out of it depressed. Then I got worried.' If the USA is a technological trendsetter, then the juridification of human relationships will be the next rib to strengthen the technological corset. It then won't be possible any more to take a step without a juridical recommendation.

7. THE ENVIRONMENT IN THE TECHNOLOGICAL UNIVERSE

The technological universe is threatened by different crises. One of them is the crisis of the environment. Without any doubt science and technology play an important role in this crisis. It does not go without saying that they can overcome this crisis. However, we have nothing better than science and technology to meet these problems. Probably we cannot manage our problems either with or without science and technology.

It is a constituent of this crisis that in the technological universe the 'natural' environment has been controlled, dominated and sometimes pushed aside, if not eliminated. People who live in a city have hardly any access to this 'natural' reality. When they look for it as tourists, they will be disappointed even in the countryside, which owing to 'advanced' agriculture has become monotonous. They smell sulphur when passing along the vineyard, ammonia when going for a walk along the meadow or maize field. The farmer has also become a chemical engineer.

Of course the environmental crisis is also regarded as an interesting challenge. The challenge of improving the deplorable results of the construction of *Homo technologicus* is eagerly accepted. We all know the outcome: a price tag is fixed on cleaner water, on cleaner air, on the preservation of the forests, etc. The conviction that everything can be arranged with money prevails here as everywhere. People have to make up their minds which more expensive construction they want and what they would like to give up in exchange for it. These solutions have their limits exposed by the relative impotence of the democratic decision-making process to achieve radical reforms, because citizens do not know what they are willing to abandon out of the package of goods and services they have got. Every group has its own specific interests, which can be very divergent, so that in the end we prefer to live on in the same style.

For example, the problem of waste is probably not merely incidental, but has structural dimensions. It continues to go from bad to worse. The *Homo technologicus* 'in us' does not believe that waste is inevitable. But the most audacious problem solver must admit that there is no solution, if our way of living in the West is going to expand all over the world. Does that mean that the problem of waste is proving structural? In that case we have to use harsher means in order to avert a calamity: not only another way of producing, but also another way of consuming, for producer and consumer are accomplices. As consumers we shall have to ask what conveniences we are willing to give up, which limits we are willing to accept. Speaking of 'harsher means' turns out to be rather pointless because of the intricacy of the problem. What we take for granted, our attitude, our relation to things around us, our relationships with other people, our way of posing questions and of looking for solutions, our endless ambitions and desires, all this needs to be discussed.

In the meantime, we understand that the flag of the environment will not be hoisted to the top tomorrow. Does the quasi-phenomenological approach to nature show a way out? It is in my opinion clear that quasi-phenomenology and technology are not alternative approaches to nature. Without technology I cannot even begin to think of a solution. Is there no solution either without quasi-phenomenology? To answer this question conclusively seems rather difficult, because we have got used to handling our problems in a technological way.

8. The Coherence of the Games

Van den Berg places the quasi-phenomenological and the scientific approach unrelatedly next to each other, without even mentioning his preference. It looks as if he wants to say that he likes 'poetry' as well as 'science' and that he appreciates both. Of course poetry stands for much that has been driven out of the technological universe, for example the enigmatic character of reality, the experience of its changeability, the possibility of wonder, the meeting of reality as a mystery, trust and faith as existential categories, etc. This two way policy of Van den Berg's is wise, because people suffer damage to their souls and their environment, if they cannot live in both language games and life forms.

So, merely opposing these human possibilities or even playing them off against each other is not quite sufficient. In its origin the scientific approach is a special case of the day-to-day approach. Daily experience is the starting point of all thought constructions, and this goes for science too. The scientific thought construction has been so extensively modelled that the experience of any actual individual has been filtered out. It has become the experience of nobody, as Van den Berg says. Curiously enough this experience, and in the wake of it this knowledge of reality which is focused on the constants and valid statements of everybody, are considered as being the most original. This is wrong. They are secondary, as I hope I have shown above in the section on 'utopia as technological universe'. In the technological universe, nature is articulated through different concepts of nature (physical, biological, etc.). The quasi-phenomenological experience keeps on reminding us that nature is something different from the object of the *metier* of the scientist or the engineer. In such experience, it is not prescribed what nature will be. In this experience nature is allowed to speak as a whole for itself.

Nevertheless modesty is appropriate for quasi-phenomenology. It cannot claim that it observes nature in its originality, or that it contains the standard measure for nature. Nor does the quasi-phenomenological approach have access to the finished creation on the 'seventh day'. Everywhere we meet human modelling of nature, except on the coral islands of Australia, as Marx said. In speaking of nature the assumption is often made that nature was born and developed without the agency of mankind. What original form of nature are we thinking of? Nature has always been mediated by culture. Recognition of this makes the plea for an authentic relation to nature rather unwarranted, the more so when we realize that technology is also a cultural achievement.

Moreover, the language game of the quasi-phenomenological approach has without doubt been influenced by the scientific language game. Not only has nature been transformed, but so has our day-to-day experience. Scientific meanings have installed themselves in the quasi-phenomenological language. This too is a form of cultural mediation. An intensive training is necessary to be able to observe scientifically, because we were not born with that talent. It is only with difficulty that we can distance ourselves from what we have learned to accept in a particular way. A person who stands at the coastline, remarks from the look of the ships on the horizon that the earth is round. It is remarkable that it took a very long time before we could map our organs under the skin, although our ancestors also had eyes to see. Indeed, they had eyes, but they did not always see what we see now, and it is interesting to investigate why.

It is obvious that the examples of quasi-phenomenological perception mostly refer to interaction with the natural environment, but the same perception and attitude can be assumed with regard to the technological universe. Can that technological environment also change through the quasi-phenomenological outlook, in the same way as the natural environment does? In literature there are only a few examples. One can think of the Dutch poet Gerrit Achterberg, who uses many scientific expressions in his poetic world. Probably the technological universe is less expressive and its plasticity is relatively less, because technological artefacts have their fixed script. That means that the artefact comes provided with a nearly compulsory interpretation. We have to learn to drive a car and it is not the other way round. Humanity has created the technological environment and has at the same time established the rules and regulations how to deal with it. That may be the reason why technological artefacts do not frequently occur in poems.

The technologizing process of the experience of nature is progressing. Without doubt the quasi-phenomenological relation, in which nature comes to speak for herself, has been moved to a marginal place in modern society. That does not mean there is no influence of quasi-phenomenology. In the first place the scientific experience presupposes the other experience. Secondly, the criticism of technological manipulation springs from everyday experience. Its voice is low, but does not give up speaking. The influence of the quasi-phenomenological experience on technology will probably not result in an internal scientific revolution. The internal business of science and technology can be considered as a grandiose human achievement. Its influence appears on another level. The broadly perceived insight into the destruction of nature imminent if we continue to produce and consume in the same manner is an example. If we cannot assume that we will have another science and technology which will outdate the prevailing science and technology, then we have to make serious efforts to limit the expansionist technological universe with regard to a human world. Culture has always set limits. This cultural task of limiting measureless technology and economics must be fulfilled in a new way, because the frontiers and limits are to be appropriated from what has been driven out of the technological universe.

NOTES

1. Phenomenology represents a philosophical tradition of not being afraid to be tricked, either in the field of knowledge, or in the field of acting. Since Descartes, Kant, etc. western philosophy does not trust its own observation any more. Scheler holds the conviction that in these philosophies there is a question of puritan-protestant attitude of distrust-in-principle. Cf. his remark on 'die puritanisch-protestantische Haltung des prinzipiellen Misztrauens'. In Scheler, M., 1927. *Der Formalismus in der Ethik und die materiale Wertethik*, p.63.
2. A detailed argument for and against the projection theory is beyond our scope. (*The Phenomenological Approach to Psychiatry*, J.H. van den Berg.) The projection theory of course stands 'in the tradition of distrust', to quote Scheler.
3. This development of modern behaviour, sticking to the scientific language game at the expense of the religious language game, has often been described as the story of secularization.
4. This idea was first articulated by the German philosopher Ernst Kapp (1808-1896), where he speaks of technology as 'Organprojektion' in his book *Grundlinien einer Philosophie der Technik*. (Published in 1877. Reprinted, Düsseldorf: Stern-Verlag Janssen, 1978).
5. Gruppelaar, 1988.

6. See also Ellul, 1967.

7. This way of reasoning is not untainted with ideology, because the state has always intervened with success in different sectors (defence, education, etc.) in order to prevent the workings of the market. Some years ago the result was the general and internationally accepted complaint, that the state was overburdened, on the one hand because the package of demands of society was heavy and excessive, and on the other hand because the state wanted to regulate too much. Thus increase of state involvement runs up against structural (financial) limits, so that a strong plea was made for the state's stepping back and a rehabilitation of the market mechanism.

REFERENCES

Van den Berg, Jan Hendrik, 1955. *The phenomenological Approach to Psychiatry.* Springfield, Charles Thomas.

an den Berg, Jan Hendrik, 1983.*The changing nature of man: introduction to historical psychology.* New York, Dell Publishing Co.

Van den Berg, Jan Hendrik. 1970. *Things: four metabletic reflections.* Pittsburgh, Duquesne University Press.

Van den Berg, Jan Hendrik, 1974. *Divided Existence and complex society: an historic approach.* Pittsburgh, Duquesne University Press.

Ellul, Jacques, 1967. *The Technological Society.* New York, Alfred A. Knopf.

Gehlen, Arnold, 1963. *Die Seele im Technischen Zeitalter.* Hamburg, Rowohlt.

Grupelaar, J. 1988. *Perfektie heeft een toekomst, een verkennende studie over cultuur en techniek.* I.V.A.

Merleau Ponty, M., 1948. *La Fénomenologie de la perception.*Paris, Gallimard.

Scheler, Max, 1927. *Der Formalismus in der Ethik und die materiale Wertethik.* Halle, Niemeyer.

Chapter 19

The Ethical Assessment of New Technologies: Some Methodological Considerations

Medard Hilhorst

Technological developments have to be understood and valued from within. I mean by this that developments always take place inside a specific framework: a hospital, present-day society, or state of the art technology. Within this framework one must try to balance different options. In what follows, I will demonstrate how a limited, moral reflection on the dynamics of technological developments can be usefully performed. The main task turns out to be the justification of those options which will have harmful effects.

1. A Philosophical Framework for Technology

There are two determining characteristics for the framework which I propose as a starting point. Taken together they do not form a complete philosophy of technology, but we do not need this for the sort of ethical reflection I am aiming at.

The first characteristic is the infinite nature of even our fundamental needs. This idea originates with David Braybrooke, who shows that our material requirements are infinite if fundamental needs are defined as 'necessary in order to function without disorders'. In this case one must allow for many medical claims to high quality medical care. The second characteristic is an idea put forward by Etienne Vermeersch amongst others, that human beings have shown 'a dual dynamics' from the very beginning: that is, an uninterrupted improvement of techniques and a progressive expansion to new fields.

Both characteristics give insight into technology as a dynamic human activity which is not neutral but purposeful. It is aimed at the fulfilment of probably infinite human needs and it is not foreign to people, but is characteristic of human nature and development.

2. ETHICS AND ITS TASK

Taking this framework as the starting point for ethical reflection, I suggest that it is somewhat forced upon us in our culture and that ethical reflection cannot easily extract itself from its grip. I do not claim that a culture can view technology in any other way, or that no other cultures except our own are possible. But nor can I swallow it just like that. Not all dynamics and not all bottomless needs are morally acceptable. Not all goals are good and sometimes the option of doing nothing is better than any other options.

I do believe that it is not effective or appropriate to deny people's needs and their dynamic striving toward fulfilment (which some would call 'progress'). It is not so much the denial but the testing and evaluation of it, on the basis of what is seen as humane, just and good, to which we should pay attention. To put it another way: both characteristics of technology depict human beings as active and aspiring. I cannot think of any moral arguments to reject such an initial description of a normative image of humanity from the very start, even though other characteristics may also be conceivable. By stepping into this framework I believe that I have taken a fruitful step, even though it is not the only possible one. The move I propose has been described here but has not been justified. Finally I would apply an adage: 'the proof of the pudding is in the eating'. My intention is to help ethical methodology and analysis a little bit further.

At this point, the task of ethics should be described. I do not believe that it is the task of ethics to propose an alternative normative image of man. In doing so one can too easily avoid the framework which is making itself plain in our society. The dynamic striving for the fulfilment of needs unavoidably leads to conflicts between people and parties. Behind these conflicts lies the struggle over values and interests. The task of ethics here is to see how interests and values can be distinguished, and to see what it means to give everyone his or her share, and own rightful place. In the case of environmental ethics one must particularly think about a just place for nature and the environment. As far as ethics is concerned there are two central questions: Where do people cause suffering or harm to themselves? and, Where do people behave at the cost of the interests of other people, nature and the environment or future generations?

3. The Framework is Tested

How is technology related to the environment? There is a twofold answer to this. Even though on the one hand technical processes and the consumption of manufactured products have a large and negative effect on the environment, on the other hand 'clean' technology is used to develop a better environment. However it is impossible to maintain this ambivalent answer in our culture as a whole. Without a doubt our society places too great a claim on the carrying capacity of its natural surroundings. Only just beginning to sink in is the real scale of that claim: (a) globally in a spatial context, (b) far-reaching and perhaps irreversible in time, and (c) unequalled in speed.

It is apparent that our society has undergone critical changes which have led to an environmental crisis. We can now ask the question, whether these changes can be characterized and typified in moral terms. In what circumstances can we talk of caused damage or harm and of wrong behaviour? It is impossible to avoid stepping into a philosophical framework here either. People who have a biocentric view of life and consider all life to be equal will take human dominion and use of nature and of the environment very seriously. Only what people really need is supposed to do no harm and only that will pass the moral test. In this view, human desires are interpreted through their biological meaning as much as possible. Such an interpretation uses a normative image of humanity as embedded in its natural surroundings and as one among many species. Dynamics is barely mentioned, since a person can (must) be satisfied with a limited (that is, appropriate) area to live in.

As a result of the environmental crisis, the framework I used as a starting point is being tested, and alternative, normative, images of humanity are coming to the fore. The need for a more explicit, justified place for nature and the environment, has a central position in the environmental philosophical debate on anthropocentrism and its interpretation and limits. The human self-image will undoubtedly change with respect to nature and the environment, and this will lead to a different interpretation of the present, dominant normative image.

I believe that ethical analysis does not need to wait for the outcome, and neither is it necessary to use a totally different framework and alternative image of humanity as the starting point. One can remain close to what is current in our culture without the analysis becoming unusable. Even though we generally think anthropocentrically about nature and the environment, in terms of their value for people, this does not necessarily imply crude utilitarianism. The natural environment is seldom seen purely in terms of raw material and its usefulness to humanity. This in turn means that that sort of use is no longer permissible in itself and can no longer be accepted without moral justification. The value of nature and the environment is being recognized more forcefully by connecting it with people in ethical, scientific or recreational terms etc., or with the larger circle of future people, which underlines the value of diversity of species and the conservation of a complete, livable environment. Sometimes the value of an animal, nature or ecosystem in itself is advocated. From a moral point of view, this broader perspective does not necessarily mean the introduction of a totally different image of humanity, but it does mean the obligation to search for moral justification for each far-reaching intervention in nature.

In general one can say that critical and decisive changes take place when nature and the environment are reduced to nothing but raw materials, to be used only for human benefit, when there is no moral sensitivity about species, ecosystems and variation, when future living situations are not taken into account from a moral point of view, and when the surroundings can no longer be experienced in their 'being' as such. To put that in terms of an image of humanity: changes are exceeded when a person is seen purely as an active and goal-orientated being, and when he places himself as the only goal opposed to his surroundings. Firstly, a human being is more than an agent or actor and secondly, he does not exist in isolation.

4. ETHICAL ANALYSIS

Any ethical analysis will have to examine carefully where changes are excessive, according to the present moral intuitions. I shall briefly attempt to do so, to indicate what sort of questions, dilemmas and considerations, humanity is confronted with.

In our society, many products, and the infrastructure related to them, generate great interest: luxury articles, disposable products, IVF (test-tube) techniques, new cancer therapies, the fax and personal computer, holidays by plane and winter sports, direct information about the Gulf War or international conferences. Moral questions can develop along one of two courses, and either refer to ourselves or to others. First, do we attack our own humanity, via this technology? In what respect do we damage ourselves, or in other words, have we really become happier and progressed? Is it possible the goal we have been pursuing has become more one-sided and one-dimensional and has our culture become flatter? In this case we will have estimated the costs and benefits wrongly. Secondly, at the cost of whom and what has this pursuit been carried out? It is possible that the effects on others have not been taken into account, that costs and benefits have not been fairly divided and that some parties are damaged. Ethical analysis, in which the principles of doing no harm and doing justice must provide help, appears to give priority to harmful effects. What does an ethical cost-benefit analysis look like?

5. ANALYSIS 1: BALANCING PERSONAL VALUES

The first question relates to the harm which we most probably cause to ourselves. In a personal consideration of technological developments, objective and subjective aspects appear to play a role, which means that there is no clear image of what is at stake. Studies indicate people's concern about certain technologies, such as biotechnology and arms technology, and their concern for a society which is most probably becoming less personal; however at the same time there is optimism about what technologies can do in the environmental field.

Nicholas Rescher asks whether a person has become 'so much happier' because of it? Using an American study lasting forty to fifty years, he indicates how personal assessment works.

a. People admire the 'progress' of some aspects of their own, limited surroundings. It is valued that negative things, such as poverty, illness and unsafeness have been reduced by production processes, housing, hygiene and medical progress. The result of this has been to shed a lot of physical pain and suffering. (The fact that negative effects can occur elsewhere will be discussed later on).

b. At the same time it appears that people do not at present feel subjectively happier, more free of worries and better in comparison with the past, despite an objectively improved physical situation and a higher standard of living. A negative correlation between 'progress' and happiness appears to exist. Furthermore it is possible to back this statement with objective information: compared with the past, the percentage of suicides has remained the same, but psychiatric help and admission have increased sharply. Apparently certain vulnerable groups are less capable of coping in this society.

c. When asked if one would rather have lived in the past, in the 'good old days', the majority of people paradoxically express their preference for today. This appreciation is understandable if one realizes that happiness and contentedness are subjective categories. We think, 'I should be satisfied with my present situation, compared with others in their previous situation, but I do not actually feel this.' The most obvious explanation is that people do not employ a fixed, objective criterion which applies to both today and the past, such as physical protection or living standards, but that people continually derive their standards according to the time they live in. The standard for happiness shifts along with this. We see that – using present day possibilities – things can still be done very differently and much better. Apparently we shift standards and aspirations as a matter of course, and they are adapted according to the perspectives of the age. We make projections towards a better future. We are unsatisfied because we still have not achieved what we wanted to achieve: 'We are in the midst of a revolution of rising expectations.'

d. It is naturally possible to interpret this dissatisfaction as a never finished, sick culture of unsatisfiable narcissism, which is tied up in itself and which damages people. In this interpretation, needs are false and expectations are ungrounded and self-defeating. However it is also possible to see dissatisfaction and impatience as yearning for freedom, emancipation, justice and true happiness. Does a moral argument exist which could exclude this second interpretation? High expectations which are not fulfilled when they are realized lead to unhappiness. This may be due to expectations, but may just as easily be due to what 'is' and should not be like that. Progress does not exist in an automatic sense, solid and general, but it is possible in a limited, local sense, and in this case it may even be seen as a moral obligation. For example, someone who begins the exploration of a personal computer sees it as an option, tries it out, curses it regularly and finally establishes that he 'could not do without it any more'. Others have dumped their darkroom equipment by the rest of their rubbish, to be collected by the dustbin man. Apparently this is how the exploration goes. Perhaps the actual question is whether we cannot waste less.

e. In summary: 'the' human measure is not fixed. In this sense one can speak of measurelessness. Technology will not automatically lead us into the blessings of the twentyfirst century, but one does not want to leave untouched the possibilities it promises. People want to move on, rather than go back to the past, and no fixed scale of values can assist them. The dynamics of development would then become a search for humanity and for what determines a good life. We know that things may be better tomorrow. Science and technology form a necessary if not sufficient precondition for happiness.

Without moral arguments which concentrate on the harmful effects that occur along with the dynamics, it is not possible to resist this development forward.

6. ANALYSIS 2: BALANCING SOCIAL VALUES

The social consideration of the side effects which accompany each new technology is a tricky one. It is possible to differentiate between two sorts of consideration. The one is related to values, the other to people. The latter consideration will be discussed in the following section. The following dilemma is linked to values:

a. Many negative side effects are inherent in technology, that is, they are inextricably linked to a new technology. In general, new options are created within society because of technology. However at the same time, other existing options including their positive values are cut off. Thus in warm countries where asphalt has been laid, it is no longer possible to walk on bare feet; where the clock has been introduced to fix precise times for appointments, it is no longer possible to cope without a watch; and where money is being replaced by electronic or plastic cards, people can no longer do without an ID card. 'Not being able to do without' means that there is a social necessity to acquire whatever is necessary to function properly. Social choices related to technology become socially fixed and lay down a certain pattern of living which no-one can avoid. Such choices lead to dependence and cannot be undone. One cannot rectify the situation which has been imposed, or distance oneself from it, just like that. To a certain extent one has to comply with it, be swallowed up by it and be controlled by it. There is generally no simple way back as far as such developments are concerned.

b. On a social level we are therefore continually confronted with complicated considerations. We know – in as far as we can review this – that all sorts of things which we has valued are lost: sensitivity to the natural environment, personal freedom, small-scale structures and perspectives, clarity and human contact. We must then compare these with those options and values which can be won: a higher standard of living, more opportunities for recreation, greater social security or longer good health. These other, often dissimilar values, make comparison difficult and the result will not be a matter of course. Sometimes the situation seems even more complicated and one can almost speak of a paradox. Even though people are capable of freeing themselves of existing dependence by means of technologies, they seem to be willing to give this freedom up again for new dependence and lack of freedom. A certain abstractness and generality which is inherent in science and technology, can lead to people who experience society as having become stale and alienated, even while recognizing what has been won.

c. A global, unequivocal, ethical, judgement is obviously not possible. The study mentioned above (see note 4) indicates that people are concerned that a society which becomes increasingly marked by technology, also becomes increasing more impersonal. In the context of environmental issues and the concern for future generations, it is sometimes said that it is not unthinkable that for us – for the first time in history – the following generation may be worse off than this generation. One can think of limited welfare or less good natural living conditions, but also of limited freedom or increasing inequality. Such warnings do not gain moral weight and the force of argument until empirical data is available to act as backing. This is because people rapidly choose new options and are satisfied with compensating measures ('flanking' policy) which may soften negative effects: extra pay or free time, a lower price or an automatic answering machine which kills the time one has to wait with music.

d. It is true that society does not merely pursue new options without looking at the consequences. However the inclination to try out new projects and let them weigh more heavily is powerful when it is not plausible that the leaving behind of old options or the embracing of new options is really harmful. For that matter, the advantages of new developments are often less well known and therefore seem less important if an ethical assessment is involved. The pursuit of the fulfilment of new desires can be lessened by specific questions about what can be achieved: greater welfare, more freedom, a higher quality of life? If this is not clear, and this is often the case, then the harm linked to this pursuit often weighs more heavily. Seen from an moral viewpoint, the principle of avoiding harm or suffering is most important here. This can also be seen in the following analysis.

7. ANALYSIS 3: WHAT RIGHT DO WE HAVE TO LIVE AT THE COST OF FUTURE PEOPLE?

In the environmental crisis, damage is evidently a byproduct of our production methods and modes of life. I plead in favour of a description as precise as possible, which is often all too easily set aside. The moral burden of proof should lie with those who cause the damage. Minister Ed Nijpels (former Dutch minister for the environment) once mentioned this in connection with car use: anyone who drives pollutes and causes harm to others. What right does any individual have to do so? He should provide reasons for it. Are the benefits comparable with the costs? Who is benefited by it and who bears the cost? Is there no better alternative?

'All things considered' says the politician, to motivate his choice for three tunnels, a Gulf War or a power station, but what precisely has he considered? It is of great importance that a war or an energy policy are also considered from a moral point of view. Elsewhere I have demonstrated, taking radioactive waste from nuclear power as an example, that a moral evaluation of public policy concentrating on harmful effects can avoid the discussion becoming unnecessarily broad. A Dutch report on energy policy hides behind broad vagueness when it says:

> In the energy debate it sometimes appears as if participants have totally different values and norms. The debate then becomes a dispute between convictions about life and patterns of values which are more or less unbridgeable... Everyone believes that society has some responsibility for the welfare and well-being of future generations. The [i.e. our] welfare is in conflict with the environment and the safety of future generations here [i.e. in the discussion being held]. A different level of confidence in technology will be decisive.

In this case public policy withdraws from rational discussion, and custom and power rapidly beat moral arguments. In my view the quote finishes at the point where ethics should start. The job of the ethicist is to come up with much more precise argumentation: which considerations, confidence, values, parties and interests are actually involved? Nature and future generations especially, which have no voice, would benefit from this. The much more narrow discussion which I conducted, led to the following conclusions:

a. Radioactive waste constitutes a long term burden for future people with the special characteristic that it has a long existence, it is irreversible and linked with cumulative risks. This is why the moral burden of proof is to justify that its production rests with this generation.

b. This burden is too easily ignored, or one believes wrongly that future people can be compensated for it. The burden's characteristic makes it difficult to compare with other, everyday risks. The (positive) compensation of 'buying off' future people's disadvantage with, for example, money, energy or culture is morally difficult to justify, because the burden of nuclear waste is concerned with values such as safety and health. The argument for negative compensation, namely that future generations would be worse off if we continue to burn fossil fuels and hence burden them with the greenhouse effect, ignores the fact that in both alternatives totally *different* generations would be harmed by us. In fact different costs and benefits are being confused with one another. Furthermore the argument presumes that we can sacrifice far off future generations for the benefit of generations in the near future. What right do we have to play this game of 'gambling with futures'?

c. There is only a small way left to justify the waste. The present generation should make it plausible that it has no other alternatives except for those which would harm itself. Then we must appeal to a sort of 'moral nuke': without nuclear energy the light would be switched off and our culture would collapse. This clearly indicates how weak this position is. Less energy production, and hence less luxurious use of energy would not harm us, but would at the most give us less advantages. Pure disadvantages to future generations should weigh more heavily then energy advantages to us. Our tendency to use a time preference, by giving more weight to people near to us in time, can be effectively criticized in such an ethical analysis. What right have we to do so? From a historical viewpoint the claim of one or two generations as opposed to thousands of future generations is also difficult to justify.

NOTES

1. Braybrooke, David, 1987. *Meeting Needs*, in the series *Studies in Moral, Political, and Legal Philosophy*, Chapters 7 and 8. Princeton, Princeton University Press.
2. Vermeersch, Etienne, 1988. *De ogen van de panda. Een milieufilosofisch essay*. p.10. Brugge, Marc Van de Wiele.
3. 'People would cultivate love for a particular region and structure their style of life so as to live gently without that place.' Nash, Roderick F., 1989. *The Rights of Nature. A History of Environmental Ethics*, p.148. London/Wisconsin, University of Wisconsin Press.
4. According to a study among people in the Netherlands. Knulst, W. and Van Beek, P., 1988. *Publiek en techniek; opvattingen over technologische vernieuwingen. Sociaal en Cultureel Planbureau*, **57**, pp. 33-44. Den Haag, Rijswijk.
5. Rescher, Nicholas, 1980. 'Technological Progress and Human Happiness', pp. 3-22. In *Unpopular Essays on Technological Progress*. Pittsburg.
6. Attfield, Robin, 1983. *The Ethics of Environmental Concern*, the chapter: 'Belief in Progress'. Oxford, Blackwell.
7. Rapp, Friedrich, 1981. 'The benefits of technology and their costs', in *Analytical Philosophy of Technology*, pp. 165-71. Dordrecht, Reidel.
8. Buchanan, James, 1986, in an interview, 'De spelregels van de economie', in *Intermediair*, **22**, pp. 37-51.
9. Hilhorst, Medard, 1987. *Verantwoordelijk voor toekomstige generaties?* Kampen. (Dissertation, with summary in English).
10 de Brauw, M.L., et al, 1983. *Het tussenrapport: basis voor de brede maatschappelijke discussie*. pp. 131, 132. Publikatie van de stuurgroep maatschappelijke diskussie energiebeleid, Lange Voorhout 14, Den Haag. This report describes the discussion on future energy policy in the eighties among large numbers of people in the Netherlands. This discussion was initiated and organized by the Dutch government, in a situation in which too much opposition existed against the building of (three) new nuclear power stations. Since than a decision about it has still not been made.
11. Goodin, Robert E., 1980. 'No moral nukes'. *Ethics*, **90**, pp. 417-49.

Chapter 20

THE FUTURE OF ENVIRONMENTAL PHILOSOPHY

Etienne Vermeersch

1. INTRODUCTION

Philosophy studies those problems for which there are no adequate scientific methods of solution. The questions that relate to individual and social acting belong to this field, as do the all-embracing questions that result from uncertainty about ourselves, about our place in the world and about the potential sense or nonsense of our conduct in that world.

Uncertainty and questioning may arise from wonder, but they may also emerge because of an awareness of danger. In the first case that may lead to a cosmology or an anthropology that locate people in their world in a more or less harmonious way: their view of the world and the way they deal with it are then usually justified and confirmed. In the second case, which very often goes with doubt – or despair – the idea of harmony is being discarded: there is a realization that something is going wrong and that thinking and acting have to strike out on a new course.

Environmental philosophy, a quarter of a century old now, certainly belongs to the second category. It has grown from many people's conviction that our civilization is on the wrong track. The first symptom of this awareness is a farewell to optimism. The thinking, feeling and acting of western humanity since the Enlightenment – 'modernity' as it is called – were marked by an enthusiasm for progress: western science, technology and economy were thought to guarantee a better 'world' (actually meaning a better human existence). The first hole in that optimism was made by Marx: science and technology remained promising, but not within a *capitalist* order. The second disappointment came after World War II, with the atomic bomb and nuclear armament: *science*, too, proved problematic. Yet in spite of all this a majority remained convinced that western civilization had sufficient resilience to solve the problems it had itself generated. The real awareness of crisis, however, was only awakened completely during the sixties when the ecological or environmental issue started to impose itself in all its dimensions on an ever growing number of people.

Problems cannot be dealt with, let alone be solved, when they are not expressed with full clarity. Since environmental philosophy has its roots in the ecological crisis, it is useful to specify its exact nature once again. Its essential characteristics are (a) the depletion of energy sources; (b) the finite nature of resources whose supplies are limited (raw materials, fresh water, farmland); (c) the increasing production of waste, which leads to the pollution and poisoning of the garbage dumps (among them air, soil, rivers and seas); (d) the extinction of species of animals and plants and the destruction of ecosystems.

The factors that boost these processes directly are: the growth of the world population, the increasing demand for ever more and more different consumer goods and, along with that, the extension of the technical potential for production (and destruction). In addition to the growing awareness of all this there is the insight that such development does not always create welfare but also causes a lot of suffering by widening the gap between rich and poor, and also growing sensitivity towards animals' suffering.

Environmental philosophy has the following assignments:

(i)   to find out whether a series of processes is at issue that really shows enough connection to be considered as one total problem;

(ii)   to discover where both the essence and the cause of this derailment can be found; and

(iii) to investigate how the global problem can be solved, for instance by removing the basic causes.

Obviously the answer to the question about causes will determine the direction in which one must look for solutions.

2. ENVIRONMENTAL PHILOSOPHY AS AN ANALYSIS OF CAUSES

There is a broad consensus among ecophilosophers that the core of the ecological problem can be reduced to something like the following. During the nineteenth and twentieth centuries, perhaps even a little sooner, a production and consumption system has arisen in the West, under the impetus of science and technology, that is gradually spreading across the world and has a destructive effect on nature by its impact on the processes (a) through (d). The question now arising is how this macroprocess has come into being, and why that development has happened in the West. Consensus disappears when one reaches the stage of answering that question. However, some general types of approach can be distinguished.

a. Idealistic approaches

The most 'popular' way to deal with this problem so far is what we may call the *idealistic* one. The derailment of western civilization is explained by means of a characteristic *way of thinking* or mentality that has determined individual and social acting so strongly that a nature-destructive praxis was an almost inevitable result.

As early as 1967 Lynn White launched the thesis that western civilization is characterized by *anthropocentrism*, the belief that man is central in the world, an attitude he also calls 'Christian arrogance' against nature, and that, according to him, originates in the Bible, more particularly in the book of Genesis. For there man is commissioned by God to function as the master of nature. The earth has no sacral character and man, as God's 'image', has the right to place all earthly things in his service. This desacralization of creation is the basis of the typically western science and technology, which in their turn have caused the ecological crisis. Therefore White concludes that either we need a new religion or we have to rethink the old one.

The importance of White's thesis is evident, if only from the fact that between 1970 and 1983 more than 160 articles were published that were inspired by the famous 1967 article. The thesis was attacked by Lewis Moncrief, who minimized the part of Christianity and who mentions the political and socioeconomic development of the West as a cause. William Coleman does see an influence from Christianity but looks for it in theological justifications that accompanied and stimulated its evolution in the seventeenth and eighteenth century. John Passmore recognizes the significance of anthropocentrism in the West, but considers that it has both a Greek (stoic) and a Christian origin. C.J. Glacken stays closer to White's thesis, and even argues that Christian anthropocentrism clearly remains an influence, citing Pope Paul VI's encyclical letter, *Populorum Progressio*. Robin Attfield, on the other hand, finds that the Christian attitude towards nature is approached too partially by White: in the Bible one can also find the beginnings of a recognition of an intrinsic value of nature. Some theologists have argued from a comparable point of view that, as well as the idea of *dominion*, another interpretation is possible, which sees man as God's *steward* on earth – still an administrator, but one who will have to account for his conduct.

This short enumeration is taken from a wide range of articles. It makes clear that within the limited scope of this paper it is a hopeless task to hold a thorough discussion about even this very specific aspect of environmental philosophy, the debate about 'Christian arrogance' as the cause of our problems. If, however, we wanted to treat the whole body of 'idealistic' attempts at explanation, it would become even more so.[1]

For there are also people who claim to recognize the root of all evil in Galilei's mathematization of the world, still others who see it in Descartes' rationalism and mechanicism, in the western ideal of aiming at theoretical knowledge, in the Enlightenment's way of thinking in general and positivism as an extreme expression of it. Part of this 'culture criticism' arose as early as the nineteenth century as a reaction against the grip science and technology threatened to get on human life, but the adjustment of it in the direction of what has now become environmental philosophy, dates from the middle of our century and is mainly to be found in the works of Adorno/Horkheimer and Heidegger.[2]

In more recent environmental philosophy there are also thinkers who are less concerned to shed light on the historical aspects of western mentality than to analyse the new mentality that has to come into being. Very influential in this respect were Arne Naess and Devall & Sessions (anthropocentrism) and Richard Routley ('human chauvinism'). In some related studies the historical approach is replaced by comparison with the mentality of non-western cultures (see for instance Ton Lemaire) and eventually this may end in an investigation of several 'fundamental attitudes' one can have towards nature (cf. mainly Wim Zweers).[3]

b. Socioeconomic approaches

In the 'idealistic' type of explanation, one takes for granted, explicitly or not, that it is primarily concepts or attitudes which determine our interaction with nature. At the bottom of the non-idealistic point of view, which one can characterize as a *socioeconomic* or *institutional* one, lies the conviction that it is rather social processes and their forms of organization which shape human acting and finally human thoughts. Marx, with his 'historical materialism', no doubt broke new ground in this approach, but the somewhat biased emphasis on the part played by production relations and the class struggle has weakened his influence on recent discussions.

The philosophy of scarcity, almost simultaneously developed by Hans Achterhuis and Nicholas Xenos, independently of each other, is in the transition area between idealistic and non-idealistic approach. Under the influence of R. Girard's ideas they consider the socioeconomic processes we experience nowadays as a consequence of the extension of the scarcity phenomenon and see the expansion of western civilization as the spreading of scarcity across the whole world. The process is paradoxical, because this civilization has in fact embraced the extirpation of scarcity as a principle, and it is absurd, because expansion of scarcity must eventually lead to self-destruction. Their approach is a rather idealistic one because an attitude towards fellow humans and the object of their needs, termed 'mimetic desire', is the moving force behind the production of scarcity; but there is also a socioeconomic pole, because it is argued that some institutional changes (family structure, property, etc.) have led to the reinforced action of mimetic desire which is typical of modernity.[4]

We find a radically institutional approach to environmental problems with Niklas Luhmann. He believes that society as a system is composed not so much of persons, as of subsystems like politics, law, science, technology, etc. which carry out operations according to autonomous patterns, meanwhile influencing other subsystems. It is not persons and their ideas or 'attitudes' that are the bearers of the social event, but those subsystems and their operations. Investigation of the 'causes' of the environmental crisis must therefore consist in analysing the possibilities and limitations of the evolution of such 'autopoietic' systems and the solution must come from a better competence in the self-rule of these systems, within the limitations imposed by the surroundings.[5]

My preferred approach, the socioeconomic, departs from the irrefutable fact that, whatever people's concepts or mentality may be, the real oppression of nature and the destruction of it that we witness nowadays has only become possible through the introduction of means with highly productive and destructive power, in short through modern *technology*. This type of technology is based on the application of *scientific* results, and the use on a large scale of both science and technology was established within an organization of the economy that we call *capitalism*. We must add to this that a limited, stationary use of this arsenal of means would not need to have disastrous consequences on its own: it is especially its unrestrained *expansion* that makes up the core of the ecological problem.

From historical investigations into the origin and substantial features of science, technology and capitalist economy we learn that they have not just sprung from the anthropocentric mentality as one coherent whole. Science arose first in the shape of mathematics, more specifically geometry, but these abstract studies of constructions built with straight lines and circles had, on their own, nothing to do with human chauvinism or control over nature. The experimental method, which gave the final go-ahead for the development of natural science, was itself so strongly determined by mathematical thinking that it cannot simply be a result of the anthropocentric mentality either. The idea of control over nature though, which we find with Francis Bacon, may have provided an incentive for the dissemination of the new method. As early as the fourteenth century, the development of technology was accelerating, a tendency which may be explained in part by geographical and political factors, but which was also due to the gradual formation of the capitalist way of managing the economy - the reinvestment of a considerable part of the profits.

Science, technology and capitalist economy were characterized already at their origin by their own internal dynamism, but the enormous process of acceleration that was the result of their mutual influence only got into its stride in the eighteenth century. Even this growing interaction was not the result of an idea or a specific vision of the relation between man and nature: it was a spontaneous, gradually increasing process that imposed itself as it were automatically. No doubt the absence of diffidence towards a sacral nature may have played a promoting role here, but one can also argue that the consciousness of control over nature was reinforced by this growing power itself.[6]

I shall term this typical system brought about by the growing interaction of science, technology and capitalist economy the STC complex (scientific, technological, capitalist complex). It came into being – at least in part – in an undirected, accidental way, and hence it is less important for environmental philosophy to investigate its roots in western culture than to ask the question why this complex is now evolving in a negative, destructive way. The beginning of an answer to this question seems to lie in the fact that it links micro-rationality to macro-irrationality. At the solution of particular problems it shows an amazing efficiency – which is why it was welcomed with so much optimism – but the totality of the system is irrational: its development itself has no goal, and especially it is characterized by an unlimited urge for expansion, though it is functioning in a finite world. Therefore sooner or later it will have to collide with the limits of this finiteness.

c. Ways to a solution

If it happens to be true that this expansion leads us headlong to catastrophe, then the most urgent task of environmental philosophy is to look for means to impose some restraints on it. In this context the fundamental difference between an 'idealistic' and a 'socioeconomic' approach emerges clearly. Even if it were true that the crisis in our civilization is caused by western anthropocentrism, one might wonder if we really can move over to another attitude in the short term. And even if we could bring about such a 'metanoia' among the masses, the concrete (socioeconomic) problem remains how we can get this macro complex itself under control, and in which direction, if any, we would have to guide it.

Consequently, the priorities in environmental philosophy are clearly fixed.

(i) We must get a better insight in the functioning of the STC complex (which could possibly lead to the conclusion that the subsystems STC have to be complemented with a P (political), J (juridical) or E (educational) subsystem).

ii) We must develop methods to impose restraints on the dynamics of the system; this means that we get to know mechanisms in both the technological and the economic sphere which can bring about stationary production and consumption: which implies among other things halting the population explosion.

(iii) In order to motivate people into reform in that direction we must devise an environmental ethics. Here insight into the anthropocentric nature of our civilization may clarify matters, but we would miss the mark if we neglected the fundamental importance of *consumption orientation;* this mentality has been created by the STC complex, but it now exerts a paralysing influence on efforts to restrain it.

3. ENVIRONMENTAL PHILOSOPHY AS NEW ETHICS

The above-mentioned studies of the historical causes and the socioeconomic solutions of the crisis in our civilization are hardly mentioned in many essays on environmental philosophy, where environmental philosophy is often identified downright with environmental ethics. This results from the conviction of many environmental philosophers that the attitude of western man towards nature is the core of our problems: they seem to underrate the power and the proper dynamics of the social processes involved. That does not mean that from my point of view I want to minimize the importance of environmental ethics, but I do want to emphasize that one cannot expect any good to come of it in itself if we neglect the importance of the structural means that could tackle the social processes as a whole.

a. A basic dichotomy?

Anyway, there is still a lot of work on hand in this more restricted field of environmental ethics, for discord and confusion are considerable. To begin with there is the dichotomy between *deep* and *shallow ecology* which was introduced by Arne Naess, but which he himself characterized in different ways in 1973 and 1983. Even if one considers as the central feature that the advocates of a *deep ecology* reject anthropocentrism radically, there is still a clear distinction to be made between those who, like Naess, want to found their ethics on a vague metaphysics (for example an 'ecosophy') and for instance Richard Sylvan (Routley), a logician who departs from a critically rationalistic position to found his attack on *human chauvinism.* as well as differing in methodology, these ethicists also take different positions on the evaluation of humanity's place in the world and its order of ranking in the scale of values.[7]

b. Nature and hierarchies of values

To begin with, there is the traditional *theological* or *metaphysical anthropocentrism*, in which the axiom that the world was created for the benefit of man led to the opinion that many characteristics of plants and animals were accounted for by noting that they were actually meant for man's use (thus the fleece of sheep was there not so much to protect them from the cold, as to let them produce wool).

Current *radical anthropocentrism* or *anthropocentric humanism* does not have this rather naive overtone: it postulates that by belonging to the species *Homo sapiens* we automatically possess a superior status. By virtue of a number of unique qualities human beings would have absolute priority over all other creatures. Starting from this anthropocentrism one tries to justify each intervention in and exploitation of nature if it happens to the advantage of individuals, or groups of (currently existent) humankind.

This basic assumption may further, according to the nature of the ethics one wishes to work in, get an *axiological* phrasing (with regard to values): the value of an object depends on its functionality for human purposes; a *deontological* phrasing (with regard to duties): we only have duties to people and to those objects that help humans in the realization of their aims; and a *juridical* phrasing (with regard to rights): only people have rights.

As a radical alternative to this anthropocentrism an ecocentrism has been proposed, which is typical of the 'deep ecology' movement. Its definitions, though, are liable to some variation. Some people adhere to a *biocentrism*: all living creatures have an intrinsic value (or, respectively, rights). This opinion may involve either 'biocentric egalitarianism' which awards all organisms the same rights, or various hierarchies of values, in which the value of humans is sometimes emphasized so strongly that one unconsciously ends up in a kind of anthropocentrism again. One can also attribute value to inanimate objects like mountains, rivers, etc., so much so that this tendency could better be called *cosmocentrism*; in it several kinds of hierarchies are possible as well.

On the other hand biocentrism has also been limited or made more specific by various authors. They attribute intrinsic value to those beings that can have '*interests*' (e.g. certain plants need a lot of sun), or those that show a '*preference*' (e.g. by expressing in their behaviour what they experience as interest or damage). A very special place, as far as social impact is concerned, is occupied by what one can call *pathocentrism*: this is an extension of anthropocentrism to all animals that can suffer *pain* (here, too, there is an axiological, a deontological and a juridical version).[8]

All these efforts to escape from radical anthropocentrism have apparently been confronted with the difficulty that no position imposes itself through sufficient evidence connected with solid rational argumentation, so much so that one is rather making an appeal to spontaneous intuitions that can differ from person to person. But radical anthropocentrism is itself hardly justifiable: it does not offer any suggestion or motivation to action against the nature-destructive operation of our complex, and, for that matter, it cannot be maintained internally in a consistent way either: for each characteristic that one claims to be uniquely human, it can be argued that not all human beings possess it, and for many qualities it can be upheld that there are animals that show them to a larger extent than some people (e.g. animals suffer more than comatose patients).

Therefore, the most reasonable approach seems to me an *enlightened* form of *anthropocentrism*. After all, one cannot avoid recognizing the following facts. Human beings are the only creatures on earth capable of reflective thinking and able to inform others of the contents of this thinking. Human beings are the only ones who can act on the basis of decisions taken after rational consideration, possibly under the influence of rational persuasion. Human beings' decisions may provoke others' reaction, and hence, when human beings wield power over other human beings, they must take into account the fact that some day the balance of power may be changed. Both the former and the latter characteristic mean that between human beings there exist relations that are not possible with any other living creature. Consequently, human beings have a special reason to take into account each other's wishes and decisions.

In all these respects human beings form a closed community. This means that only human beings can have access to it, not that they all do have access to it. Children, mentally handicapped persons, comatose patients are accepted into this community not for logical but for other reasons. From a historical point of view, anthropocentric humanism is rather the result of a progressive extension of forms of egoism, of group egoism, of chauvinism, to a wide community of which the bounds are not arbitrary but biologically unambiguously fixed.

When one considers this type of humanism as a positive achievement, openings to new forms of sympathy may be looked for, such as the extension of our solidarity to the human beings of future generations. Indeed the conception of ethics that we propose here does not suppose that values, standards and rights exist in an abstract heaven from where they are dropped onto human society. They rather come into being within societies under the influence of individual and collective needs, of the interactions between individuals and groups and of the adaptation of groups to their ecosystem. That certain peoples will rather kill human enemies than the totem is not a consequence of an ecocentric attitude but of a specific form of adaptation to the surroundings. What may be expected from us as ecophilosophers is, therefore, not that we are going to impose on our fellow humans values they have neglected, but that we try to persuade them to introduce new values, standards and rights, because the new world situation prompts us all to that.

In order for there to be a fair chance of acceptance – and without that acceptance there is no point to it at all – we must set up an argumentation that leans as far as possible on the hierarchy of values that is now already prevailing.

Two extensions of anthropocentric humanism which are accepted to some extent nowadays meet this condition. These are the extension of human solidarity to future generations and to a sympathy with all animals that can suffer. These extensions are sufficient to motivate all measures that are needed to get the STC complex under control and to pass on the preserved species and ecosystems unaffected to our descendants. Indeed this enlightened anthropocentrism considers nature as a patrimony which we have received, but which we have to hand on intact as well; the pathocentrism that has been coupled with it gives our care for fellow humans an authenticity which it would lack if we were moved by one expression of suffering and not by another.

The essential advantage of this approach over, say, a biocentric or a cosmocentric one, is that it provides us with criteria to make decisions when values come into conflict. For example to assess the greater or lesser importance of the suffering of some species of animals we can take into account the fact that their susceptibility to suffering depends on the complexity of the central nervous system. As far as the value of ecosystems and species is concerned, we can take into account their relevance to future generations: it is better to protect orchids than the smallpox virus.

Although our approach seems the most appropriate one it does not exclude the possibility of analysing the ethical positions set out above from the point of view of man's fundamental attitude towards nature. For instance, when we are guided by Wim Zweers' classification, the attitude of the 'despot' corresponds with that of a blind, radical anthropocentrism. The 'enlightened despot' is a little more 'sensible' but does not yet include future generations in his perspective. That may be the case, though, in one of the interpretations of the 'steward'; but in order to correspond fully with our proposal he must still add a 'partnership', at least with respect to animals that can suffer pain.

A sense of 'partnership' and 'participation' towards the rest of nature seems to be a rather emotional and aesthetic experience, which one can go through occasionally, but which can hardly form a well reasoned basis for acting in nature. For instance the notion of the 'own purposes' of nature seems to be a rather odd one: I wonder whether we can still speak about 'participation' when we realize that since the Neolithic era agriculture and cattle breeding have depended on an ever-increasing deterioration and destruction of original ecosystems. The most sensible 'fundamental attitude' seems to be that of 'firefighter': someone who knows what is lost year after year, but who still tries to make the most of a hopeless situation.

4. WHERE IS ENVIRONMENTAL PHILOSOPHY GOING TO?

Is environmental philosophy useful, does it have a future? It seems to me that the task of environmental philosophy should be the current task of philosophical anthropology. Questions about humanity show a rather peculiar characteristic. In this area facts are no longer any more respectable than a Lord Mayor: the determination of facts is not necessarily the most relevant activity. For example the eradication of poverty, famine or smallpox happens to be much more important than a thorough study of these phenomena. Human misery, suffering and survival itself are more urgent problems than purely theoretical questions concerning human nature and its characteristics. At a time when we are on our way to destroying the ecosystem in which and on which we live, the central question is consequently no longer which is 'Die Stellung des Menschen im Kosmos' (Scheler). We must find out if humanity still has enough resilience to escape from the fatal dynamics and we must also try to know which processes of thinking, acting and social organization we have to get going to realize that purpose.

The question how we can live in a harmonious relation with nature as individuals and as a society is, however, very difficult to answer because it touches the core of our existence and acting. Hippocrates once said: 'Biological life has been given to us by nature, but the beautiful, valuable life is a question of culture.' What distinguishes humans from other organisms consists in culture, in modelling nature: everywhere man has set foot ashore, spontaneous, freely developing nature is restrained. For millennia humans were able to do this because their numbers and their means of production were limited. The destruction of nature is not the result of a despotic attitude towards nature which is a characteristic attitude of humans, and of humans only: grasshoppers too completely eat bare the areas they settle on. Modern humanity and its relation to nature is essentially characterized by power: a capacity for interfering and also for destroying on a planetary scale. But on the other hand we also have the advantage over all other animals of possessing the ability to anticipate the catastrophe.

The first and most urgent assignment of an environmental philosopher, therefore, consists in clarifying this power of foresight and for this purpose it is necessary that one relinquishes all scientific-technological optimism: each claim that our STC complex will solve the problems automatically, is a contribution to the blinding; each enthusiastic announcement about the 'way out' – cold fusion or elephant grass – jeopardizes our vigilance again. There is no 'royal road' to the solution of environmental problems. Only gaining control over the expanding STC complex by halting population growth and by introducing a stationary production and consumption system may bring a solution for the earth and for humanity.

To realize this aim, further investigation must be carried out into the mechanisms that accelerate the expansion of our complex and into the means that can restrain the system. We must also get a better insight into the factors that stimulate the current consumption orientation and into the attitudes that can bring about alternative patterns of need; without a fundamental change of attitude all measures to try and change the actual functioning of the STC complex will run into strong opposition. Along with this type of research we can continue working at devising environmental ethics and possibly new fundamental attitudes and cosmologies that may encourage a willingness to accept social changes. We must, however, constantly realize that attitudes and ethics alone cannot produce a direct effect on the processes, but only by providing the motivation to accept changes in the way of production and consumption. Economically speaking we must look for a new macro-economic system in which the value of a commodity must also be a function of its 'ecological relevance', which means taking into account the impact its production and consumption have on energy, raw materials, pollution and attacks upon ecosystems.

Furthermore we badly need a fresh political philosophy that can form the theoretical preparation for the new political and juridical organization. To promote further knowledge of the mechanisms of our STC complex historical investigation may still be necessary. For example: where exactly is the origin of capitalism? May political or juridical aspects of our society have possibly played a part?

Because of the great importance of people's motivation it is advisable that the different schools of thought in environmental ethics come to a broader consensus. For that purpose a renewed study of the theory of values is needed, and also a weighing of the respective merits of cosmocentrism, biocentrism, pathocentrism and anthropocentrism, especially with respect to their capacity to offer an adequate basis for these ethics, and especially concerning their capacity of motivating the population.

Finally it seems very important to investigate the possibilities of changing the structure of the human hierarchy of needs, the ideal being that people are ever less attracted by products with a high energetic or material value and a low form and informational value. In contradistinction to the production and consumption of matter and energy the production of form or information has a rather negligible impact on the ecosystems. Those who have replaced the need to drive fast cars with setting their minds on writing poems or computer programs, may gain equal joy and equal public recognition and self-esteem from this, but ecologically speaking this behaviour is a lot more favourable.

Environmental philosophy is certainly the anthropology of the future, but perhaps it is also the philosophy of the future in general: when this philosophy, this critical thinking fail, when our acting keeps running out of control, there will probably be no more future to philosophize on, no future at all...[9]

NOTES

1. White, L., 1967. 'The Historical Roots of our Ecological Crisis', *Science*. **155**:1203-7.

White, L., 1973. 'Continuing the Conversation', in I.G. Barbour, *Western Man and Environmental Ethics*, pp.55-64. Reading Mass., Addison Wesley.

Moncrief, L.W.,1970. 'The Cultural Basis of our Environmental Crisis', *Science* **170**: 508-12; Coleman, W., 1976. 'Providence Capitalism and Environmental Degradation. English Apologetics in an Era of Economic Revolution', *The Journal of the History of Ideas*, **1**.

Coleman's point of view, however, is contrary to R.H. Tawney's (see Tawney, R.H., 1926. *Religion and the Rise of Capitalism.* Harmondsworth, Penguin)and to D.S. Landes's (see Landes, D.S., 1969. *The Unbound Prometheus: Technological Change and Industrial Development in Western Europe from 1750 to the Present* Cambridge, Cambridge University Press).

Passmore, J., 1974. *Man's Responsibility for Nature: Ecological Problems and Western Traditions.* p.39. London, Duckworth.

Glacken, C.J. 1967. *Traces on the Rhodian Shore: Nature and Culture in Western Thought from Ancient Times to the End of the Eighteenth Century* Berkeley, University of California Press; also C.J. Glacken, 1970. 'Man Against Nature: An outmoded Concept', in H.W. Helfrich jr. (ed.), *The Environmental Crisis: Man's Struggle to Live with Himself.* London/New Haven..

Attfield, R., 1983. *The Ethics of Environmental Concern.* Oxford, Blackwell.

For a complete picture of the relations between Christianity and environmental crisis. see De Temmerman, Wim, 1987. *Milieucrisis en Christendom* (Ghent, 860 pp., unpublished licentiate's thesis). Also useful is Nash, Roderick Frazier, 1987. *The Rights of Nature: A History of Environmental Ethics,* chapter 4, 'The Greening of Religion'. University of Wisconsin Press.

2. For an exhaustive survey of the positive and negative attitudes and reactions towards the scientific-technological developments, see Van der Pot, Johan H.J., 1985. *Die Bewertung des technischen Fortschritts, eine systematische Uebersicht der Theorien* Assen, Van Gorcum, 2 vols.; Almond, G.A., M. Chodorow & R.H. Pearce, 1977. *Progress and its Discontents.* Berkeley: University of California Press.

3. Naess, Arne, 1973. 'The Shallow and the Deep, Long-Range Ecology Movement: A Summary', *Inquiry* **16**: 95-100; also 1989, *Ecology, Community and Lifestyle: Outline of an Ecosophy.* Cambridge, Cambridge University Press.

Bill Devall & George Sessions (eds.), 1985. *Deep Ecology: Living as if Nature Mattered.* Salt Lake City, Utah.

Routley, R. & Routley, V., 1980. 'Human Chauvinism and Environmental Ethics', in D.S. Mannison, M.A. McRobbie & R. Routley, *Environmental Philosophy.* pp.96-189. Monograph Series no. 2, Dep. of Phil., Australian National University. For Ton Lemaire see his contribution, 'De Indiaanse houding tegenover de natuur: Indiaanse ecologie als uitweg voor onze milieucrisis?', in W. Achterberg and W. Zweers (eds) 1984. *Milieucrisis en Filosofie.* Amsterdam: Ecologische Uitgeverij.

For W. Zweers cf. his contribution to this colloquium. One finds a general survey of this environmental philosophy in R.F. Nash, op. cit., chapter 5, 'The Greening of Philosophy'.

4. Achterhuis, Hans, 1988. *Het rijk van de schaarste.* Baarn, Ambo.
    Xenos, Nicholas, 1989. *Scarcity and Modernity.* London, Routledge.
5. Luhmann, Niklas, 1986. *Ökologische Kommunikation.* Westdeutscher Verlag.
6. This analysis of characteristics of the STC complex was elaborated at greater length in Vermeersch, E., 1988, *De Ogen van de panda.* Bruges, Van de Wiele; and also 1990 in 'Weg van het WTK complex: onze toekomstige samenleving', in *Het milieu: denkbeelden voor de 21st eeuw,* pp.17-40. Commissie Lange Termijn Planning Milieubeleid, Kerkebosch, Zeist.
7. Routley's attack on *human chauvinism* is found especially in Richard & Val Routley's article mentioned above; his (Routley = Sylvan) criticism of *deep ecology* in Sylvan, R., 1985, 'A Critique of Deep Ecology, Part I', *Radical Philosophy,* summer 1985, p. 212, and 'A Critique of Deep Ecology, Part II' *Radical Philosophy,* autumn 1985, p. 10-22.
8. As a predecessor of 'biocentrism' Albert Schweitzer may rank. Apart from that it is often difficult to find out an author's exact position. He who sees 'life' as an autonomous value, may mean individual organisms by that, but also ecosystems; with many authors non-living natural objects are included too, like rivers and mountains. Clearly and exclusively 'pathocentric' is Singer, Peter, 1973. 'Animal Liberation', in *New York Review of Books,* April 5. 'Biocentric' is Taylor, Paul W., 1986. *Respect for Nature: A Theory of Environmental Ethics.* Princeton. 'Cosmocentric' are Naess, Devall & Sessions: further Stone, Christopher D., 1972. 'Should Trees have Standing? Toward Legal Rights for Natural Objects', *Southern California Law Review* **45**: 450-501. For further discussion of these positions see for instance Achterberg, W., 1986. *Partners in der natuur.* Utrecht, Van Arkel.
9. The author wishes to thank Wim Zweers for some useful suggestions.

Contributors

(book-titles etc. translated in English)

WOUTER ACHTERBERG (1941) teaches environmental philosophy and ethics at the Faculty of Philosophy (Department of Ethics) of Amsterdam University and is Socrates Professor of Humanistic Philosophy at Wageningen Agricultural University. With Wim Zweers he co-edited the first two Dutch readers on environmental philosophy (*Environmental Crisis and Philosophy*, 1984, and *Environmental Philosphy between Theory and Practice*, 1986) and is author of *Partners in Nature* (1986) and of numerous articles on environmental ethics and on philosophical aspects of environmental policy. He is now preparing an introductory book on environmental philosophy.

HANS ACHTERHUIS (1942) has a theological and philosophical background. He was formerly Socrates Professor of Humanistic Philosophy at Wageningen Agricultural University, and is now professor of philosophy and chairman of the Department of Philosophy at Twente Technical University. He is author of, among others, *The Market of Welfare and Happiness* (1980), *Labour: a Strange Remedy* (1984), *The Realm of Scarcity* (1988). His main focus is on social philosophy, health care and philosophy of technology: in recent years these interests have been partly directed at environmental problems.

JAN J. BOERSEMA (1947) studied biology and ethology, and is now at the Department of Environmental Science of Groningen University. He has done much research in the field of agriculture and nature. He is editor-in-chief of the Dutch standard textbook on environmental science, *Introduction to Environmental Science*, now in its fourth, revised and enlarged edition (1984-1991), and is author of numerous articles on environmental science. His current special interest is in the historical roots of the humanity/nature relationship, on which he is finishing a Ph.D. thesis.

MAARTEN COOLEN (1943) is a mathematician and a philosopher, and is now – as a philosophical anthropologist – at the Faculty of Philosophy (Department of Anthropology and Metaphysics) of Amsterdam University. He has written several articles on the anthropological background of modern technology and on the implicit presuppositions of artificial intelligence, as well as on environmental philosophy. He is author of *Beyond the Machine: on Human Self-Understanding in the Age of Information Technology* (1992).

PAUL VAN DIJK (1933) has a theological background, and teaches ethics at the Department of Philosophy of Twente Technical University, where he is involved with the teaching of philosophy to technical students. He is author of *For Heaven's Sake, What are We Getting Into? Nuclear Armaments, Church and Culture in the Work of*

C.J. Dippel (1983) and *On the Borderline between Two Worlds: An Inquiry into the Ethical Thought of Scientist C.J. Dippel* (1985), as well as of numerous articles.

MEDARD HILHORST (1951) finished studies in technology, theology and ethics. He is now a lecturer in health ethics at the Centre of Applied Ethics of the Faculty of Philosophy, and the Section for Medical Ethics of the Faculty of Medicine, both at the Erasmus University, Rotterdam. He is author of *Responsible for Future Generations?* (1987) and of several articles on this subject, as well as of *Environmental Ethics* (1991), a course written for the Open University at Heerlen.

FRANS JACOBS (1943) is a philosopher, a former member of the Faculty of Philosophy of Amsterdam University (Department of Ethics) and now a senior lecturer in the Department of Philosophy of Law at the Faculty of Law, Amsterdam University. He published *In the Presence of All: On Universalism in Ethics* (1985). His other publications are in the fields of ethics, including medical ethics, philosophy of labour, political philosophy and philosophy of law.

PETRAN KOCKELKOREN (1949), philosopher, is at the Department of Philosophy of Twente Technical University. His field of study is philosophical anthropology, and his research focuses on environmental philosophy, specializing on hemeneutics of nature (after Dilthey and Plessner), the relationship between corporality and culture, and the relationship between technology and culture. He is author of, among others, *The Nature of the Good Interpreter* (1992) and *From a Vegetable to a Plantworthy Existence: Ethical Aspects of Biotechnology with Plants* (1993, commisioned by the National Department of Agriculture, Nature, and Fisheries).

CHUNG LIN KWA (1953) studied biology and philosophy. In 1985 he received a scholarship at Pennsylvania University from the Dutch Organization for Academic Research. In 1989 he obtained his Ph.D. on an inquiry into the history of American systems ecology, and now he is at the Department of the Dynamics of Science of Amsterdam University. He has published on philosophy and on fundamentals of ecology. He is editor of the *Newsletter of the European Association for the Study of Science and Technology.*

SUSANNE LIJMBACH (1953) studied plant pathology and philosophy and is now at the Department of Applied Philosophy of the Agricultural University of Wageningen. Her research and publications focus on the socio-cultural position of animals: either as socio-cultural subjects or as objects of socio-cultural research.

BERT MUSSCHENGA (1950) was educated as a theologian, and is director of the Centre for Reflection at the Free University, Amsterdam, besides having a chair in social ethics in the Faculty of Philosophy at the same university. His most important publications are *Necessities and Possibilities of Morality* (1980) and *The Quality of Life: Criterion for Medical Action?* (1987). He has several publications and editorships in the field of applied ethics.

HANS OPSCHOOR (1944) is an economist and has a doctorate in the field of environmental economics (1974). From 1982 until 1990 he was director of the Institute for Environmental Studies at the Free University, Amsterdam, and now he is chairman of the National Council of Research in Environment and Nature, as well as professor of environmental economics at the Free University. His most recent publications are *Persistent Pollutants: Economics and Politics* (in English,1991, with David Pearce); *Economic Instruments for Environmental Protection* (in English, 1989, with Hans Vos); *After Us No Deluge: Preconditions for Sustainable Use of the Environment* (1989).

PIETER SCHROEVERS (1930) is a biologist and ecologist, who has worked for many years at the National Institute for Nature Management. Convinced of the necessity for politicization of environmental issues, he became an active member of left wing environmental movements. He was co-founder of *Aktie Strohalm* and of the Foundation for Environmental Education. He has published extensively in the fields of limnology, landscape ecology, environmental philosophy and environmental education.

JAN VAN DER STRAATEN (1935) is an economist and teaches environmental economics and leisure sciences at the Catholic University of Tilburg. Author of *Acid Rain: Economic Theory and Dutch Policy* (1990). His other publications are on economic theory applied to the environment and nature, tourism and the environment, environmental policy in the EU and in the Netherlands, the relation between environmental-economic theory and environmental policy, and the relation between landscape and birds.

HENK TENNEKES (1936) studied aviation technology at Delft Technical University, then taught for 12 years in the United States. In 1977 he became research director at the Royal Dutch Meteorological Institute and professor of meteorology at the Free University of Amsterdam. Since 1990 he has been director of strategic policy development at the Meteorological Institute. His most important publications are *A First Course in Turbulence* (in English, 1972, MIT Press), *Lorenz's Butterfly* (1990), and *Persistently Warm* (1990). He is especially interested in turbulence, chaos, predictability and self-organizing systems, as well as in an 'ecologization of science'.

PIETER TIJMES (1936) is a social and political philosopher at the Department of Philosophy of Twente Technical University and participates in the Research Programme on Cultural Philosophy of Technology. His main focus is on problems concerning scarcity and technics. He edited *Labour Does Not Ennoble Man* (1989) and has published articles on philosophy of technology, philosophical anthropology and environmental philosophy.

ETIENNE VERMEERSCH (1934) was educated in classical philology and philosophy, and since 1967 he has been professor of philosophy at the University of Gent in Belgium, specializing in modern philosophy and philosophical anthropology. At first his interest was mainly in the philosophical implications of information technology, cybernetics and electronic brains, but for the last ten years he has been concentrating on bioethics and environmental philosophy. On this last subject he published *The Eyes of the Panda: An Essay on Environmental Philosophy* (1988). He has also contributed a philosophical chapter to the advisory report of the National Commission on Long Term Environmental Policy *The Environment: Thoughts for the 21st Century* (1990).

KOO VAN DER WAL (1934) studied philosophy, theology and German literature Until 1978 he was professor of philosophy at Amsterdam University, and now holds the same position at Erasmus University, Rotterdam, with an emphasis on ethical theory, metaphysics and philosphical anthropology. He is author of several books and articles, among them *Wordview: Thinking as a Philosophical Problem* (1968). In recent years he has published principally in the areas of environmental philosophy, philosophy of technology and ethics of science.

WIM ZWEERS (1937) studied sociology, and until 1970 he was director of a research institute for the sociology of art. In 1971 he joined the Faculty of Philosophy of Amsterdam University where he turned to social aesthetics and philosophy of culture. From 1980 he engaged in the development of environmental philosophy in the Netherlands. He is author of *Theatre and Public in the Netherlands* (1970) and *Marxism and the Sociology of Art* (1982). He co-edited, with Wouter Achterberg, *Environmental Crisis and Philosophy* (1984) and *Environmental Philosophy: Between Theory and Practice* (1986) and has published numerous articles in the field, mainly on attitudes towards nature, participation, intrinsic value of nature, and ecological spirituality. Currently he is finishing a major work on ecological theory for a 'postmodern' culture.

INDEX

GE
40
E26
1994

WITHDRAWN
From Library Collection

WITHDRAWN
From Library Collection

Reinsch Library
Marymount University
2807 North Glebe Road
Arlington, Virginia 22207